Tolley's Taxation in Corporate Insolvency

Second Edition

A practical guide to the taxation of
insolvent companies, their creditors and shareholders

by
Anthony C R Davis MA FTII Solicitor
of Lovell White Durrant

With chapters on administration and compliance contributed by
Richard Setchim BA MSPI ACA
of Price Waterhouse

Tolley Publishing Company Limited
A UNITED NEWSPAPERS PUBLICATION

Published by
Tolley Publishing Company Limited
Tolley House
2 Addiscombe Road
Croydon Surrey CR9 5AF
081-686 9141

Index and tables compiled by
Indexing Specialists, Hove, East Sussex

Typeset by
Phoenix Photosetting, Chatham, Kent

Printed and bound in Great Britain by
Biddles Ltd, Guildford and King's Lynn

Preface to Second Edition

The first edition of this book (published under the title Tolley's Taxation of Insolvent Companies) was completed on 1 May 1986 when the *Insolvency Act 1986* had been enacted but the most relevant parts of it were not yet in force. The new edition is based on the law in force on 15 May 1991, taking into account proposals made in the 1991 Finance Bill as presented to the House of Commons on 17 April 1991. In the intervening five years practitioners have developed considerable experience in dealing with the new law and the new insolvency procedures of administration and company voluntary arrangements which it introduced. Unfortunately, despite the considerable thought and care which went into the 1986 Act, it has become apparent that the tax implications of these procedures were not addressed in any useful way during the legislative process, with the inevitable and unsatisfactory result that uncertainties abound. Many of these are addressed in the new edition of this book, but there are no doubt an ample number of problems left to solve in any future edition.

Since 15 May 1991, the judgment of Millet J in *J Sainsbury plc v O'Connor* (referred to in 6.11, 8.5, 8.6, 18.11 and 18.12 below) has been upheld unanimously by the Court of Appeal although it is not yet known if the case will proceed to the House of Lords. The case of *Collins v Addies Ch D, 12 June 1991* (unreported) also considers the meaning of the word "release" in the context of *ICTA 1970, s 287* (now *ICTA 1988, s 421*).

The basic material of the first edition has been left intact apart from necessary updating. Six new chapters have been added which deal with not only the new insolvency procedures but also the increasingly important international element of insolvency taxation; national insurance contributions; and BES companies. The sections dealing with the taxation of creditors in and shareholders of insolvent companies have been considerably expanded. I am also especially grateful to Richard Setchim for the two chapters which he has contributed—his considerable practical experience of the compliance aspects, in particular, adds a new dimension to the book.

As with the first edition, there are a large number of individuals who deserve mention for having contributed to the book in various ways, although the responsibility for the text and for the views expressed is mine alone. Of my partners at Lovell White Durrant, Chris Hanson has again given of his valuable time to comment on the new material in the book with the benefit of his great experience in insolvency matters, and Chris Major has helped to pursue a number of the tax issues introduced in the second edition. David Williams helpfully suggested the introductory chapter on insolvency procedures generally. In addition to contributing two chapters, Richard Setchim has made numerous constructive comments on other parts of the book. Most importantly, Elaine Davies has done a substantial part of the routine work needed to update the first edition as well as researching some of the new chapters. Greg Sinfield assisted in updating the VAT chapters and Adrian Brettell reviewed the stamp duty section.

I would also like to record thanks to the individuals at the Inland Revenue, Department of Social Security and Customs & Excise who have been very generous with their time in answering my irritating questions in the middle of their more important duties, particularly the writer of the letter setting out the Revenue's views on the legal basis of distress for taxes, reproduced with the permission of the Controller of Her Majesty's Stationery Office in 4.5 below.

Others who have helped include Richard Raper and his team at Indexing Specialists who prepared the tables and index; Christine Monaghan who helped with many detailed enquiries about references; Pat Probetts who typed (and retyped) the manuscript; and, last but definitely not least, my wife Mary who has given unfailing support to me in producing both editions.

Anthony C R Davis

Lovell White Durrant
65 Holborn Viaduct
London EC1A 2DY

5 July 1991

Contents

Contents

Contents

Contents

Contents

Abbreviations and References

ABBREVIATIONS

ACT .... Advance Corporation Tax
Appx .... Appendix
Art .... Article
B .... Baron
BES .... Business Expansion Scheme
BTR .... British Tax Review
CA .... Companies Act (in statutory references); Court of
Appeal (in case references)
CAA .... Capital Allowances Act
CCA .... Court of Criminal Appeal
CCAB .... Consultative Committee of Accountancy Bodies
C & E Commrs .... Commissioners of Customs & Excise
CEPR .... Customs & Excise Press Release
CGT(A) .... Capital Gains Tax (Act)
Ch .... Chapter
Ch D .... Chancery Division
CIR .... ~ Commissioners of Inland Revenue
CJ .... Chief Justice
CS .... Court of Session
CWR 1949 .... Companies (Winding-Up) Rules 1949,
SI 1949 No 330
D(H)SS .... Department of (Health and) Social Security
EC .... European Communities
ESC .... Inland Revenue Extra-Statutory Concession published
or proposed to be published in booklet IR1
FA .... Finance Act
FCA .... Federal Court of Australia
F(No 2)A .... Finance (No 2) Act
HL .... House of Lords
IA .... Insolvency Act
ICAEW .... Institute of Chartered Accountants in
England and Wales
ICTA .... Income and Corporation Taxes Act
Ins R 1986 .... Insolvency Rules 1986, SI 1986 No 1925
IRPR .... Inland Revenue Press Release
ITC .... Commissioner of Income Tax, Jamaica ·

ITER 1973	Income Tax (Employments) Regulations 1973, SI 1973 No 334
J	Mr Justice
KB	King's Bench Division
KB (NI)	King's Bench Division, Northern Ireland
LC	Lord Chancellor
LJ	Lord Justice
LPA	Law of Property Act
NIC	National Insurance Contributions
OECD	Organisation for Economic Co-operation and Development
p	page
para	paragraph
PAYE	Pay As You Earn
PC	Privy Council
Pt	Part
QB	Queen's Bench Division
QB(NI)	Queen's Bench Division, Northern Ireland
Reg	Regulation
RSC	Rules of the Supreme Court
s	section
SA	Stamp Act
SCE	Supreme Court of Eire
Sch	Schedule
SDRT	Stamp Duty Reserve Tax
SI	Statutory Instrument
SP	Inland Revenue Statement of Practice
SSA	Social Security Act
SSCR 1979	Social Security (Contributions) Regulations 1979, SI 1979 No 591
t/a	trading as
TMA	Taxes Management Act
TR	Technical Release
VAT	Value Added Tax
VATA	Value Added Tax Act
VAT Gen R 1985	Value Added Tax (General) Regulations 1985, SI 1985 No 886
Vol	Volume

REFERENCES

AC	Law Reports, Appeal Cases
All ER	All England Law Reports
ALR	Australian Law Reports
B & C	Barnewall & Cresswell's King's Bench Reports
BCC	British Company (Law) Cases
BCLC	Butterworths Company Law Cases

B & CR	Reports of Bankruptcy and Companies (Winding Up) Cases
BTR	British Tax Review
Burr	Burrow's King's Bench Reports
Ch	Law Reports, Chancery Division [1891 onwards]
Ch App	Law Reports, Chancery Appeal Cases
Ch D	Law Reports, Chancery Division (1875–1890)
Cl & Fin	Clark & Finnelly's House of Lords Cases
Cmnd	Command Paper
EDN: see note below	
Eq	Law Reports, Equity Cases
HKLR	Hong Kong Law Reports
ILRM	Irish Law Reports Monthly
KB	Law Reports, King's Bench
LEE: see note below	
LJKB	Law Journal Reports, New Series, King's Bench
LON: see note below	
LR	Law Reports
LT	Law Times Reports
MAN: see note below	
M & W	Meeson & Welsby's Exchequer Reports
QB	Law Reports, Queen's Bench
QBD	Law Reports, Queen's Bench Division
SLT	Scots Law Times Reports
SLT (Notes)	Scots Law Times Notes of Recent Decisions
STC	Simon's Tax Cases
TC	Reports of Tax Cases
TLR	Times Law Reports
VATTR	Value Added Tax Tribunal Reports
WLR	Weekly Law Reports

Note: References to VAT Tribunal cases not reported in VATTR are by case number, e.g. EDN/83/68 (1234).

Table of Cases

Cases are listed alphabetically under the first-named or only party unless the Crown ('R'), CIR or C & E Commrs are the first-named party, in which circumstance the case is listed under the second-named party.

Table of Statutes

Table of Statutory Instruments

Chapter 1

Introduction

General

1.1   This book is intended as a practical summary of the tax-related aspects of corporate insolvencies in the UK. Apart from a few paragraphs in this chapter, it is exclusively concerned with taxation matters and assumes a basic knowledge of the relevant insolvency and tax law. The law discussed is that in force in England and Wales on 15 May 1991, taking into account proposals made in the 1991 Finance Bill as presented to the House of Commons on 17 April 1991.

Insolvency procedures

1.2   Although the rest of this book concentrates on the tax-related aspects of corporate insolvency, it may be helpful to readers with a tax background to give a brief summary of the basic types of insolvency procedure which can arise, and to describe the differences between them. Readers should, however, appreciate that this summary cannot be more than a drastic simplification of these complex areas of law. Particularly in view of the technical nature of the discussion in the remainder of this book, a tax practitioner dealing with insolvency who is not familiar with insolvency law and practice should take care to obtain appropriate specialist advice.

1.3   The law relating to corporate insolvency is largely found in the *Insolvency Act 1986* (*IA 1986*) and the *Insolvency Rules 1986, SI 1986 No 1925* (*Ins R 1986*). There are four formal insolvency procedures, which are, in the order used in the Act, company voluntary arrangements, administration orders, receivership and winding up. Two other situations also recur in this book: sales by mortgagees (see 1.9 below) and striking off without a liquidation (see 1.11 below).

Company voluntary arrangement

1.4   This is a procedure for agreement between a company and its creditors for a composition in satisfaction of its debts or a scheme of arrangement of its affairs. *IA 1986, s 1* introduced a simplified procedure whereby a proposal can be made to the company and its creditors by the directors (or liquidator or administrator where relevant) for a voluntary arrangement which, if approved by the necessary majority (essentially, over 75 per cent in value of creditors and over 50 per cent in value of shareholders) is binding on all those who had notice of the meeting. The proposal must appoint an insolvency practitioner as nominee to obtain the necessary approval of the arrangement and then as supervisor of the implementation of the voluntary arrangement. The company normally continues to trade after the arrangement has been approved.

Administration order

1.5   This is a court order under the procedure introduced by *IA 1986*, *s 8* whereby, on petition by a company, its directors or one or more of its creditors, the court appoints an insolvency practitioner as administrator to manage the affairs, business and property of the company. The court must be satisfied that the company is, or is likely to become, unable to pay its debts and that the order would be likely to achieve the survival of the company or any part of its undertaking as a going concern, the approval of a voluntary arrangement or a compromise or arrangement under *CA 1985*, *s 425*, or a better realisation of the assets than a winding up. While the petition is being considered, and then while the administration order is in force, the company cannot be wound up, and the consent of the administrator or the court is needed for any security to be enforced, goods to be repossessed, other proceedings, execution or legal process to be commenced or continued, or any distress to be levied. If the company already has an administrative receiver, this will block the making of an administration order (unless the appointor's security is open to attack or the appointor consents) but, once an administration order is in force, no administrative receiver may be appointed. The company may continue to trade under the management of the administrator.

Receivership

1.6   A company goes into receivership where a creditor, holding a charge over a company's assets as security for a debt, appoints a receiver to realise the assets to repay the debt. The form of security may be a fixed charge over specific assets, which prevents the company from dealing with those assets except with the creditor's consent, or may be a floating charge over any part or all of a company's assets with which the company may deal freely in the ordinary course of business. A floating charge will crystallise on the occurrence of certain events set out in the deed constituting the charge, or upon appointment of a receiver or liquidator, whereupon it becomes a fixed charge and the assets can no longer be dealt with freely.

1.7   The term "administrative receiver" was introduced by *IA 1986*, and means:

'(a) a receiver or manager of the whole (or substantially the whole) of a company's property appointed by or on behalf of the holders of any debentures of the company secured by a charge which, as created, was a floating charge, or by such a charge and one or more other securities; or

(b) a person who would be such a receiver or manager but for the appointment of some other person as the receiver of part of the company's property.' [*IA 1986, s 29(2)*].

Before 1986, the term "receiver and manager" was used somewhat similarly. The company frequently continues to trade under the management of the administrative receiver. It is worth noting, also, that the primary responsibility of a receiver is to the creditor(s) appointing him, to realise the assets in the most efficient manner, and not to the company or other creditors though he does have some duties towards them.

1.8   The court may also appoint a receiver to protect or preserve property for the benefit of persons with an interest in it, but this will not necessarily be connected with a company's insolvency.

Sale under power contained in mortgage

1.9   The powers of a mortgagee are not limited to appointment of a receiver. He may also be entitled under an express provision in the mortgage deed or under the statutory power contained in *LPA 1925, s 101(1)(i)* to exercise a power of sale of the mortgaged property. The power of sale cannot be exercised after an administration order has been made except with the leave of the court or the consent of the administrator. [*IA 1986, s 10(1)(b)*].

Winding up (liquidation)

1.10   Liquidation and winding up are terms used to describe the process whereby a liquidator is appointed to collect in a company's assets, and to distribute the proceeds in satisfaction of the company's liabilities and then, if there is a surplus, to the company's shareholders. There are various forms of liquidation.

(a) *Winding up by the court (compulsory liquidation)*. Under *IA 1986, ss 117 162* a winding up petition may be presented by a company, its directors or any of its creditors or contributories for the court to order that the company be liquidated. The court initially constitutes a civil servant, the Official Receiver, as liquidator to administer the winding up [*IA 1986, s 136(2)*]; provided that the assets are sufficient, the liquidation will usually then be completed by an insolvency practitioner appointed for the purpose.

(b) *Voluntary liquidation.* Under *IA 1986, s 84* the members resolve to put the company into liquidation. If the directors make a statutory declaration that the company can pay its debts in full within one year (or less) the process will be a members' voluntary winding up governed by *IA 1986, ss 91–94*. If no such declaration can be made it will be a creditors' voluntary winding up governed by *IA 1986, ss 97–106*. If the liquidator in a members' voluntary winding up forms the opinion that the company will not be able to pay its debts within the stated period, the winding up is converted to a creditors' voluntary winding up under *IA 1986, ss 95–96*.

A petition for a compulsory winding up may be presented where a company is being wound up voluntarily. If the court makes a winding up order on this petition, the voluntary winding up is superseded by a compulsory winding up.

Striking off without a liquidation

1.11 By *CA 1985, s 652*, the Registrar of Companies may strike off the register a company which he has reasonable cause to believe is no longer carrying on business or in operation. On publication of the name of the company in the Gazette for the second time, the company is dissolved by *section 652(5)*. This does not absolve the directors and members of the company from any liability or prevent the court from winding up the company (subject to prior reinstatement). However, the effect will usually be dissolution without liquidation. Any member or creditor aggrieved by the dissolution can apply within the next 20 years for restoration of the name on the grounds that the company was in fact carrying on business or in operation, or that it would be otherwise just to do so. [*CA 1985, s 653*].

The nature of tax claims in an insolvency

General

1.12 Uniquely in the context of tax law, a liquidator, and frequently an administrator or administrative receiver, has a dual responsibility regarding tax. Like any person concerned with a business, his activities give rise to continuing obligations to make tax returns and comply with other procedural formalities, paying tax where it is exigible; but he may also be concerned with the Crown (represented by the Inland Revenue, Customs & Excise and Department of Social Security) as a creditor in the insolvency (and, to an extent, as a preferential creditor). Moreover, the liabilities to the Crown as creditor or preferential creditor proving in a liquidation or administrative receivership derive not from the taxing statutes familiar to the tax practitioner, but from what was once the royal prerogative and is now a separate statutory duty, in certain cases enforceable as such against an administrative receiver or liquidator personally. The Crown also has recourse to special measures to enforce its

4

claims for tax, notably the statutory rights of Crown set-off and distress (discussed below in Chapters 3 and 4 respectively).

Crown as preferential or unsecured creditor

1.13   The distinction between the Crown's right to recover tax unpaid at the date of appointment of a receiver or to prove for tax unpaid at commencement of a liquidation, and the Crown's right to recover tax liabilities arising after those dates, is of fundamental importance for other reasons also. Tax liabilities (including corporation tax as well as deduction taxes such as PAYE and sub-contractors' payments) in respect of pre-liquidation periods will be provable in the liquidation irrespective of when they are due and payable and whether or not assessed at the date of liquidation, and will rank according to the statutory rules. This point is expected to be confirmed in relation to companies in compulsory liquidation in regulations, to be issued jointly by the Department of Trade and Industry and Inland Revenue, some time later in 1991 after the date of writing. These regulations are intended to replace the previous regulations made under *CWR 1949, Rule 224* reproduced in Appendix I of the first edition of this book. If (and only if) taxes fall within the statutory categories considered in Chapter 2 below, they will be preferential and rank for payment *pari passu* with other preferential claims. Those claims which are not preferential will rank as unsecured claims. It should be noted that preferential tax claims can arise both in a liquidation and (if the date of appointment of a receiver precedes the date of liquidation) also in a receivership where a receiver is appointed under a floating charge or if a floating chargee goes into possession. [*CA 1985, s 196*]. Non-preferential tax claims, however, are only provable in a liquidation; there are no non-preferential claims for tax against a receiver in respect of periods before his appointment.

Tax liabilities arising after date of liquidation

1.14   The treatment of tax liabilities arising after the date of liquidation is different. Liabilities then arising for corporation tax will normally fall to be discharged pre-preferentially as expenses of the liquidation. By contrast, a receiver will not normally be concerned with corporation tax or income tax liabilities at all, as (except in a few cases such as income tax deductions from payments and, possibly, Schedule A income such as rents) these will remain the liability of the company, to be proved in a subsequent liquidation or, if the company is already in liquidation, to be recovered from the liquidator (*Re Regents Canal Ironworks Company, ex parte Grissell CA 1875, (1876) 3 Ch 411*). The exceptional case is where the receiver is appointed under a floating charge which had not crystallised at the time that the winding up of the company began, in which case tax arising after the liquidation may be payable in priority to the debts secured on the charged assets as an expense of the winding up, under *Ins R 1986, Rule 4.218* (*Re Barleycorn Enterprises Ltd CA, [1970] 2 All ER 155* and *Re*

Christonette International Ltd Ch D, [1982] 3 All ER 225). These questions are discussed generally in Chapters 5 and 8 below. Both receivers and liquidators may, however, be liable for VAT chargeable on supplies made after their appointment (see Chapter 9 below).

Administrators

1.15   The position of administrators is different again. During an administration, corporation tax liabilities cannot be enforced (except where the Crown can avail itself of a set-off) although they continue to accrue. If the administration is followed by a liquidation, then the tax before the date the liquidation begins will rank either preferentially or as an unsecured claim. If, however, the company is to survive, then it will be necessary for the administrator to arrange for the corporation tax debts to be paid or compromised (e.g. in a voluntary arrangement). These aspects are discussed in detail in Chapters 6 and 7 below. Administrators will have to account for VAT chargeable on supplies made after their appointment (see Chapter 9 below).

Chapter 2

Preferential Debts for Tax

The historical background

2.1   The Crown, by virtue of the Royal Prerogative, originally enjoyed a priority in bankruptcy for all taxes (*Re Henley & Co CA 1878, 1 TC 209*). This priority was first cut down by the *Bankruptcy Act 1849*, and analogous provisions were subsequently introduced into and extended by the Companies Acts. The Crown now only ranks preferentially where the legislation provides, and is otherwise an unsecured creditor. See, for detailed discussion, *Food Controller v Cork HL, [1923] AC 647* and *Re Pratt CA 1950, 31 TC 506*. Arguments based on the Royal Prerogative have been rejected by the courts as inconsistent with modern provisions for recovery of tax in insolvency quite recently in *Re Herbert Berry Associates Ltd (in liquidation) HL 1977, 52 TC 113* (a case on distress for unpaid tax) and *Re Cushla Ltd Ch D, [1979] STC 615* (a case on Crown set-off).

2.2   The logic of Crown preference for unpaid tax was considered in detail by the Cork Committee, in Chapter 32 of their Report (Cmnd 8558). They rejected the argument that debts for taxes, being debts owed "to the community", should be paid in priority to debts owed to private persons, on the convincing ground that the loss of a bad debt is likely to be felt far less keenly by the national exchequer, a view supported by judicial authority in Scottish law. However, they accepted that different considerations apply to tax claimed in circumstances where the insolvent party has acted as a kind of tax collector, as in the case of PAYE or national insurance contributions. The Committee also included in this category the Crown's claim for VAT, a point which has subsequently caused some controversy.

2.3   The chief result of the Cork review was the introduction of *IA 1986*, which made a number of major changes to the law relating to preferential debts. Most notably, the Crown's preference for assessed taxes was abolished while the preferential period for VAT was reduced from twelve months to six months. The Crown's preference for "collected" taxes was, however, largely preserved.

The present position

2.4   The law relating to preferential debts is contained in *IA 1986, ss 175, 176, 6 Sch. IA 1986, ss 175(1), 386(1)* provide that the preferential debts listed in *IA 1986, 6 Sch* are to be paid 'in priority to all other debts'. It applies to every mode of winding up, thus including both voluntary and compulsory liquidation. It also applies to certain receiverships by virtue of *IA 1986, s 40*. The specific receivership provisions are mentioned further in 2.21 below.

2.5   Preferential debts rank in a liquidation after the expenses of the winding up, which include for example the costs of realising the company's assets and the liquidator's remuneration. Where assets are insufficient to meet the preferential debts in full, they rank equally among themselves and abate in equal proportions. [*IA 1986, s 175(2)(a)*].

Statutory charge where distress has been levied

2.6   It is specifically provided in the case of compulsory liquidation that, where distress has been levied on the company's goods or effects during the three months ending with the date of the winding up order, the chattels in question or the proceeds of sale of them are to be charged for the benefit of the company with payment of the preferential debts to the extent that the company's property is for the time being insufficient to meet them. [*IA 1986, s 176(2)*]. A person who has, accordingly, surrendered goods or effects or made a payment to the company ranks as a preferential creditor in respect of the amount of the proceeds of sale of the goods or of the payment, except as against so much of the company's property as is available for preferential creditors by virtue of the surrender or payment. [*IA 1986, s 176(3)*]. This includes distress levied by the Inland Revenue or Customs & Excise as is evident from the *Memco* case, discussed in the following paragraphs. The provisions in *IA 1986* differ from *CA 1985, s 614(4)* (and indirectly *CA 1948, s 319(7)*), which they replaced. *CA 1985, s 614(4)* referred to persons 'distraining or having distrained' within the three-month period; while what is now *IA 1986, s 176(3)* was formerly expressed as follows:

> 'In respect of any money paid under such a charge, the landlord or other person has the same rights of priority as the person to whom the payment is made.'

The Memco case

2.7   The old wording was considered in *Re Memco Engineering Ltd Ch D, [1985] 3 All ER 267*. The case concerned a distress levied by Customs & Excise for unpaid VAT which had been made, but not completed, at the time that liquidation began. In addition to considering the nature of an incomplete distress for tax generally in the context of a compulsory liquidation (a point discussed in 4.24 below), the court had also to consider whether the distress fell within the periods affected by *CA 1985, s 614(4)* and, if so, how the claim by Customs should be treated, in view of the special rights of priority conferred by the provision. Distress had been levied on the goods in question more than three months before the winding up order, but they had not been sold until some months after it had been made.

2.8   The court held that the distress was within *CA 1985, s 614(4)* since the words 'distraining or having distrained' denote a continuous process. The new wording refers only to a person who has "distrained", and in view of the judge's comments, *IA 1986, s 176(2)* will now apply even where a distress has been completed (i.e. the goods have been sold) within the three months before the winding up order. This is without prejudice to *IA 1986, s 128*, which provides that a distress put in force after commencement of the winding up is void (and see also the discussion of *IA 1986, s 126*, in 4.24 below, concerning distress made but not completed at the time of commencement of the winding up).

2.9   On the final point considered, the judgment was more controversial. There are two possible views, of which the first is that the proceeds of sale of the goods are to be treated as a fund for payment of the preferential creditors and the distrainor, *pari passu*. In the *Memco* case, Customs & Excise were anyway a preferential creditor so that on this argument the whole of their claim would have ranked preferentially to the extent of the distress. The other view, rejected in the *Memco* case, is that the distress fund should be used to pay out only the original preferential claims, so that the distrainor would then stand in the shoes of the preferential creditors to the extent of the distress, in the words of the judge, as a "postponed preferential creditor". On that view, Customs would have proved against the distress fund for the part of their claim that was originally preferential; but to the extent of the distress, they would have proved for the balance of their claim as "postponed preferential creditors". The latter view is supported by a Hong Kong case, *Official Receiver v Ho Shui-Wah, [1967] HKLR 116*, concerned with an analogous provision of the Hong Kong Bankruptcy Ordinance. In the *Memco* case, Mervyn Davies J took the first view, preferring not to complicate the rules of priority by introducing a further class of creditor. It is submitted that this is a surprising result, in view of the wording of the provision, and it is a pity that the principle of subrogation (whereby a third party meeting a claim may, in some circumstances, stand in the shoes of the original claimant) was not dealt with expressly as this would on the face of it have met the judge's objections to the "postponed preferential creditor" solution. The wording now contained in *IA 1986, s 176(3)* purports to deal with the point arising in the *Memco* case. It states that the distrainor *is* a preferential creditor to the extent of his distress, but *not* against the distress fund. The Revenue's practice in compulsory liquidations under the new legislation is expected to be set out in regulations made by the Department of Trade and Inland Revenue some time in 1991 after the date of writing (these regulations will replace the previous regulations made under *CWR 1949, Rule 224* reproduced in Appendix I of the first edition of this book). See 4.25 below.

The "relevant date"

2.10   *IA 1986, s 387* defines the "relevant date" which is relevant in determining the periods in respect of which the Crown ranks preferentially for taxes under certain different corporate insolvency procedures, under *IA 1986, 6 Sch.* The relevant date depends on the type of insolvency concerned. In relation to a company which is being wound up:

'(a)   if the winding up is by the court, and the winding-up order was made immediately upon the discharge of an administration order, the relevant date is the date of the making of the administration order;

(b)   if the case does not fall within paragraph (a) and the company—

(i)   is being wound up by the court, and

(ii)   had not commenced to be wound up voluntarily before the date of the making of the winding-up order,

the relevant date is the date of the appointment (or first appointment) of a provisional liquidator or, if no such appointment has been made, the date of the winding-up order;

(c)   if the case does not fall within either paragraph (a) or (b), the relevant date is the date of the passing of the resolution for the winding up of the company.' [*IA 1986, s 387(3)*].

In relation to a company in receivership, the relevant date is (in England) the date of appointment of the receiver by debenture holders. [*IA 1986, s 387(4)*].

Types of preferential debts for tax

Income and corporation tax

2.11   The preferential claim for assessed tax (i.e. income tax and corporation tax) was abolished by *IA 1986*. The fact that pre-insolvency tax liabilities do not now rank preferentially has significant consequences in receivership and liquidation since the income and corporation tax liabilities are merely unsecured claims unless they relate to periods after commencement of a liquidation when they may fall to be paid as an expense of the liquidation or, in the case of corporation tax on chargeable gains, after the liquidator's remuneration up to the Official Receiver's scale, under *Ins R 1986, Rule 4.218(1)(p)* (see further 8.37–8.42 below). Non-assessable taxes due to be withheld from payments never have ranked preferentially (see *Lang Propeller Ltd CA 1926, 11 TC 46*), except for certain PAYE deductions and amounts under the construction industry tax deduction scheme, discussed in the following paragraphs.

Tax deductions: PAYE and sub-contractors' payments

2.12 The only preferential debts due to the Inland Revenue are those due at the "relevant date" (see 2.10 above) in respect of income tax deductions required under PAYE and the construction industry sub-contractors' scheme. These debts are set out in *IA 1986, 6 Sch 1–2* and are the amounts due in respect of the twelve months next before the "relevant date". It should be noted that PAYE deductions made by a company are not themselves impressed with any trust in favour of the Revenue (see *Attorney General v Jeanne Antoine KB 1949, 31 TC 213*).

2.13 PAYE may have to be deducted from payments made to employees in satisfaction of their own separate preferential claims for remuneration under *IA 1986, 6 Sch 9–12*. This is, however, a liability arising in the receivership or liquidation itself, and is a separate matter from the preferential claim for PAYE. Although the point may not be free from doubt, the statutory limit for employees' preferential claims for wages (currently £800) is, accordingly, taken as the figure before deduction of PAYE tax. It is understood that the Inland Revenue consider that the preferential claim applies to income tax on emoluments actually paid in the twelve month period, not income tax which has been payable in that period, consistent with the treatment of NIC described in 2.20 below.

VAT and other debts due to Customs & Excise

VAT

2.14 The VAT preferential debt is now set out in *IA 1986, 6 Sch 3*. This reads concisely:

'*Debts due to Customs and Excise*

Any value added tax which is referable to the period of 6 months next before the relevant date . . .'

The definition of "relevant date" set out in 2.10 above applies. Unlike the preferential claim for assessed tax (now abolished), the VAT claim *must* be in respect of tax for the six month period immediately preceding that date. The VAT "referable to" the preferential period is defined in *IA 1986, 6 Sch 3*, which states that:

'(a) where the whole of the prescribed accounting period to which any value added tax is attributable falls within the 6-month period, the whole amount of that tax is referable to that period; and

(b) in any other case the amount of any value added tax which is referable to the 6-month period is the proportion of the tax which is equal to such proportion (if any) of the accounting reference period in question as falls within the 6-month period.'

"Prescribed" in (a) means prescribed under *VAT Gen R 1985, Reg 58(1)*. The effect of (b) is that the preferential part of the VAT for the first accounting period falling across the start of the six months is to be computed on a time-apportionment basis. The final accounting period is dealt with very neatly by *VAT Gen R 1985, Reg 58(3)(a)* which provides that an accounting period ends on the day before that on which control of the assets of a registered person passes to, *inter alia*, a receiver or liquidator who is then responsible for filing a return in respect of that period not later than the last day of the month next following the end of the period (see 9.11–9.12 below).

2.15 The question of how group registration affects the preferential debt was raised in *Re Nadler Enterprises Ltd Ch D, [1980] STC 457*. That case concerned two companies, both in liquidation, which had been members of a group VAT registration. Customs & Excise sought to prove preferentially in the liquidation of Nadler Enterprises Ltd (which, presumably, had the money) for VAT unpaid by the representative member of the group, its parent Elizabeth Nadler Ltd (which, one assumes, did not). What is now *VATA 1983, s 29* provides that all members of a group registration 'shall be liable jointly and severally for any tax due from the representative member'. At issue was whether the VAT so due fell within the terms of the preferential claim. The liquidator's concern is understandable, since it is at first sight strange that a VAT liability for which the company was not required to account during the preferential period, and which was owed in the first instance by another legal person, can on demand be incorporated into the preferential claim. But, unsurprisingly in view of the clear wording of *section 29*, the judge held that it could be. The same result would follow in similar circumstances where the preferential claim arose in a receivership.

2.16 The situation in the *Nadler* case does not by any means exhaust the complexities which can arise with preferential claims and group registrations. For example, the provisions give no indication how VAT input tax recovered or credited or output tax paid by a representative member should be allocated within the group. This will have to be done (if at all) on a "just and equitable" basis if on the facts there is no basis for asserting a prior contractual course of dealing or (still more unlikely) a quasi-contractual remedy. It is, however, considered that another group member which has paid tax for which the representative member was primarily liable can be subrogated to Customs' preferential claim. Another difficulty arises where there are different preferential periods for different companies which do not correspond, in which case a possible view is that it is the latest six months of tax which is "referable to" the relevant period for each company.

2.17 Customs & Excise have, however, confirmed that they do not regard VAT due in respect of periods before a company joined a group registration as capable of falling within *VATA 1983, s 29(1)* and being recoverable from other group members.

Taxes on imports

2.18   The other point which arises in relation to the VAT preferential claim is whether it includes VAT due on importation. *VATA 1983, s 2(4)* provides that 'tax on the importation of goods shall be charged and payable as if it were a duty of customs'. This on the face of it excludes such VAT from all the usual collection procedures for VAT including the preferential claim. However, it is still VAT. Customs & Excise have no fixed practice on this point but are known to have accepted in individual cases that VAT on importation cannot be claimed preferentially. The point arises more frequently in considering whether the import agent or a bank guaranteeing the VAT is subrogated to the preferential claim than it does against Customs directly. There is no preferential claim for import duties.

Other debts due to Customs & Excise

2.19   Other preferential debts due to Customs & Excise include certain car tax [*IA 1986, 6 Sch 4*]; and certain other excise duties [*IA 1986, 6 Sch 5*]. (Under proposals contained in the Finance Bill published on 17 April 1991, excise duty on beer is to be included in the latter from an appointed day.)

National insurance contributions

2.20   Certain NIC also rank as preferential debts under *IA 1986, 6 Sch 6–7*. Those relevant to insolvent companies are the sums due on the "relevant date" on account of Class 1 contributions, which will include both primary and secondary contributions, and which became due in the twelve months next before the "relevant date". The same definition of "relevant date" applies as for the Inland Revenue and Customs & Excise debt under *IA 1986* (see 2.10 above). Both kinds of Class 1 contributions become payable in any tax week where earnings are paid [*SSA 1975, s 4(2)*], so that the preferential claim will apply to contributions that have become payable on earnings paid in the previous twelve months. Contributions will accordingly only be due preferentially in respect of emoluments actually paid before the "relevant date". There will be no contributions payable in respect of earnings which have accrued but are unpaid at that date, or which are suffered by reimbursing the Department of Employment when subrogated to the employee's preferential claim.

Preferential debts in receiverships

2.21   An administrative receiver appointed (or person taking possession) under a floating charge before commencement of liquidation must also discharge the preferential debts. [*IA 1986, s 40*]. The "relevant date" to be taken is then the date of appointment of the receiver (see 2.10 above). As will be appreciated, this different date can be a point of some

13

importance when the liabilities are computed for the period in question. If assets are insufficient to discharge preferential creditors in an earlier liquidation, recourse may be had to assets subject to a floating charge—see further 5.4 below. [*IA 1986, s 175(2)(b)*].

Duty to pay preferential debts

2.22   An administrative receiver or liquidator who fails to discharge preferential debts may be held personally liable for a breach of statutory duty, and the funds may be recoverable from the actual payee. So, in *CIR v Goldblatt Ch D 1971, 47 TC 483*, a receiver, who had been removed, delivered assets back to the company which passed them to the debenture-holder without discharging the preferential claim for income tax and profits tax of which all parties were (or should have been) aware. Both the receiver and the debenture-holder were held liable to pay the tax. Similarly, in *The Watchmakers' Alliance and Ernest Goode's Stores Ltd Ch D 1905, 5 TC 117* liquidators paid away the assets to the contributories without making any provision for a Crown debt for income tax and were held liable to pay the amount in question. In *Re Aidall Ltd CA 1932, 18 TC 617*, a liquidator failed to pay a preferential claim for super-tax and distributed the available funds to a person claiming to be entitled in the liquidation as a contributory. The court acknowledged the liquidator's personal liability and considered that it was entitled to make an order for repayment to the liquidator by the person who had received the funds, so that the tax liability could be discharged.

Interest and penalties

2.23   Interest and penalties for unpaid taxes do not normally rank as preferential claims as they are not "tax" within the meaning of *6 Sch 1, 2*. The position is discussed more fully in Chapter 16.

Chapter 3

Crown Set-Off

Crown set-off in a liquidation

General principle

3.1   The principle of set-off in bankruptcy and liquidation, now enshrined in *Ins R 1986, Rule 4.90*, is a very old one, having been in existence according to Brightman J in *Re D H Curtis (Builders) Ltd Ch D 1977, [1978] 2 All ER 183* for more than 300 years. It is to be distinguished from the type of set-off sometimes available in contract law. Its different purpose was expressed in a frequently quoted judgment of Parke B in *Forster v Wilson 1843, 12 M & W 191* at pp 203–204:

> 'The right of set-off in bankruptcy does not appear to rest on the same principle as the right of set-off between solvent parties. The latter is given by the statutes of set-off . . . to prevent cross actions . . . But, under the bankrupt statutes, the mutual credit clause has not been so construed. The object of this clause . . . is not to avoid cross actions, for none would lie against assignees, and one against the bankrupt would be unavailing, but to do substantial justice between the parties, where a debt is really due from the bankrupt to the debtor to his estate . . .'.

Rule 4.90 is made pursuant to *IA 1986, s 411, 8 Sch 12*. It substantially re-enacts *Bankruptcy Act 1914, s 31*, formerly applied to liquidations by *CA 1985, s 612*. It is not applicable to administrative or other receiverships. Its effect is to provide that, where there have been mutual dealings, before liquidation, between the company and a creditor, the mutual obligations resulting from those dealings are to be set off against each other and the creditor is to be entitled to prove only for the balance (if any). The particular difficulty encountered in the context of tax liabilities is the requirement for mutuality of dealings.

3.2   *Ins R 1986, Rule 4.90* is as follows:

'*Mutual credit and set-off*

(1)   This Rule applies where, before the company goes into liquidation there have been mutual credits, mutual debts or other mutual dealings between the company and any creditor of the

company proving or claiming to prove for a debt in the liquidation.

(2)   An account shall be taken of what is due from each party to the other in respect of the mutual dealings, and the sums due from one party shall be set off against the sums from the other.

(3)   Sums due from the company to another party shall not be included in the account taken under paragraph (2) if that other party had notice at the time they became due that a meeting of creditors had been summoned under section 98 or (as the case may be) a petition for the winding up of the company was pending.

(4)   Only the balance (if any) of the account is provable in the liquidation. Alternatively (as the case may be) the amount shall be paid to the liquidator as part of the assets.'

The date at which set-off is to be taken is, in the case of a company, the date of commencement of the liquidation. Where a company is wound up voluntarily this means the date of passing of the resolution. In the case of a compulsory winding up, the date is the presentation of the petition (not the date of the winding up order). (See *Re City Equitable Fire Insurance Co Ltd (No 2), [1930] 2 Ch 293* per Lord Hanworth at p 310; *Re Dynamics Corporation of America (in liquidation) Ch D 1975, [1976] 1 WLR 757* per Oliver J at p 769). The application of *Rule 4.90* is mandatory: that is to say, the parties cannot contract out of it.

Application of set-off to the Crown

The early cases

3.3   It was long held, in a series of cases dating from the nineteenth century, that the principle of set-off could only apply to claims arising out of contract, because of the reference in what is now *Rule 4.90(1)(2)* to 'mutual credits, mutual debts or other mutual dealings'. This requirement of mutual dealings was regarded as of the essence of a claim for set-off and in its absence, no set-off was thought to arise. The two most important cases in which this principle was expressed were *Palmer v Day & Sons, [1895] 2 QB 618*, where a set-off by a firm of auctioneers between fees owed to them and the proceeds they held from the sale of some pictures was permitted; and *Re Mid-Kent Fruit Factory, [1896] 1 Ch 567*, where a claim by a company's solicitors to set off their outstanding fees against money they held on behalf of their clients to be applied for a special purpose was refused. In a key judgment in the latter case, Vaughan Williams J summarised the law as it then stood and affirmed that the indebtedness must arise out of contract. As will be appreciated, tax liabilities are not contract debts. See, for example, the speech of Lord Somervell of Harrow in *Government of India v Taylor HL, [1955] 1 All ER 292*, at p 301, where he said:

'Tax gathering is an administrative act, though, in settling the quantum, as well as in the final act of collection, judicial process may be involved. Our courts will apply foreign law if it is the proper law of a contract, the subject of a suit. Tax gathering is not a matter of contract, but of authority and administration as between the state and those within its jurisdiction'.

A similar point was made in *R v Vaccari CCA, [1958] 1 WLR 297* at p 299. The application of Crown set-off to tax liabilities was therefore thought to be doubtful.

The Curtis case

3.4   The line of authority summarised in the preceding paragraphs was not followed in what is now the leading authority in this area, *Re D H Curtis (Builders) Ltd Ch D 1977, [1978] 2 All ER 183*. The facts of the case were straightforward. The company went into voluntary liquidation in October 1974. At that time, it owed tax of £106.65 to the Inland Revenue and also owed £112.80 to the Department of Health and Social Security. A VAT refund was due of £219.45, which the Crown wished to set off under what is now *Rule 4.90*. The liquidator sought a declaration that they could not do so. Brightman J (as he then was) felt as he put it an "overwhelming conviction" that the judgment of Vaughan Williams J was wrong. He based this on the statement of the purpose of set-off in bankruptcy, as expressed in the *Forster* case (and set out in 3.1 above), as 'to do substantial justice between the bankrupt and his creditors', and said, at p 190:

> 'If that is the purpose of set-off in bankruptcy, one would expect to find that any mutual demands capable of being proved in bankruptcy can be the subject-matter of set-off whether or not arising out of contract'.

Support was found for this view in the original wording of the *Bankruptcy Act 1825* and the *Bankruptcy Act 1849* which referred to 'every debt or demand hereby made provable'. Thus, in the *Curtis* case, the VAT refund was set off against the PAYE and NIC claims.

The Cushla case

3.5   The *Curtis* case was approved in a subsequent High Court judgment of Vinelott J in *Re Cushla Ltd Ch D, [1979] STC 615* where he referred to the reasoning of Brightman J as "lucid and compelling". This company was an Isle of Man incorporated company, in compulsory liquidation following a court order on 24 February 1975. The sum of £4,726 was, again, due to the Inland Revenue (after deducting a preferential claim of £200) and a balance of £951 to the Department of Health and Social Security. There was a VAT input of £4,055.42 owed to the company at the date of winding up and, as in the *Curtis* case, the

Crown sought to set these obligations off against each other. However, through a computer error £3,651.28 was accidentally paid to the liquidator by Customs & Excise. The liquidator pursued the issue in the *Curtis* case, as to whether the right of set-off could apply; and also argued that, as the payment made to him in error did reflect an actual debt, he should be entitled to keep the money. The liquidator's first argument was on a different basis from those addressed by Brightman J in the *Curtis* case. The liquidator in *Cushla* argued that, apart from these issues, the question was whether the right of set-off could apply to the Crown at all. He based his case on the old right of unrestricted priority for its debts enjoyed by the Crown under the Royal Prerogative and suggested that the set-off provisions were inconsistent with this and could never have been intended to apply to Crown debts. This argument was firmly dismissed, as was another argument that Crown debts are of a particular nature in that there is no true mutuality in dealings between the Crown and a subject. For instance, the same rights and remedies are not available to the taxpayer in proceedings against the Crown under the *Crown Proceedings Act 1947* (discussed further in 3.8–3.11 below). On this point, the judge held that there was no authority to support the arguments and that the 1947 Act could not apply. Perhaps unsurprisingly, the liquidator was also unsuccessful in his second submission, that he should be entitled to keep the money paid to him in error. This was held to be money paid under a mistake of fact and recoverable at law, to which the liquidator had no right by reason of the mandatory operation of the set-off provisions.

The Cullen case

3.6 The *Curtis* case has now been considered by the Court of Appeal in *R A Cullen Ltd v Nottingham Health Authority CA, The Times, 1 August 1986* where the company in liquidation had provided plumbing services to a hospital and its bill had been set off against arrears of NIC. The main issue in the case was whether (as the court in fact found) the Health Authority was to be regarded as an agent of the Secretary of State for the purpose of determining whether Crown set-off should apply but Sir Denys Buckley, in his judgment, observed that no suggestion was raised that Brightman J's decision was wrong, though it was referred to in argument in support of the application of the right of set-off to the particular facts.

Extent of Crown set-off

3.7 In the *Curtis* case Brightman J did not consider whether the right of set-off will necessarily apply to all amounts owing between an insolvent company and the Crown. In both the *Curtis* and *Cushla* cases, the amounts at issue were payments of a tax-like nature and in *Cullen* they were debts from and to the same Government Department. It is frequently assumed in practice that Crown set-off is generally available but, in fact, it is not absolutely clear from the cases referred to in this chapter whether the same set-off principle would necessarily apply in liquidation to all payments of different kinds. This might be doubted if the purpose of set-off is indeed to do substantial justice between the bankrupt and his creditors (but see the Scottish cases cited in 3.10 below for a similar question in receiverships). It would seem somewhat less than just that the body of creditors should be affected by the principle, in a sense an historical accident, that the Crown in all its departments is to be treated as a single indivisible entity. This was certainly the view of two independent review bodies, the Blagden Committee, which reported in 1957 (Cmnd 221), and the Cork Committee (Cmnd 8558). As the Cork Committee observed (Report, p 306), there is no mutuality between different taxes which are of a different nature or other impositions and contractual liabilities; while the practice can only operate in favour of the Crown, never against it (see further 3.9 below). The latter point was, as has been seen in 3.5 above, discussed (and rejected) in the *Cushla* case, and the issue is now in practice an academic one.

Relevance of Crown Proceedings Act 1947 to set-off in liquidation

3.8   In the context of administrative receiverships, questions may arise as to whether leave of the Court is necessary for the Crown to apply set-off, under the *Crown Proceedings Act 1947, s 35* (as discussed in 3.9) below. This point was not taken in the *Curtis* case, apparently because it was taken for granted that the leave would be given. The question was, however, discussed in *Cushla* and the *Cullen* case and these judgments confirm that the 1947 Act is irrelevant in a liquidation in England and Wales where the right of set-off is governed by *Rule 4.90* (not by "proceedings") and where it also appears that the Rules of the Supreme Court (discussed in the following paragraphs) are inapplicable. [*RSC Order 2, Rule 2*].

Crown set-off in administrative receivership

Crown Proceedings Act 1947 and Court Rules

3.9   As has already been noted, *Rule 4.90* is inapplicable to a company in administrative receivership. The position in administrative receivership is governed exclusively by the *Crown Proceedings Act 1947* and the general law of set-off as against assignees. It would seem that, in relation to tax liabilities, set-off will only be allowed to the Crown, and then only in respect of debts due at the date of appointment if the debts relate to the same Government Department, or the court grants leave. The Act requires Rules of Court to be made providing that a person should not be entitled without leave of the court to avail himself of any set-off or counterclaim in any proceedings by the Crown if either the subject matter of the set-off or counter-claim does not relate to the Government Department in the name of which the proceedings are brought, or the proceedings are brought in the name of the Attorney-General. [*Crown*

Proceedings Act 1947, s 35(2)(g)(ii)]. The Rule in question relating to the Supreme Court (i.e. High Court and above) is *RSC Order 77, Rule 6*, which is as follows:

'(1)   Notwithstanding Order 15, Rule 2, and Order 18, Rules 17 and 18 a person may not in any proceedings by the Crown make any counterclaim or plead a set-off if the proceedings are for the recovery of, or the counterclaim or set-off arises out of a right or claim to repayment in respect of, any taxes, duties or penalties.

(2)   Notwithstanding Order 15, Rule 2, and Order 18, Rules 17 and 18, no counterclaim may be made, or set-off pleaded, without the leave of the Court, by the Crown in proceedings against the Crown, or by any person in proceedings by the Crown—

   (a)   if the Crown is sued or sues in the name of a Government department and the subject-matter of the counterclaim or set-off does not relate to that department; or

   (b)   if the Crown is sued or sues in the name of the Attorney-General.

(3)   Any application for leave under this rule must be made by summons.'

The corresponding provision for the County Court is *County Court Rules 1981, Order 42, Rule 9*. For the purposes of *section 35(2)(g)(ii)* of the 1947 Act and the corresponding court rules, "tax" includes (*inter alia*) interest charged under *TMA 1970, Pt IX*. [*TMA 1970, s 69(b)*]. *RSC Order 77, Rule 6(1)* above is an interesting provision: it prevents an individual from, for example, setting off a debt due from the Crown which is totally unconnected with tax (say a premium bond win) against a tax liability. It also prevents set-off by a taxpayer between taxes (VAT and income tax for example) and in the present context prevents a receiver from himself claiming set-off in connection with proceedings by the Crown for the recovery of VAT. A rather inconclusive case where a taxpayer failed even to show that he was entitled to a tax repayment to set off was *Collis v Cadle Ch D 1955, 36 TC 204*.

Decided cases on equivalent Scottish legislation

3.10   There is no reported English authority on the question as to when leave will be given under *RSC Order 77, Rule 6(2)* set out in 3.9 above. There are, however, three cases on the Scottish equivalent, which derives from the *Crown Proceedings Act 1947, s 50*. In the first of these, *Atlantic Engine Co (1920) Ltd (in liquidation) v Lord Advocate CS, [1955] SLT 17*, the set-off arose out of the requisitioning of a company's business by the Ministry of Supply. The company owed money to the Ministry and also to the Admiralty and the Air Ministry representing overpayments on contracts for the supply of war materials. Set-off was permitted. The Lord President put it in this way:

'. . . but in this case I can discover no reason for not granting leave. The three Departments concerned were all contracting with the same company for the supply of the same class of war requirements, and it is difficult to conceive of a situation more favourable for treating the three administrative agencies as one for the purposes of the section.'

In *Laing (Liquidator of Inverdale Construction Co Ltd) v Lord Advocate CS, [1973] SLT (Notes) 81*, the Crown claimed in a liquidation for unpaid PAYE, and the company claimed for refunds and for regional premiums under the *Selective Employments Payments Act 1966*. As Lord Keith put it, 'both claims arose out of legislation of a fiscal character', and leave was again granted, on the basis that there was 'sufficient similarity between the nature of the claims on either side to make it appropriate to grant leave'. (As appears from these cases the *Crown Proceedings Act 1947* does apply to liquidations in Scotland, though not in England as discussed in 3.8 above.) The third and most recent case is *Smith v Lord Advocate (No 2) CS 1980, [1981] SLT 19*, where the company's claim was for payments due from the Ministry of Defence in respect of the construction of and repairs to naval works. The Crown claimed for repayment of loans and loan stock in favour of the Secretary of State for Industry and also for NIC and tax due to the Inland Revenue (the type of tax is not specified in the report). The court referred to the two earlier Scottish cases and adopted the approach in the *Atlantic Engine* case:

'. . . there seems considerable force in approaching a decision on the request for leave by asking firstly:— "Why should leave not be granted?" and then considering the other circumstances arising from the case.'

3.11 How far the Scottish cases are relevant to the English law is not clear. Certainly, the court in the *Smith* case stressed the distinctions between the Scottish and English legal system, and this point was also made by Vinelott J in the *Cushla* case where he referred to the *Laing* decision (at p 622h). It does, however, seem likely that the English courts will adopt a similar approach. Certainly, if the wide test in the *Smith* case is applicable, it is difficult to imagine circumstances when leave would not be given to the Crown.

Set-off and preferential claims

The Morel case

3.12 In *Re Cushla Ltd* (see 3.5 above), the Inland Revenue's preferential claim was deducted before the Crown's claim for outstanding tax and NIC was made. There is, however, more direct authority on the question whether a set-off should be applied first in satisfaction of the Crown's preferential or non-preferential claims. The leading case in this area was *Re E J Morel (1934) Ltd Ch D, [1961] 1 All ER 796* which concerned a company in compulsory liquidation. A bank had advanced certain money for payment of employees' wages and was, accordingly, subrogated to their preferential claim in respect of that money, as well as certain unsecured claims. The bank sought to set off money held on a different account against the non-preferential part of its claim, and it was held that it could not do so. Buckley J (as he then was) reached his conclusion in the following terms, at pp 804–805:

'In my view, the right solution for this problem is to treat the balance which results from the set-off as being non-preferential except to the extent that it can be demonstrated that the credit is insufficient to discharge the preferential claim in full. The result of the set-off is to give the creditor payment in full of his claim to the extent of the set-off, and in that way he is better off than creditors who merely have to rely on their right to prove and get a dividend. If he obtains, by set-off, payment in full, it seems reasonable that that payment in full should be treated as being in respect of that part of his debt which would rank first in priority. Moreover, the fact that if the preferential claim exceeds the amount of the credit to be set off against it, there would be some part of the preferential claim which demonstrably had not been paid off, and could still claim preference, is a circumstance that seems to demonstrate that my method of approaching the solution is the right one.'

The Unit 2 Windows case

3.13   Although the decision in the *Morel* case is an attractive one, it has now been rendered very doubtful following another High Court decision in *Re Unit 2 Windows Ltd Ch D, [1985] 3 All ER 647*, where this point was considered further. There, three possible solutions to the problem were proposed:

(a)   that the set-off should be applied against the non-preferential claim first (naturally enough, the preferred view advanced by what was then the DHSS, now the DSS);

(b)   that it should be applied rateably between the non-preferential and preferential claims; and

(c)   that it should be applied first against the preferential claim (the *Morel* approach).

Walton J rejected the first solution on the ground that Counsel for the Crown could offer no argument more substantial than that it favoured his client. But he also rejected the third argument, based on the *Morel* case, and the reasons he gave for it are interesting:

'Now it is to be observed (i) that that judge did not have the benefit of a full argument on the point. In particular, the "rateable" solution was not put forward by either counsel. (ii) The judge speaks of the result of set-off being to give the creditor payment in full of his claim to the extent of the set-off. As we have already seen, this is a somewhat dangerous simplification of the position. What [*section*] *31* [*Bankruptcy Act 1914*, now *Rule 4.90*] is directed towards is to establish precisely what was the claim of the creditor, and to the extent of the set-off he has no claim at all: it is not that that claim, or portion of a claim, has been paid off. (iii) The judge speaks of the solution he suggests being "reasonable". The question, however, is not whether it is a "reasonable" solution; reasonability often depends on the point of view of the person considering it: here both the Crown and the liquidator consider their own preferred solutions "reasonable". It surely is whether it is consistent with the terms of the section, which is entirely silent on the point, and which therefore cannot properly be construed, in effect, as giving the company the right of appropriation. (iv) And lastly, rather like the thirteenth stroke of the clock, which by itself casts doubt on all that has preceded it, the only circumstance relied on by Buckley J as demonstrating that his method of approaching the solution is the right one is one which cannot possibly, by any stretch of the imagination, do so. It happens to be a purely arithmetical result in the case before him that some part of the preferential claim could not be said on any footing to be extinguished.'

The judge held that the middle course was the correct one, that the set-off should be applied rateably, on the basis that 'equality, proportionate equality, is, in the circumstances of the silence of the relevant section, equity'. While issue might perhaps be taken with the "arithmetic" approach to the set-off provisions—having regard to the judgment of Parke B quoted in 3.1 above and also the points made in 3.7 above—it seems that the *Unit 2* decision must now be regarded as the leading authority on this question. Both it and the *Morel* case concerned companies in liquidation. In the past, the Crown departments accepted the application of the *Morel* case to receiverships also; the *Unit 2* decision is, it appears, now normally accepted as applicable to receiverships in its place although it is theoretically open to receivers to raise contrary arguments. Customs & Excise have, however, stated that they do not accept that the *Unit 2* decision applies to set-off made under *FA 1988, s 21* (see 20.11 below).

Pre- and post-insolvency debts

3.14 A set-off between obligations entered into before and after a liquidation is precluded by *Ins R 1986, Rule 4.90* and the statutory scheme for discharge of debts. The question is somewhat less clear in an administrative receivership, but it is considered that set-off is not available to the Crown across the date when a floating charge crystallises, e.g. by appointment of the receiver. The reasons are, first, that it is objectionable (and contrary to the intention of *IA 1986*) that a particular creditor should be entitled to obtain payment of a debt in priority to the order for payment prescribed by statute, such priority resulting only by virtue of events occurring after appointment. A principle can also be extracted from decided cases that a company's position should be frozen at the date of appointment of a receiver so that no set-off can in normal circumstances be raised as between activities before and after that date. In *Business Computers Ltd v Anglo-African Leasing Ltd Ch D, [1977] 1 WLR 578* set-off was claimed between debts one of which arose before, and the other after, notice of appointment of a receiver. Templeman J (as he then was) held that a set-off could not be permitted unless the second debt arose before notice was received, or arose out of the same contract, or was connected with it. The judgment does not in terms encompass tax liabilities but it seems likely that a set-off would be refused in respect of VAT. While other cases have found against receivers, it is submitted that these may be distinguished. *Rother Iron Works Ltd v Canterbury Precision Engineers Ltd CA, [1973] 1 All ER 394* is one of these, where the right of set-off accrued under a pre-existing contract out of rights which had already arisen at the date of appointment. Customs & Excise, in particular, formerly made an argument that VAT input tax repayments due after receivership should be set off against VAT due in respect of periods before that date. This argument was abandoned soon after what became *VATA 1983, s 14(7)* was introduced in 1982 which gave a similar statutory right. *Section 14(7)* has now been repealed but Customs in certain circumstances rely on *FA 1988, s 21* discussed further in 20.9–20.13 below.

Fixed charges on book debts

3.15 A further complication arises in relation to the fixed charges on book debts now commonly included in standard form floating charges. On the basis that a charge takes effect as an assignment of the assets it includes to the chargee, set-off should not be available in this case either. Both Inland Revenue and Customs & Excise now accept that a fixed charge on book debts will cover tax repayments where the date of registration of the charge precedes the date the entitlement to a tax credit arose, but this is subject to *FA 1988, s 21* where there are subsequent VAT liabilities unpaid and *VATA 1983, s 14(7)* where not all VAT returns have been made. See further 20.9–20.13 below. Debts included in the fixed charge would not therefore be eligible for Crown set-off.

Crown set-off in administration

3.16 As stated in 3.8 above, set-off is not a "proceeding" and nor is it a "legal process". Accordingly, the restriction in *IA 1986, s 11(3)(d)* on commencement or continuation of 'proceedings. . . or other legal process' during the period for which an administration order is in force is irrelevant to Crown set-off. The Crown is, therefore, entitled to set off debts it is owed against money which it would otherwise itself owe to the company in administration. Such amounts will be irrecoverable by the company or its administrator, as discussed in connection with administrative receiverships in 3.9–3.11 above.

Chapter 4

Distress for Unpaid Tax

Background

4.1   Distress (also called "distraint") is a summary remedy whereby, as an alternative to a court action, a creditor may seize the chattels of a debtor to satisfy the debt (or compel him to perform some other duty). This remedy was available to landlords and some others under the common law long before the introduction of income tax and has its roots in feudal times. A statutory power of distress for unpaid income tax, modelled on the common law, was included in the earliest taxing statutes. Its terminology survived largely unchanged in *TMA 1970* until 1989 but has now been a little modernised, both in that Act and in the corresponding VAT provisions.

4.2   Despite its feudal origins, evidence was given to the Keith Committee that distress is still regarded as an important weapon by the Inland Revenue and Customs & Excise against recalcitrant taxpayers. The Keith Committee considered the modern distress powers in some detail and made three recommendations. These were, first, that the terminology of *TMA 1970* should be brought up to date; secondly, that the powers of forcible entry for distress by the Revenue and Customs should be subject to "judicial overview"; and thirdly, that statutory penalties should be introduced for breaches of walking possession agreements (Report, Ch 24.2, Vol 2). These recommendations were implemented as regards VAT (although the powers of forcible entry have since been revoked). The Revenue initially accepted all three recommendations in their December 1986 consultative document 'The Inland Revenue and the Taxpayer', and drafted proposals to put the three recommendations into effect. In their July 1988 consultative document 'Keith: Further Proposals', they withdrew the proposal introducing a penalty for breach of walking possession agreements, because it appeared 'doubtful that the penalty would be effective or could be collected'. The remaining proposals were introduced in *FA 1989, s 152* but have not at the time of writing been brought into effect by an appointed day order, the intention being to bring the amendments into effect at the same time as regulations to be made by the Treasury for costs, some time in 1991.

4.3   The Crown's powers of distress were also considered by the earlier Cork Committee which recommended total abolition of the remedy on the same grounds as, and consistently with, its recommendation for abolition of the Crown's priority for assessed taxes (see 2.2 above) (Report, p 374). The recommendation for the abolition of distress was not accepted by the Government, although the corporation and income tax preferential claim was abolished by *IA 1986*.

4.4   As well as the power of distress still enjoyed by landlords, statutory powers of distress are available to local authorities for arrears of community charge and business rates, but these powers, and the Scottish remedy of "poinding" under *TMA 1970, ss 63, 63A* and *VAT Gen R 1985, Reg 66* are outside the scope of this book. It should, however, be noted that under the old law, i.e. before the *Debtors (Scotland) Act 1987*, tax charged in England was held to be recoverable under the Scottish process (*Rutherford v Lord Advocate CS 1931, 16 TC 145*). The statutory powers of distress for taxes apply in Northern Ireland (as well as England and Wales).

Comparison with other distress powers

4.5   Interpretation of the statutory powers of distress for unpaid taxes relies heavily on the model of the common law remedy which it resembles in many respects (for example, both require a five-day minimum period of retention of impounded goods). Perhaps for obvious reasons, there is a relative lack of legal authority on distress for taxes although such reported cases as do exist are referred to below. However, the statutory provisions regulating landlords' distress, notably the various Law of Distress Amendment Acts and subordinate legislation, do not apply to distress for unpaid taxes, and, despite their resemblance, it seems that the two remedies are different in their nature. The courts will prefer to rely on the words of the statute where these are clear in themselves, and may refuse to import the common law reliefs and restrictions into the statutory power. So, it was held under the early law relating to distress for tax, by Lord Mansfield, that a distress for taxes is really in the nature of an execution (*Hutchins v Chambers 1758, 1 Burr 579*). This dictum was quoted with approval more recently by Bray J in *MacGregor v Clamp & Son 1913, [1914] 1 KB 288* at p 291. How far this difference applies is, however, unclear. For example, in two recent cases, it was stressed that Lord Mansfield's dictum does not apply in the context of the Companies Acts (*Re Herbert Berry Associates Ltd (in liquidation) HL 1977, 52 TC 113* and *Re Memco Engineering Ltd Ch D, [1985] 3 All ER 267*). The Revenue have, however, confirmed to the author that they consider that a distress for taxes is comparable with a landlord's distress and not with an execution by a judgment creditor, for the following reasons:

'(a)   There is no statutory definition of the word "distress" in the *TMA 1970* (which, at *ss 61–62*, governs distress for taxes). The procedure provided for by the Act—i.e. a "self-help" remedy, rather than a process founded on a judicial or quasi-judicial decision—is very similar to landlord's distress. Both these factors strongly suggest that "distress for taxes" connotes distress as at common law. The *TMA 1970* does, of course, have its origins in a time when landlord's distress was a more common event than it is today.

(b) It is clear that a distress cannot be described as an execution. In *Potts v Hickman HL, [1940] 4 All ER 491*, it was argued that distress for rates was in law an execution. Both the Court of Appeal and the House of Lords accepted that "execution" meant "execution under a judgment":

> "An execution is essentially the process of a court; it is the final step in a cause, and proceeds from a judgment". (Goddard LJ, delivering the Court of Appeal's judgment).

The Court of Appeal thought that the decision of the Justices (to issue a distress warrant) was a judgment—the House of Lords held it was not. It is significant that the claim that a distress was an execution failed even in connection with distress for rates, which is a process of a judicial nature. Distress for rates requires the issue of a summons, requiring the ratepayer to appear before the Justices, at which hearing the rating authority must prove the liability. The procedure laid down by *TMA 1970, s 61* is quite different and has nothing even resembling a judgment: a Collector is empowered to levy distress on his own initiative following a bare demand as a "self-help" remedy. He only needs to resort to the General Commissioners (or Justices of the Peace once *FA 1989, s 152* is implemented) if he requires in addition a warrant to break open premises.

(c) The view that there is any distinction between the effect of a distress by a landlord and that of a distress for taxes was rejected in *Re Herbert Berry Associates Ltd, supra*—see e.g. Lord Russell at p 135D. The argument that a distress for taxes was a form of execution was raised (and failed) before Templeman J: it was abandoned altogether on appeal.

The basis for this distinction between distress and execution is not merely accidental or historical. It is grounded in the fundamentally different natures of the remedies. Execution consists of the taking of chattels so that they may be sold to satisfy a debt due. Until sale, the property in them remains in the debtor (*Giles v Grover HL, (1832) 1 Cl & Fin 72*, cited at 45/1/9 in *RSC Order 45*).

Distress on the other hand, is a taking of goods by way of pledge. (Halsbury's Laws 4th ed, Vol 13, para 201). As a result, the distrainor obtains, from the moment when possession is taken a special property in the goods (*ibid*, Vol 36, para 123). This right is more than a mere right of retention.

A floating charge, whilst a present security, does not become a charge on particular assets unless the charge has "crystallised". Until that time, it is only a charge on a "fund" of assets, which may increase or decrease. If, before crystallisation, the fund has been depleted, the charge can only fix on the residue. See, for example, *Evans v Rival Granite Quarries Ltd, [1910] 2 KB 979* at p 999 per Buckley LJ:

> "A floating security is . . . a floating mortgage applying to every item comprised in the security, but not specifically affecting any item until some event occurs . . . which causes it to crystallise into a fixed security."

Execution does not have the effect of depleting the fund of assets within the scope of the floating charge until sale:

> "When in these cases (*Re Standard Manufacturing Co Ltd, [1891] 1 Ch 627* and *Re Opera Ltd, [1891] 3 Ch 260*) the goods were seized in execution, the goods were not by such seizure finally alienated from the company (for the company might have paid out the execution), so that time was left for the rights of the debenture-holders to develop into a fixed charge . . .". (Fletcher Moulton LJ in *Evans v Rival Granite, supra* at p 996).

Distress, however, does deplete the fund of assets: the debenture holder's charge can only crystallise on goods which are not already subject to prior rights, namely the special property of the distrainor.

At Halsbury's Laws 4th ed, Vol 13, para 204 it is said that:

> "The right to distrain for unpaid rates or taxes or under the summary jurisdiction of Magistrates are more analagous to execution than to the common law right of a landlord to distrain for rent . . .".

This statement is derived from four cases: *Hutchins v Chambers 1758, 1 Burr 579*; *MacGregor v Clamp & Son 1913, [1914] 1 KB 288*; *McCreagh v Cox and Ford KB, (1923) 92 LJKB 855*; and *Swaffer v Mulcahy 1932, [1934] 1 KB 608*.

The first point to note is that only *MacGregor v Clamp* concerned distress of poor rate or tithe rentcharge. Both the latter were governed by a distress warrant procedure which was of a judicial nature, and did not involve a "self-help" remedy. Lord Mansfield's dictum that distress for poor rate was 'more analagous to an execution than a distress at common law' in *Hutchins v Chambers* makes sense in context: as applied to distress for taxes it does not. The same comment applies to *McCreagh's* and *Swaffer's* cases.

In *MacGregor's* case, there was a distress for income tax. Bray J repeated Lord Mansfield's dictum in *Hutchins v Chambers*, and Lush J also said that 'the process is readily analogous to execution on a judgment'. These dicta are inconsonant with *Potts v Hickman*, and moreover they are, as a matter of fact, inapplicable to distress for taxes. Further, in all four cases, the real issue was the extent to which statutory restrictions on distress for rent applied to statutory distresses. The distinction drawn by Lord Mansfield between a common law distress and a statutory distress was not one derived from their respective procedures, or from the nature of the rights given to the distrainor *vis à vis* third parties, but was between a distress to enforce a right to money *simpliciter*, (as in statutory distresses) and a distress to enforce a right issuing out of land, (i.e. the right to rent). The question of the rights conferred by a distress was never considered. In the result, I do not think the passage in Halsbury which I quoted is a reliable guide to the answer to that question.'

Inland Revenue distress

Extent of the power

4.6   The Inland Revenue's power of distress for unpaid tax is conferred by *TMA 1970, s 61(1)*, which has been modernised by *FA 1989, s 152* in accordance with the Keith Committee's recommendations, with effect from a date in 1991 which at the date of writing has yet to be appointed. The Revenue's intention is that the modernised wording should not alter the powers contained in the provisions except in two respects, noted below. See IRPR 14 March 1989, para 34, Tolley's Official Tax Statements 1989–90, 5.329. *TMA 1970, s 61(1)* (as modernised) now reads as follows:

'If a person neglects or refuses to pay the sum charged, upon demand made by the collector, the collector may distrain upon the goods and chattels of the person charged (in this section referred to as "the person in default").'

The power of distress applies to income tax, capital gains tax, corporation tax and development land tax [*TMA 1970, s 118(1)*] as well as to interest on tax. [*TMA 1970, s 69(a)*]. It is extended to PAYE deductions [*ITER 1973, Reg 28*], to NIC [*SSCR 1979, Reg 46*], to deductions from payments to sub-contractors [*Income Tax (Sub-Contractors in the Construction Industry) Regulations 1975, SI 1975 No 1960, Reg 9*] and to SDRT. [*Stamp Duty Reserve Tax Regulations 1980, SI 1986 No 1711, Sch Pt II*]. The power of distress does not apply to stamp duty, capital transfer tax or inheritance tax.

Demand and refusal

4.7   Before distress can lawfully be levied, there must be both a demand for tax and a neglect or refusal to pay. [*TMA 1970, s 61(1)*]. The demand required is the familiar application for the payment of tax which must be served at the "place of last abode" of a taxpayer under *TMA 1970,* *s 60*. In an old case where a Collector of Taxes distrained immediately after making demand when the occupier of the premises was absent (*Gibbs v Stead 1828, 8 B & C 528*) it was held that a reasonable time must elapse between the time a demand is made and the distress. In a later case also, where an assessment for tax due under Schedule E from a company's employee was made at the company's office which he rarely attended, and was not received before distress was levied at his home, it was held that the assessment was invalid so that the distress was not properly made and the taxpayer was entitled to damages for wrongful distress (*Berry v Farrow 1913, [1914] 1 KB 632*). However, a taxpayer cannot raise any objection to the assessment in respect of which demand is made in distress or other recovery proceedings (*Simpkin v Robinson 1881, 45 LT 221, CIR v Pearlberg CA 1953, 34 TC 57*). Such matters can only be dealt with on an appeal against the assessment.

Time limits

4.8   There is no time limit for distress specified in the Act and the remedy is available at any time when recovery proceedings can be instituted generally. The Collector is restricted by common law to carrying out distress only between the hours of sunrise and sunset. Distress is not undertaken on a Sunday, Bank or Public Holiday. In fact, the Revenue's practice is rather more generous than the cases quoted in the foregoing paragraphs require. Normally, a tax demand is followed by a special letter mentioning the Revenue's powers of distraint, and after a further interval (which may vary) a personal visit is made by the Collector himself. An exception to this is where a defaulter has had distress levied on him within the two previous years. In that case, unless he is an employer owing PAYE deductions, a telephone call will usually be made instead. The purpose of the visit or call is to ensure that the taxpayer is aware of his debt and that there are no special circumstances justifying non-payment. Such calls may well also make it difficult for a taxpayer to argue at a later stage that he was unaware of the liability. They provide an opportunity for the defaulter to settle his liabilities before the weapon of distress is used, and he becomes liable for payment of costs.

Role of Collectors of Taxes

4.9   The persons responsible for levying distress under *TMA 1970, s 61(1)* are Collectors of Taxes. Formerly, a warrant had to be issued to enable a Collector to distrain in an individual case. Now, he is entitled to rely on his ordinary warrant of appointment under *TMA 1970, s 1(2)* except where it is necessary to break open premises, when a warrant must be specially obtained for the purpose. In the past, such a warrant needed only to be signed by the General Commissioners. In evidence to the Keith Committee, the Inland Revenue said that only one application for such a warrant had been made between 1960 and 1980, and was then refused. Notwithstanding this, the Keith Committee recommended the introduction of a judicial overview of this power, and both Customs & Excise and, more recently, the Revenue have agreed to implement this recommendation. (Customs introduced this safeguard although their power of forcible entry has been subsequently revoked.) The Revenue have introduced an amendment to *TMA 1970, s 61(2)* by *FA 1989, s 152(3)*, expected to be brought into effect some time in 1991 after the date of writing, which provides that:

'a justice of the peace, on being satisfied by information on oath that there is reasonable ground for believing that a person is neglecting or refusing to pay a sum charged, may issue a warrant authorising a collector to break open, in the daytime, any house or premises, calling to his assistance any constable.'

There is no legal necessity for a Collector to be accompanied, but the instructions issued to Collectors by the Board of Inland Revenue require a bailiff to be present whenever distress is levied. This has obvious advantages for the Collector (and a bailiff's expertise in valuation may also prevent an excessive distraint).

Manner of distress

4.10   A distress is made by seizure of the chattels distrained. Seizure may be actual (e.g. taking one or more items and declaring the distress made) or constructive (e.g. walking around the premises so as to demonstrate the intention of distraining). For cases on rent, see, *inter alia, Cramer & Co Ltd v Mott QB 1870, LR 5 QB 357* and *Swann v Falmouth 1828, 8 B & C 456*. No particular words, or form, are required, provided the intention is clear. In the case of rent, a notice or memorandum of seizure must also be left at the premises, and this practice is also followed by the Revenue who use a standard Distraint Notice and Inventory (Form C204A). This notice is not a legal requirement in the case of distress for taxes, but serves as the necessary evidence of intention and has obvious practical benefits, as well as being capable of constituting notice to third parties. The notice sets out the tax liabilities in respect of which distress is levied and the address at which the assets are situated and is completed with details of the items impounded and signed by the Collector. The notice also provides for the Collector to insert the name of the person who gave verbal confirmation that the distrained goods are the absolute property of the defaulter.

Impounding and walking possession agreements

4.11   Once distress has been levied, the goods must be kept for five days, at the cost of the person in default. [*TMA 1970, s 61(4)*]. The Revenue as a matter of practice adopt *The Distress for Rent Rules 1988, SI 1988 No 2050* as the basis for their costs. Specific regulations governing the Revenue's costs are to be made pursuant to *FA 1989, s 152(6)* and *TMA*

1970, s 61(6), but this has not occurred at the time of writing although it is expected later in 1991. The scale is set out in the standard Distraint Notice, and VAT may be added. Rather than taking the goods into close possession (i.e. removing them, which occurs very rarely), the Revenue will normally leave them on the defaulter's premises provided the debtor (or a responsible person in the case of a company) signs a "walking possession" agreement with the debtor. Unlike distress for rent, there is no statutory basis for such an agreement, but the Revenue have a printed form (Form C204B) which provides that in consideration of the goods not being removed, the debtor acknowledges that the distress has not been abandoned and agrees to pay the fee for walking possession. He also agrees to give the Revenue access to the goods while the distress is in force, to keep them in his possession, and to inform any other person seeking to levy distress or execution that the Revenue have already done so. A walking possession agreement has no statutory force but is, nonetheless, binding on a taxpayer in the same way as any other contract he may enter into, and does not of itself prejudice the Revenue's powers of distraint. An argument that it did prejudice the Revenue was made in *Re Herbert Berry Associates Ltd (in liquidation) HL 1977, 52 TC 113*, at first instance, but Templeman J held firmly that it did not constitute an abandonment of the distress and it is clear from an earlier case that an abandonment of a walking possession agreement must be properly demonstrated as a matter of fact (*Lumsden v Burnett CA, [1898] 2 QB 177*). It has also been held in connection with an alleged breach of a landlord's distress that such agreements bind a tenant, but not a third party unaware of the impounding (*Abingdon RDC v O'Gorman CA, [1968] 3 All ER 79*). The Revenue's remedies for breach of a walking possession agreement continue to be the same as those normally available for breach of contract: an action for damages or civil recovery proceedings. They may also levy a second distress, or, where there is an element of dishonesty, take criminal proceedings. The Keith Committee recommended introduction of a statutory penalty for breach of walking possession agreements, and the Revenue did at first propose to introduce provisions similar to those contained in *FA 1985, s 16* for walking possession agreements entered into with Customs & Excise (see 4.21 below). However, in their consultative document of July 1988, 'Keith: Further Proposals', the Revenue changed their view and decided not to proceed with this aspect of their proposals on distraint:

'Because it now appears doubtful that the penalty would be effective in preventing breaches or could be collected where this occurred'.

Sale

4.12   If the person does not pay the tax due together with the costs and charges, the distrained goods are to:

'be appraised by one or more independent persons appointed by the collector [and] sold by public auction by the collector for payment of the sum due and all costs and charges.'

Any surplus after deducting that payment is to be restored to the owner of the goods. [*TMA 1970, s 61(5)*]. This wording as set out incorporates amendments made by *FA 1989, s 152(5)* following the Keith Report recommendation as to the modernisation of *TMA 1970, s 61*, which at the time of writing is expected to be implemented by an appointed day order later in 1991. The obligation under the pre-existing law for the distrained goods to be sold immediately after five days was not followed in practice, but once this point has been reached the debtor will not normally be allowed to negotiate some other agreement to pay the debt. As will be appreciated, distress is an expensive process for the taxpayer and he (or a receiver or liquidator) will do better to agree at an earlier stage other terms on which the liability is to be discharged.

What may be distrained

4.13   The amended *TMA 1970, s 61(1)* no longer distinguishes between taxes charged in respect of "lands, tenements and premises" and taxes charged in respect of a "person". The former category included tax charged under Schedule B (commercial woodlands) which was abolished in 1988, and the old Schedule A, until its abolition in 1963. This distinction was once important, in theory, since a distress upon premises, etc. could be levied on any goods on the premises (including those of third parties) (see, *inter alia, Reading v Chew QB 1898, 78 LT 681*; *MacGregor v Clamp & Son 1913, [1914] 1 KB 288*). In contrast, distress for tax charged on a person may only be levied on his own goods (*Shaftesbury v Russell 1823, 1 B & C 666*). The amended *TMA 1970, s 61(1)* makes it clear that distress may only be levied 'upon the goods and chattels of the person charged'. In any event, in the case of a company, it seems that corporation tax would be chargeable on the company since the income tax rules only apply for the purposes of computation. Consequently, distress could only be levied on the company's assets and a third party's goods would be protected in any event. [*ICTA 1988, ss 8(1), 9(1)*]. The common law protection from distress of "tools of the trade" does not apply to a distraint for taxes (*MacGregor v Clamp*, above), but in practice the Inland Revenue state that they would not seize any "tools of the trade".

Priority of tax claims

4.14   The Inland Revenue have a special priority for unpaid tax, contained in *TMA 1970, s 62*, which was amended with immediate effect by *FA 1989, s 153*, as part of the modernisation of the distraint legislation with a view to making *section 62* consistent with the Revenue's preferential claims (see 2.11–2.13 above). See IRPR 14 March 1989, para 36, Tolley's Official Tax Statements 1989–90, 5.329. *TMA 1970, s 62* now determines the priority of certain tax debts over a distress or execution levied for other causes (apart from a distress for rent), or over other forms of assignment (e.g. bills of sale), including distress by Customs & Excise. The third party making the distress, execution, etc., may be called on by the Revenue to pay the tax debt. *TMA 1970, s 62(1)* provides that:

'If at any time at which any goods or chattels belonging to any person (in this section referred to as "the person in default") are liable to be taken by virtue of any execution or other process, warrant, or authority whatever, or by virtue of any assignment, on any account or pretence whatever, except at the suit of the landlord for rent, the person in default is in arrears in respect of any such sums as are referred to in subsection (1A) below, the goods or chattels may not be so taken unless on demand made by the collector the person at whose suit the execution or seizure is made, or to whom the assignment was made, pays or causes to be paid to the collector, before the sale or removal of the goods or chattels, all such sums as have fallen due at or before the date of seizure.'

The sums referred to in *section 62(1)* are defined in *TMA 1970, s 62(1A)* as:

'(a)   sums due from the person in default on account of deductions of income tax from emoluments paid during the period of twelve months next before the date of seizure, being deductions which the person in default was liable to make under ICTA 1988, s 203 (pay as you earn) less the amount of the repayments of income tax which he was liable to make during that period; and

(b)   sums due from the person in default in respect of deductions required to be made by him for that period [of twelve months next before the date of seizure] under ICTA 1988, s 559 (sub-contractors in the construction industry).'

If these sums are not paid within ten days of the demand made by the Collector to the person seizing the goods, the goods may be distrained by the Collector in accordance with the provisions already discussed, notwithstanding the earlier distress, execution, etc. [*TMA 1970, s 62(2)*]. The period of ten days was introduced by *FA 1989, s 153* to clarify the timescale upon which the Collector may operate.

4.15   *TMA 1970, s 62* is confined to taking (or, as this is called later in the section, "seizure"). It would not prevent, say, appointment of a receiver, or his dealing with the goods since this would not be by virtue of a taking of a kind mentioned in the section, although just arguably it might be by virtue of an assignment. It is also confined to goods "belonging to" a person. Thus, on the face of it, a prior fixed charge would prevail over *TMA 1970, s 62*. The time to be considered is the time when the process of taking is initiated, not the time the right to take is conferred on the creditor. This provision has not in the past been used particularly extensively, although notices are served by the Inland Revenue on persons with interests in assets on which they have distrained, such as mortgagees, with a view to preventing dealings with the assets. As is noted in 4.23

below, the Revenue normally withdraw an incomplete distress where a receiver is appointed under a floating charge, provided an undertaking is given, and recognise the priority of a fixed charge.

Customs & Excise distress

Extent of the power

4.16   Customs & Excise are empowered to distrain for unpaid VAT by *VATA 1983, 7 Sch 6(4)* and *VAT Gen R 1985, Reg 65* (as amended). *Reg 65(1)* (as amended) says:

> 'If upon [written] demand a person neglects or refuses to pay tax [or any amount recoverable as if it were tax] which he is required to pay under the Act or any regulation made thereunder, a Collector or an officer of rank not below that of Senior Executive Officer may distrain on the goods and chattels of that person and by warrant signed by him direct any authorised person to levy such distress, provided that where an amount of tax is due under paragraph 4(9) of Schedule 7 to the Act (other than an amount assessed as due under paragraph 4(1) of the said Schedule upon failure by a person to make a return) no distress shall be levied until 30 days after that amount became due.'

The word "written" first in square brackets above was added by the *Value Added Tax (General) (Amendment) (No 3) Regulations 1987, SI 1987 No 1916, Reg 11* with effect from 1 January 1988, which at the same time deleted the requirement that the demand be made by an authorised person, to facilitate the issue of demands automatically by computer without need for signature by an authorised person. The second set of words in square brackets was added by the *The Value Added Tax (General) Amendment Regulations 1986, SI 1986 No 71* and apply with effect from 19 February 1986. They aim to clarify the position regarding the use of distress to recover penalties and surcharges under *FA 1985*, in respect of which distress can now be levied. Similar though not identical powers are conferred separately for unpaid car tax [*Car Tax Act 1983, 1 Sch 3(2)(a)(b)*], general betting duty and bingo duty [*Betting & Gaming Duties Act 1981, s 28*]. There is no general power to distrain for customs or excise duties.

Manner of exercise: comparison with Inland Revenue power

4.17   The power is in broadly similar terms to the power contained in *TMA 1970, s 61*, although there are some significant differences. As with a distress for assessed tax, there must be a demand and refusal to pay. It is likely that the same legal requirements for a reasonable time to elapse before a distraint is made would apply to Customs & Excise. However, it is specifically provided that in respect of tax due under an assessment under *VATA 1983, 7 Sch 4(9)* (other than an assessment under *7 Sch 4(1)*, i.e. one made on a person who has failed to render a return) no distress shall be levied until 30 days after the amount becomes due. [*Proviso to VAT Gen R 1985, Reg 65(1)*]. The exception for *7 Sch 4(1)* assessments took effect from 1 January 1986 in line with the stronger powers available to Customs for use against VAT offenders following implementation of the Keith Committee's recommendations. At the same time a judicial safeguard was introduced for Customs' powers (now revoked) to obtain distress warrants to break open premises. [*Value Added Tax (General) Regulations 1985 (Amendment) Regulations 1985, SI 1985 No 1650, Reg 12*].

4.18   The practice followed by Customs & Excise regarding demands for tax is somewhat less generous than that of the Inland Revenue. A formal demand is made after the normal reminders have failed to produce payment, and according to evidence put to the Keith Committee, it was normal for a distress warrant to be issued only by the principal of the VAT office concerned. Responsibility for issuing demands and levying distraint may now legally be given to a lower grade of officer, and it is unclear whether the old practice will still apply, though it is understood that in practice it is the Surveyor who signs the warrant. It has been held in the specific context of distress for VAT that a taxpayer could not challenge an assessment in recovery proceedings (*C & E Commrs v Holvey QB, [1978] STC 187*), although it is true to say that the judge did not regard the income tax case of *CIR v Pearlberg CA 1953, 34 TC 57* as particularly helpful to his construction of *FA 1972*. The Tribunal may, however, hear a late appeal against an assessment even where distress has been levied in respect of the unpaid tax (*P J Davies v C & E Commrs, [1979] VATTR 162*).

Impounding and sale

4.19   Distress may be levied by a Collector or an officer not below the rank of Senior Executive Officer, who may by a warrant signed by him direct any authorised person to levy the distress. [*VAT Gen R 1985, Reg 65(1)*]. As with the Inland Revenue, a bailiff normally accompanies the distraining Customs officer. Although in accordance with the Keith Committee's recommendations (referred to in 4.2 above) the power to issue warrants to break into premises was transferred to magistrates with effect from 1 January 1986 by the *Value Added Tax (General) Regulations 1985 (Amendment) Regulations 1985, SI 1985 No 1650, Reg 12(b)*, this power was revoked completely with effect from 1 April 1986. [*Value Added Tax (General) (Amendment) (No 2) Regulations 1986, SI 1986 No 305, Reg 2*]. The reason for this was explained in CEPR 9 April 1986, that Customs had received Parliamentary Counsel's opinion that the express authority of an Act of Parliament is needed for the entry into premises by force for this purpose, and that VAT law does not provide such authority.

4.20   Distress by Customs & Excise is clearly confined to the goods belonging to the person failing to pay the VAT. [*VAT Gen R 1985, Reg 65(1)*]. Otherwise, the legal requirements for impounding and sale are virtually identical to those for assessed tax (see 4.11–4.12 above). Thus, the goods must be kept for five days, following which they are to be appraised and then sold by public auction. [*Reg 65(4)–(5)*]. One anomaly has, however, arisen in the context of costs, rectified with effect from 26 July 1984 by an amendment to *VATA 1983, 7 Sch 6(4)* (made by *FA 1984, s 16(1)*).

Walking possession agreements: FA 1985, s 16

4.21   One difference between Inland Revenue and Customs & Excise powers of distress, which continues now that the Revenue has decided not to proceed with the implementation of this Keith Committee recommendation, is that a statutory sanction has now been introduced for breaches of walking possession agreements made where distress has been levied for unpaid VAT on the chattels of a "person in default". It is understood that it was the ineffectiveness of the Customs' power, however, which led the Revenue to decide not to do so. "Walking possession agreement" is specially defined as an agreement under which in consideration of the property distrained upon being allowed to remain in the custody of the person in default, and of the delaying of its sale, the person in default:

(a)   acknowledges that the property is under distraint and held in walking possession; and

(b)   undertakes that except with the consent of the Commissioners and subject to such conditions as they may impose, he will not remove or allow the removal of any of the specified property from the premises named in the agreement. [*FA 1985, s 16(2)*].

If the person in default is in breach of an undertaking contained in the walking possession agreement after 24 July 1985, he is liable to a penalty of one half of the tax due, or amount recoverable as if it were tax due, unless he satisfies the Commissioners (or a Tribunal on an appeal) that there is a reasonable excuse for his breach. [*FA 1985, s 16(3)(4)*].

Particular problems

Charged assets

4.22   As has been seen, both Inland Revenue and Customs & Excise rights of distress are confined to the property of the person charged with the tax. There is, however, a lack of clear authority on the interaction between the law of priorities of charges and the statutory powers of distress. The Revenue's and Customs' practice is to acknowledge the priority of a fixed charge, and this is apparently consistent with the limitation on the statutory powers of distress to property "belonging to" or "of" the person owing the tax (see 4.13 and 4.16 above). See further the passages set out in 4.5 above.

4.23   The position is less certain where there is a floating charge. In practice, both the Inland Revenue and Customs & Excise withdraw an incomplete distress where an administrative receiver is appointed, provided an undertaking is given to account for the proceeds of sale of the goods up to the amount of their debt. Problems can still arise, however, since it is far from clear when the distrainor obtains an inalienable right to the property. In the case of execution levied by a judgment creditor, it has been held that a floating charge which has not crystallised at the time of sale of the assets after execution has been levied cannot confer any rights on the debenture-holders (*Evans v Rival Granite Quarries Ltd, [1910] 2 KB 979*); but where the charge has crystallised before sale it has been held that the rights of the charge-holders will prevail over those of the execution creditors to whom the sheriff must account for the proceeds (*Re Opera Ltd CA, [1891] 3 Ch 260*). Following Lord Mansfield's dictum that 'distress for taxes is really in the nature of an execution' in *Hutchins v Chambers 1758, 1 Burr 579* (see 4.5 above), it may be arguable that these cases apply. This is not, however, the Revenue's view. As they state (see 4.5 above), they regard a properly levied distress as taking priority over a floating charge which has not crystallised.

Effect of liquidation

4.24   Although the point has not been satisfactorily determined in a decided case (and has been found "surprising" by a number of judges), it appears that distress is treated as a "proceeding" for the purposes of the Companies Acts. This was accepted by the Crown in the House of Lords in *Re Herbert Berry Associates Ltd (in liquidation) HL 1977, 52 TC 113* following a long line of authority including *Re Roundwood Colliery Co CA, [1897] 1 Ch 373, Re Bellaglade Ltd Ch D 1976, [1977] 1 All ER 319* and *Re Lancashire Cotton Spinning Company ex parte Carnelley CA 1887, 35 Ch D 656*. Consequently, in a voluntary winding up, it was held that, although the court had (under what is now *IA 1986, s 126* read with *IA 1986, s 112*) a discretion to restrain an incomplete distress proceeded with after commencement of a liquidation, this discretion would only be exercised in exceptional circumstances (see, again, the *Herbert Berry* case). The Cork Committee noted (*Report*, p 333) that this rule was not apparently applicable in a compulsory liquidation, although *IA 1986, s 128* (formerly *CA 1985, s 523*) provides that in the case of a company in compulsory liquidation any "attachment, sequestration, distress or execution" put in force against the company after commencement of the liquidation is void. No legislation was introduced, but the point has now been considered by the High Court in *Re Memco Engineering Ltd Ch D, [1985] 3 All ER 267*, a case concerned with a distress for unpaid VAT. Following the authority of the cases on voluntary liquidations already cited, it was held in the *Memco* case that another section, what is now *IA 1986, s 130(2)* (and was formerly *CA 1985, s 525(2)*) applies in a compulsory liquidation so that a distress levied before the commencement cannot be proceeded with against the company except with the leave of the court and subject to such terms as the court may impose. *IA 1986, s 130(2)* thus has a different emphasis from *IA 1986, s 126*: in a case under the latter provisions the court has a discretion to restrain, while under the former it has a discretion to permit the continuation of, the proceedings. This distinction is, however, of little importance in practice since the court will apply the same principles and will normally allow distress levied, but incomplete, at the date of commencement of liquidation to continue. The approach was expressed as follows by Lord Russell of Killowen, in the *Herbert Berry* case at p 135:

> 'The Crown exercised its undoubted right to distrain, without any question of unfair conduct or sharp practice or of negligence in not pursuing the Company for its liabilities sufficiently promptly, and did so well before the winding-up was mooted by a notice. To use a phrase previously used, is there any ground for depriving the Crown of the fruits of its diligence?'

So, it was held in the *Memco* case that the fact that a company is being pursued for the VAT owed, not only by itself, but by other companies in the group, and that the liquidator may not be in a position to apportion the VAT between the various companies will not be "special circumstances" to justify the court restraining the proceedings.

4.25   The position regarding Inland Revenue distress is, in practice, normally determined by the regulations made by the Department of Trade and Inland Revenue. These were issued originally pursuant to *CWR 1949, Rule 224* and a revised version is expected in 1991 some time after the date of writing, taking account of the *Memco* case and *IA 1986, s 176*. They should provide that:

(a)   if the distress was levied after commencement of the winding up, the Revenue will abandon the distress, give up possession of the goods (or proceeds of sale) and prove for the tax as an unsecured or preferential claim, as appropriate;

(b)   if the distress has been completed by a sale before the three months immediately preceding the date of the winding up order, they will retain the proceeds to satisfy the tax in respect of which the distress was levied;

(c)   if the distress has been completed within the three months, then if the liquidator has insufficient funds on hand or there are insufficient other assets to enable him to satisfy all preferential debts, the Collector will surrender the sale proceeds but prove as a "conditional preferential creditor" under *IA 1986, s 176(3)* (see 2.6–2.9 above); and

(d)   if the distress is incomplete at the date of the order, the original regulations provided that if the liquidator requests and provides an undertaking in the prescribed form (to keep an account of the proceeds of sale of the goods, and apply the surplus after payment of the preferential debts in payment of any non-preferential tax claims included in the distress) the Collector will give up possession and again prove as a "conditional preferential creditor" as above. (It is expected that this procedure will be carried over into the new regulations.)

These regulations apply, strictly, only to compulsory liquidations, but it appears that (in their previous form) they were, in practice, observed in voluntary liquidations as well (see Touche Ross, Insolvency Technical Bulletin No 8312).

Interaction of distress and the preferential claim

4.26   In a compulsory liquidation, where any person has distrained upon the goods or effects of the company within three months before the date of a winding up order, those goods or effects (or the proceeds of their sale) are to be charged for the benefit of the company with the preferential debts to the extent that the property is for the time being insufficient to meet them. [*IA 1986, s 176(2)*]. *IA 1986, s 176(3)* provides that, in respect of any money paid under such a charge, the person levying distress will rank as a preferential creditor, 'except as against so much of the company property as is available for the payment of preferential creditors by virtue of the surrender or payment'. The meaning of these provisions (as previously enacted in *CA 1948, s 319*) was considered in the *Memco* case, and is discussed in 2.6–2.9 above.

Effect of appointment of administrator

4.27   Powers of distress generally are now subject to *IA 1986, ss 10, 11*. *IA 1986, s 10(1)(c)* protects the company's position where a petition has been presented for an administration order. During the interim period between that date and the making of the order or dismissal of the petition, no proceedings and no execution or other legal process may be commenced or continued, and no distress may be levied against the company or its property, without leave of the court. If an order is made, the company's property is similarly protected, subject to the consent of the administrator as an alternative to leave of the court. [*IA 1986, s 11(3)(c)*]. In view of the acceptance of distress as a "proceeding" for the purposes of the Companies Acts (see 4.24 above), it appears that this would also prevent completion of a distress already levied, but given the court's discretion under *IA 1986, ss 10, 11* this is likely to be academic as the court can normally be expected to apply the same principles as in a voluntary winding up. The Inland Revenue have indicated to the author that whilst they do not necessarily accept that leave of the court would be required to complete a distress, their current practice is that once the Collector becomes aware that a petition for an administration order has been presented, or an administration order has been made and an administrator appointed, the Collector will suspend the distraint action;

and that if the subsequent proposals under *IA 1986, s 24* are accepted, the Collector will then withdraw the distraint.

Remedies for unlawful distress

4.28   The victim of an unlawful distress for taxes is in broadly the same position as the victim of an unlawful common law distress. The remedies available to him include an action for damages at common law for wrongful distress or trespass, or a court order for return of the goods. In extremity, an injunction may be sought preventing distress being levied or sale of the goods although if the courts follow the approach adopted as regards distress for rent, injunctions may not be granted readily except in flagrant cases. Where a distress is wrongful from the outset (if, for example, no demand has been made), a purchaser under the distrainor, cannot obtain legal title to the goods; but if the distress is merely irregular (wrongly executed, for example) a third party purchaser can obtain a good title although an action for damages will still lie against the distrainor. The case of *James Colin Bowe and Mrs Mary Margaret Bowe v C & E Commrs 1989, MAN/87/366 (3767)* confirms that the VAT Tribunal has no jurisdiction to review the conduct of a distress levied by Customs & Excise, and that any remedy must be sought in the High Court (or other appropriate court).

Chapter 5

Income and Corporation Tax in Administrative Receivership

What is administrative receivership?

5.1   The distinction between receivership and other types of insolvency procedure has already been discussed in Chapter 1 above. "Administrative receiver" is a term introduced by *IA 1986* where it is defined in *section 29(2)* as:

'(a)   a receiver or manager of the whole (or substantially the whole) of a company's property appointed by or on behalf of the holders of any debentures of the company secured by a charge which, as created, was a floating charge, or by such a charge and one or more other securities; or

(b)   a person who would be such a receiver or manager but for the appointment of some other person as the receiver of part of the company's property.'

Put very simply, at the risk of over-simplifying, an administrative receiver is one appointed under a floating charge who normally has under his control substantially all of a company's business rather than particular assets. As this is the most frequent situation where a receiver is appointed, and the term "administrative receiver" is both longer and still a relatively new one, an administrative receiver is often referred to just as a "receiver". His position is, however, governed by *IA 1986, ss 42–49* which provide among other things that so far as consistent with the debenture under which he is appointed an administrative receiver has the powers specified in *IA 1986, 1 Sch*, that he is deemed to be the company's agent unless and until the company goes into liquidation, and that he is personally liable on any contract entered into by him in the carrying out of his functions (except in so far as the contract otherwise provides), with the benefit of an indemnity out of the company's assets. The tax implications of specific types of receivership other than administrative receivership are dealt with in Chapter 13 below.

The effect of appointment of an administrative receiver

5.2   On appointment of an administrative receiver over all or part of its assets, a company remains chargeable to corporation tax, which is

43

computed on the normal basis and by reference to the usual accounting periods. There are no special provisions comparable to those applicable to companies in liquidation under *ICTA 1988, s 342*, and the company does not cease to be the beneficial owner of its assets (see dicta of Lord Greene MR in *English Sewing Cotton Co v CIR CA, [1947] 1 All ER 679* at p 682A). Group relationships are not disturbed by the appointment of an administrative receiver but his activities may result in there being "arrangements" for subsidiaries to leave the group causing the loss of group relief (under *ICTA 1988, s 410*) and the ability to surrender ACT (under *ICTA 1988, s 240(11)(b)*). Since the receiver will almost invariably be an agent of the company (at least until liquidation) so that his acts are to be regarded as the company's own, transactions by the receiver are likely to affect the company's tax liabilities (normally by increasing its chargeable gains and trading losses).

Administrative receiver's liability for tax

General principle

5.3   As a general rule, subject to the exceptions noted below, an administrative receiver appointed over assets of a UK resident company has no liability to pay corporation or income tax on income received or gains made by the company after his appointment or as a result of his own activities. See *Re Regent's Canal Ironworks Company, ex parte Grissell CA 1875, 3 Ch D 411* (see 5.12 below). This was common ground in relation to tax on chargeable gains, in *Re Mesco Properties Ltd CA 1979, 54 TC 238*, discussed in 8.38–8.39 below, but the same principle is regarded as applicable to other forms of profits. Save in exceptional cases, discussed below, he will not even be concerned with the company's corporation tax position and will leave it to a liquidator if one is appointed to deal with matters such as, for example, the submitting of tax computations and the making of appeals against estimated assessments.

Exceptions from the general principle

5.4   There are a number of exceptions from the general rule that an administrative receiver appointed over assets of a UK resident company is not liable to pay corporation tax. One is perhaps the case of rental income and other receipts falling under Schedule A (see 5.6–5.8 below). Obligations to account for tax will also arise where payments must be made under deduction of tax—in particular, certain payments of interest, other annual payments, payments chargeable to tax under Schedule E to which PAYE applies and payments to sub-contractors in the construction industry (see 5.21–5.24 below). The following paragraphs set out the position in more detail as regards the different types of liability. It should be borne in mind that under *IA 1986, s 40* an administrative receiver appointed under a floating charge before commencement of a liquidation must discharge preferential debts (see generally Chapter 2 above) and that if the liquidation has already begun at the date of his appointment recourse may be had to assets held by an administrative receiver appointed under a floating charge to pay preferential debts (including preferential tax claims) where other assets are insufficient, under *IA 1986, s 175(2)(b)*. Finally, a receiver may make provision for tax where it is clear that there will be a surplus of realisations under the charge and funds will be passed to the company after discharging the secured debt, or may even pay tax to avoid interest running to the detriment of unsecured creditors. Although not strictly a liability to pay tax, an administrative receiver may suffer tax indirectly on his income, for example where he receives payments under deduction of tax. Normally his ability to recover such tax will depend on the company's circumstances and will often be impossible. Apart from the situations described above, and situations where a recovery of or in respect of tax may be made (see 5.26–5.27 below), an administrative receiver is likely to be unconcerned with tax liabilities and is unlikely even to have power to deal with them.

Liability under ICTA 1988

Schedule D

5.5   *ICTA 1988, s 59(1)* provides that income tax under Schedule D is to be 'charged on and paid by the persons receiving or entitled to the income in respect of which the tax is directed by the Income Tax Acts to be charged'. So, in *CIR v Thompson KB 1936, 20 TC 422*, it was held that a receiver and manager appointed under a floating charge was assessable to income tax in respect of the trading income of the company as a person receiving or entitled to receive the income. Income tax no longer applies to UK resident companies, and *ICTA 1988, s 59(1)* is expressly excluded for the purposes of corporation tax. [*ICTA 1988, s 59(4)*]. Under *ICTA 1988, s 6(2)* it is also provided that the sections of the Income Tax Acts relating to the charge of income tax shall not apply to income of a company (not arising to it in a fiduciary or representative capacity) if the company is resident in the UK or, if non-resident, the income is chargeable to tax here as profits of a branch or agency under *ICTA 1988, s 11*. Although income tax principles do apply for computation purposes under *ICTA 1988, s 9*, this is not a charging provision. Thus, corporation tax remains chargeable on a UK resident company alone. [*ICTA 1988, ss 6(1), 8(1)*]. The position of receivers of foreign resident companies is dealt with in 15.17–15.26 below.

Schedule A

5.6   *ICTA 1988, s 21(1)* is in terms similar to *ICTA 1988, s 59(1)* and states that income tax under Schedule A is to 'be charged on and paid by the persons receiving or entitled to the profits or gains' in question. Under *ICTA 1988, s 21(2)* the corporation tax provisions have effect to the exclusion of *ICTA 1988, s 21(1)*. Thus, the same arguments apply as for Schedule D income that the company alone is chargeable to tax.

5.7   There is a significant difference between the provisions of Schedule D and those of Schedule A, however, which is that there is a special collection provision applicable where a notice is served on an agent holding rents or other receipts from land on behalf of a principal who has failed to pay tax under Schedule A. *ICTA 1988, s 23(7)* provides that the agent must pay to the Collector 'any sums from time to time received . . . on account of rents or receipts from any land (including any sums so received which are in his hands when the notice is given)' until the tax liability has been satisfied. An agent failing to comply with the requirements of a notice duly served on him under *ICTA 1988, s 23(7)* is liable to a penalty of up to £300 for each failure, and non-compliance as respects sums in his hands when the notice is given or as respects any one payment subsequently received by him is to be treated as a separate failure. [*ICTA 1988, s 23(8)*]. The terms of *ICTA 1988, s 23(7)* extend to any Schedule A liability of the principal unsatisfied at the date of the notice, not only that on the rents in question. It is limited to sums representing rent, etc. in the hands of the agent at the time the notice is served, and to sums which are subsequently received by him.

5.8   The Inland Revenue have been known to argue that *ICTA 1988, s 23(7)* applies to receivers who are in receipt of rents and other Schedule A income recovered under the security. It is, however, strongly arguable that this provision does *not* apply to receivers for the following reasons.

(a)   It is, on the face of it, a subsidiary provision to *ICTA 1988, s 21* (the charging provision for Schedule A) which, as has been seen, does not apply to corporation tax. This is suggested by the opening words of *ICTA 1988, s 21(1)–(8)*, and also from the headnote to *ICTA 1988, s 23* which is 'Collection from lessees and agents'. It is hard to see that *ICTA 1988, s 23* can have an existence independently of *ICTA 1988, s 21*.

(b)   The "principal" in question here can only be the company in respect of which the receiver is appointed. As such, the receiver is only incidentally the agent of the company acting on its behalf, and indeed may not be an agent at all (e.g. after liquidation or if the charge provides otherwise): see *IA 1986, s 44(1)(a)* and *American Express International Banking Corp v Hurley QB, [1985] 3 All ER 564*. In fact, a function such as that of receiving rents may not be exercised "on behalf of" the company at all, but for the benefit of the debenture-holders (see *Gosling v Gaskell and Grocott HL, [1897] AC 575* and *Sowman v David Samuel Trust Ltd Ch D, [1978] 1 All ER 616*).

Even if *ICTA 1988, s 23(7)* does apply to receivers, it would not (on the interpretation suggested in the previous paragraph) apply to sums already paid out at the time of the notice, for example, to charge-holders on a distribution. The normal practice is therefore for a receiver to distribute rents to the debenture-holder as quickly as he can.

Chargeable gains

5.9   Chargeable gains made during the course of an administrative receivership by a person other than the receiver (e.g. the company itself or a liquidator) remain the liability of the company. [*ICTA 1988, ss 6(1)(3), 345*]. As noted in 5.3 above this means that an administrative receiver is likely to be completely unconcerned with such liabilities which cannot be recovered from him directly.

5.10   Chargeable gains resulting from disposals by a receiver are dealt with specifically in *CGTA 1979, s 23(2)*, which provides that receivers and charge-holders are to be treated as nominees of the company in their dealings with the charged property. It says:

> 'Where a person entitled to an asset by way of security or to the benefit of a charge or incumbrance on an asset deals with the asset for the purpose of enforcing or giving effect to the security, charge or incumbrance his dealings with it shall be treated for the purposes of this Act as if they were done through him as a nominee by the person entitled to it subject to the security, charge or incumbrance; and this subsection shall apply to the dealings of any person appointed to enforce or give effect to the security, charge or incumbrance as receiver and manager or judicial factor as it applies to the dealings of the person entitled as aforesaid.'

This provision must be read with *CGTA 1979, s 46* which deals with nominees. This provides that where assets are held by a person as nominee for another person, *CGTA 1979*:

> 'shall apply as if the property were vested in, and the acts of the nominee or trustee in relation to the assets were the acts of, the person or persons for whom he is the nominee or trustee (acquisition from or disposals to him by that person or persons being disregarded accordingly).'

The combined effect of the two sections is, first, that acts of a debenture-holder or receiver to whom they apply are to be treated as acts of the company itself. Secondly, no question of chargeable disposals between the company and the receiver can arise. There are no provisions imposing a liability directly on a receiver, so that it follows that the company alone will be chargeable in respect of disposals he makes. As already noted (in 5.3 above), this was common ground in *Re Mesco Properties Ltd CA 1979, 54 TC 238* (see 8.38–8.39 below).

Liability under TMA 1970

5.11   It might be thought that provisions contained in *TMA 1970* would impose a direct liabilty on administrative receivers of UK resident companies to pay tax, but this is not the case. *TMA 1970, s 108*, which

47

provides that a liquidator is to be regarded as the "proper officer" of a company for certain purposes, does not refer or apply to receivers. *TMA 1970, s 71* does provide for certain administrative acts to be done by receivers, and permits them to retain funds to pay tax, but it is only applicable to bodies of persons chargeable to income tax and, as has been seen, is thus inapplicable to receivers appointed over the assets of UK resident companies (see 5.5 above). *TMA 1970, s 75* refers to receivers appointed by a UK court but an administrative receiver is not appointed by the court (though he is in certain respects subject to its supervision). The position of court receivers is dealt with separately below in 13.13 below.

Tax as an expense of the receivership

5.12   Before the *Mesco Properties* decision (see 5.3 above and 8.38–8.39 below), an argument was occasionally made by the Inland Revenue that a receiver is required to make a provision for corporation tax as an expense of the receivership. This argument appeared difficult to justify since (in contrast to the liquidator's position in a compulsory liquidation where his expenses are governed by formal rules) the payment of expenses in receivership is made only in consequence of powers conferred by the debenture itself, or by *LPA 1925, s 109(8)*, or, now, *IA 1986, 1 Sch.* Such arguments were resisted strongly by receivers for the following reasons.

(a)   Although a debenture will commonly provide for the payment of 'costs, charges and expenses incurred' by the debenture-holder or receiver under its provisions in priority to payment of the principal and interest secured by the charge, it would be surprising if a tax liability could be imposed on a receiver or debenture-holder solely by reason of the words adopted in the charge instrument and, even if it could, the costs and charges included in this provision are probably only those which the receiver has a positive liability to pay.

(b)   *LPA 1925, s 109(8)* which obliges a receiver to provide (*inter alia*) for 'all . . . taxes affecting the mortgaged property' does not, on its face, confer any priority for taxes arising out of the activities of the company or its agents (not being taxes affecting the property) and, even if it did, there is authority that it does not confer on a taxing authority the right to sue (see *Liverpol Corporation v Hope CA, [1938] 1 All ER 492* and also *Re John Willment (Ashford) Ltd Ch D, [1979] STC 286*). This argument is now still more strongly supported by the permissive wording of *IA 1986, s 42* and *1 Sch.*

(c)   In *Re Regent's Canal Ironworks Company ex parte Grissell CA 1875, 3 Ch D 411* a receiver advanced funds to a liquidator out of the property secured by the charge to enable the liquidator to pay certain expenses, including wages, rent and insurance as well as unspecified "taxes" (possibly the old Schedule A tax and rates) and other outgoings to enable the assets to be realised more favourably. It was held that no claim could be sustained against him by the liquidator when he sought to recover these sums and, it follows *a fortiori*, those who received the various outgoings.

Such arguments are not known to have been advanced by the Inland Revenue for some years.

Effect of liquidation on an administrative receiver

5.13   The principle that an administrative receiver is not liable to tax on the company's income and gains is not affected if a liquidation commences after his appointment. Although his agency will cease in such circumstances, as is now provided in *IA 1986, s 44(1)(a)*, the funds he holds will continue to accrue for the benefit of the company, subject to the rights of the debenture-holders (see *Gosling v Gaskell and Grocott HL, [1897] AC 575*), being applied in satisfaction of its indebtedness so that the tax on the income or gains will remain the company's liability. This follows from the reasoning of Lord Greene MR in *English Sewing Cotton Co v CIR CA, [1947] 1 All ER 679*. See also dicta in (*inter alia*) *CIR v Paterson CA 1924, 9 TC 163* and *CIR v Thompson KB 1936, 20 TC 422*. Equally, the acts of a receiver who is no longer the company's agent may still result in tax liabilities falling on the company whose assets he administers (e.g. tax on capital gains).

5.14   The position where an administrative receiver is appointed under a (crystallised) floating charge at a time when liquidation has begun is different and this is an exception to the general rule that receivers are not concerned with post-appointment tax liabilities. Tax arising in the course of a liquidation is, as will be seen, an expense of the winding up (see 8.37–8.41 below). Assets of the company at the date of winding up are available for payment of these costs, as well as the preferential debts, in accordance with the priority set out in *IA 1986, s 175(2)(b)* and *Ins R 1986, Rule 4.218*. It was held in *Re Barleycorn Enterprises Ltd CA, [1970] 2 All ER 155* that property subject to a floating charge which has not crystallised at the date of winding up is an asset for this purpose; consequently, it will be available to satisfy post-liquidation tax liabilities. In *Re Christonette International Ltd Ch D, [1982] 3 All ER 225* it was held that for this purpose a compulsory liquidation begins at the time the order is made (and that the provisions of what is now *IA 1986, s 129(2)*, which make the liquidation retrospective to the date of petition, do not apply). In summary, therefore, assets in the hands of a receiver appointed under a floating charge (which crystallises on liquidation but not before) may under existing law be available to pay post-liquidation tax liabilities, as well as preferential debts, if a winding up order is made or resolution passed before his appointment.

Receiver not agent of the company

5.15   In practice, a receiver is almost invariably constituted the agent of the mortgagor company, either expressly by the charge itself or impliedly under *LPA 1925, s 109(2)* or, now, under *IA 1986, s 44(1)(a)* where he is an "administrative receiver". His agency will, however, cease if the company goes into liquidation (see *Gosling v Gaskell*, 5.8(b) above and *IA 1986, s 44(1)(a)*), and it is not impossible for a charge deed to provide that a receiver will act as the agent of a third party such as the debenture-holder. Alternatively he may become the agent of the debenture-holder (see *American Express International Banking Corp v Hurley QB, [1985] 3 All ER 564*). The position for tax purposes of a receiver who is not the agent of the company (and the company where such a receiver is appointed) is not substantially different from that of a receiver who is the agent of the company, for the same reasons as apply where the company goes into liquidation (see 5.13 above).

Interest and other annual payments

Interest, etc. received

5.16   Interest and other annual payments *received* by the company (or to which it becomes entitled) during the administrative receivership will be treated like any other receivership income and will be subject to tax, payable by the company or a liquidator under Schedule D without any liability falling on the receiver, as discussed generally above. The receiver may, of course, suffer a deduction of income tax which will not normally be recoverable by him.

Interest, etc. paid

5.17   An administrative receiver may, however, be personally liable to account for income tax where he *makes a payment* of interest chargeable under Schedule D Case III (under *ICTA 1988, s 349(2)*) or certain other types of payment falling within the categories set out in *ICTA 1988, s 349(1)*, i.e.:

(a)   any annuity or other annual payment charged with tax under Schedule D Case III;

(b)   any royalty or other sum paid in respect of the user of a patent; or

(c)   certain types of rent and other payments in respect of mines, quarries, wayleaves, etc.

This is because the administrative receiver will fall within *ICTA 1988, s 349(1)(2)* as a person 'by or through whom' the payment is made since, as appears from *Rye and Eyre v CIR HL 1935, 19 TC 164*, this term may include both a principal and an agent (and indeed any person into whose hands interest comes—see *Howells v CIR KB 1939, 22 TC 501*). In either case, the receiver is required to deduct out of the payment a sum equal to the amount of income tax on the payment at the basic rate, to deliver an account to the Inspector of Taxes, and is then assessable and chargeable himself in respect of that amount. [*ICTA 1988, ss 349(1)(2), 350(1)*]. His obligation to the payee is thereby discharged. [*TMA 1970, s 106*]. The receiver must, if requested in writing by the payee, furnish him with a statement showing the gross amount of the payment, the amount of tax deducted, and the actual amount paid. [*ICTA 1988, s 352*]. The position may be contrasted with that of a mortgagee selling under the power of sale who may apply part of the proceeds to the interest component of the secured debt without accounting for tax, as *ICTA 1988, s 349(1)* does not then apply.

5.18   The most frequent example of the requirement to deduct income tax from payments will be where a receiver accounts to the debenture-holder for an amount representing accrued interest on the secured debt. However, *ICTA 1988, s 349(2)* does not apply (so that no income tax deduction is required) in the circumstances mentioned in *ICTA 1988, s 349(3)* of which the most relevant are:

(a)   interest payable in the UK on an advance from a bank carrying on a *bona fide* banking business in the UK; or

(b)   interest paid by such a bank in the ordinary course of that business.

Administrative receivers are appointed over banking businesses relatively rarely, but the first of these situations is frequently met.

5.19   Another situation where an administrative receiver may not be liable to account for tax deductions in respect of interest is in the exceptional case where he is an agent of the person to whom the interest is paid. This appears to follow from *Hollis v Wingfield CA, [1940] 1 All ER 531*. There, a mortgagee received £9,000 from a liquidator representing the proceeds of sale of some charged shares. She retained sufficient funds to discharge the principal and accrued interest secured, without making any allowance for the tax deductions which she would have suffered if the mortgagor had paid the interest itself. The Court of Appeal held that she was not obliged to account to the liquidator for the tax, but should show the interest in her return as received gross and herself pay the income tax under the normal procedures. Since payment to a receiver as agent for a debenture-holder is, under general principles, payment to the debenture-holder himself the same should apply in such a case. This case was, however, decided under the old income tax deduction provisions.

5.20   No deduction would be required on payment of money by an administrative receiver to the company or to its liquidator or administrator, since the question of interest would not arise as such. The position is a little more complicated where a receiver accounts to a second receiver for the balance of the sale proceeds. The best view is probably that a receiver who accounts for an unappropriated sum should not make any deduction on account of tax since the money will not be "interest" when he pays it, but merely an unallocated pot which the second receiver may apply for any purpose (including payment of his own fees). If payment is made direct to a second mortgagee (other than a bank falling within *ICTA 1988, s 349(3)(a)*), however, or to a receiver who is an agent of such a second mortgagee, a deduction may well be required if an interest element is involved.

PAYE and sub-contractors' payments

PAYE deductions

5.21   The other major area where deductions can be required is in connection with payments of emoluments to employees, both when discharging the preferential claim for employees' wages (see 2.13 above) and when making payment of emoluments as such.

5.22   There is an argument that a receiver is not obliged to account for PAYE deductions, since employees will generally remain employees of the company after his appointment until he terminates their employment (*Griffiths v Secretary of State for Social Services QB, [1973] 3 All ER 1184*), and any payment made by the receiver will not therefore be made in the capacity of employer. Moreover, *ICTA 1988, s 203* only empowers the Revenue to make regulations enabling them to assess 'any person making any payment' of emoluments (contrast *ICTA 1988, s 349* which refers to persons 'by or through whom the payment is made') and arguably only the company makes the payment in any other than a mechanical sense. The PAYE liability would thus remain with the company, as it does with tax on chargeable gains. Unfortunately, tempting though this argument might be, the Revenue are likely to argue that it does not accord with *ITER 1973, Reg 2(1)* which defines "employer" not as the contractual employer but as the person actually paying the emoluments. It may also be arguable that a receiver would be an "intermediate employer", that is a person under whose general control and management an individual works, under *Reg 3* of the same regulations, or a "successor" under *Reg 34*.

5.23   The PAYE Regulations apply specifically to receivers, and others, where payments are made to former employees. [*ITER 1973, Reg 16(3) (as amended)*].

Payments to sub-contractors

5.24   If, in exceptional cases, a receiver makes a payment to which the construction industry tax deduction scheme applies, he must deduct and account for income tax in the same manner as for PAYE under *ICTA 1988, Pt XIII Ch IV* and *Income Tax (Sub-Contractors in the Construction Industry) Regulations 1975, SI 1975 No 1960*. Where such payments are made *to* a receiver under a contract entered into before his appointment, however, Revenue practice is not to require a deduction to be made, apparently on the basis that such payments are not made to a sub-contractor as *ICTA*

1988, ss 559, 560 provide: see Inland Revenue booklet 'Construction Industry Tax Deduction Scheme' IR 14/15 (1982), para 155. A receiver is, however, required to re-register under the scheme if he is to enter into contracts for the company.

Pension scheme surpluses

5.25　Where, as is not uncommon, an administrative receiver (or liquidator) receives a payment out of a pension scheme surplus from the administrator or trustee of the scheme, then, subject to certain very limited exceptions, the amount is received subject to deduction of 40 per cent tax. This is not income tax but a payment on account of the company's corporation tax liability. This tax will not be recoverable by the receiver or by the company. [*ICTA 1988, ss 601, 602* and *Pension Scheme Surpluses (Administration) Regulations 1987, SI 1987 No 352*].

Tax refunds and group relief payments

5.26　The situations discussed above in this chapter (where an administrative receiver may be faced with paying, or at least bearing, tax liabilities) are to be contrasted with the situation where the company is entitled to a tax refund, or may become so on the making of a claim. The receiver will then be under a duty to take steps to "get in" the refund, as he would be with any other property, to the advantage of the debenture-holder, even to the extent of co-operating in a "tax scheme". See *Lawson v Hosemaster Machine Co Ltd CA, [1966] 2 All ER* per Danckwerts LJ at p 950. Whether a tax refund falls under the fixed charge on book debts or under the floating charge is discussed in 13.6–13.8 below.

5.27　The tax losses of a company which is a member of a group are one of its assets, in the sense that they can be turned to account, and will normally be covered by a floating charge. Complex situations may arise where different members of a group (some or all of which may be in the course of one or more insolvency procedures) have different tax losses available for surrender and/or different amounts of tax against which they can be set and/or different creditors who may be affected by how the tax liabilities are met. Groups of companies which are solvent do not normally pay for their losses on any kind of arm's length basis but in a situation like that just described an arm's length negotiation as to the amounts payable for the losses ought perhaps in theory to take place, into which a number of factors would enter such as the certainty of establishing the losses in question and the possibility of secondary liability for the tax of a possible purchaser of the losses. In practice, it will rarely be possible to justify the expenditure of creditors' money on issues of this kind and an even split of the tax saved between surrendering company and claimant may be agreed as the most appropriate way to proceed. It may well be possible to agree with the Inland Revenue that no tax liabilities arise in the group in any event without calculating the losses. Similar issues arise with companies in administration and because of the greater concern with tax liabilities in this procedure the theoretical points may be more important. The compliance aspects of group relief, terminal loss and other claims are dealt with in Chapter 17 below.

Chapter 6

Income and Corporation Tax in Administration

Introduction to the process

6.1   The administration procedure was introduced to insolvency legislation in Great Britain by the *IA 1986* on the recommendation of the Cork Committee.

6.2   A court can make an administration order at the request of the directors, shareholders or creditors of the company. The court will need to be satisfied that the company is or is likely to become unable to pay its debts and that one or more of the purposes specified in *IA 1986, s 8* is likely to be achieved. These are:

(a)   the survival of the company *and* the whole or any part of its undertaking as a going concern;

(b)   a voluntary arrangement;

(c)   a scheme under *CA 1985, s 425*;

(d)   a more advantageous realisation of the company's assets than in a liquidation.

Consequences of administration order

6.3   An administration can start at any time when the company is not in liquidation. If an administrative receiver is in office, his charge-holder will have to agree to the order and if this happens, the receiver must hand the assets to the administrator when the order is made.

6.4   A company voluntary arrangement or a scheme of arrangement may start during an administration and continue separately after it has concluded, whatever other exit route is chosen from the administration.

6.5   It is not possible to place a company into liquidation or to appoint a receiver while the administration order is in force.

6.6   The order operates as a stay against all legal procedures including the enforcement of proprietary rights. In particular, during the administration period the enforcement of security over the company's property, and the repossession of goods held under hire purchase agreements are prohibited without the administrator's consent or leave of the court (which may be granted subject to conditions); and subject to the same consent/leave, no execution or other legal process may be commenced or continued or distress levied. [*IA 1986, s 11*]. The order gives the administrator time to call a meeting of creditors to put to them for approval his proposals for achieving the purposes specified in the court order. If the creditors agree to the administrator's proposals, the administration will continue until the objectives are achieved or the administrator decides that they cannot be achieved, at which point he will apply to the court for the administration order to be discharged.

6.7   Until such time as the order is discharged the administrator is responsible for managing the company's affairs and 'may do all such things as may be necessary for the management of the affairs, business and property of the company'. Certain specific powers are set out in *IA 1986, 1 Sch* and are the same as those of an administrative receiver. [*IA 1986, s 14(1)*].

6.8   The administrator acts throughout as agent of the company and normally (provided he acts properly) without incurring personal liability. On his release he is specifically 'discharged from all liability both in respect of acts or omissions of his in the administration and otherwise in relation to his conduct as administrator'. [*IA 1986, s 20(2)*].

6.9   On the discharge of the administration order the company may revert to the control of its directors or a further insolvency process may follow.

The effect of appointment of an administrator

Accounting periods

6.10   *ICTA 1988, s 12* sets out the circumstances in which an accounting period of a company ends for corporation tax purposes. These include the commencement of a liquidation [*ICTA 1988, s 12(7)*], but the Inland Revenue have confirmed that neither the filing of an administration order petition, nor the making of an administration order, would of itself bring about the end of an accounting period (ICAEW TR 799, para 9(b)—see Appendix 2). If the trade ceases, however, an accounting period will end in the normal way. [*ICTA 1988, s 12(3)(c)*].

Beneficial ownership

6.11   Whereas the beneficial ownership tests of the various group relationships of a parent company are no longer satisfied (apart from the capital gains group) after the commencement of liquidation (see 8.31 below), the Inland Revenue have confirmed that they would not normally regard an administration order itself as affecting the beneficial ownership tests of the various group relationships of a parent company (ICAEW TR 799, para 9(c)—see Appendix 2). However, it is possible that proposals put by the administrator to creditors which are approved under *IA 1986, s 24* might do so. Furthermore, arrangements by the administrator for the sale of the shares in subsidiaries break the group relationship for the purposes of the tests in *ICTA 1988, 18 Sch 5(3)* and could thus, *inter alia*, cut off entitlement to group relief and to set-off by the subsidiaries of surrendered advance corporation tax, by virtue of *ICTA 1988, s 410(1)(b)* and *ICTA 1988, s 240(11)* respectively (see *J Sainsbury plc v O'Connor Ch D, [1990] STC 516* discussed further in 18.11 below).

Comparison with administrative receivership and liquidation

6.12   The effect of the appointment of an administrator is similar to that of an administrative receiver. However, unlike an administrative receiver, an administrator will be concerned with the corporation tax liabilities of the company arising after his appointment (see 6.17–6.20 below) and will wish to make use of the ability to use trading losses for the period in which he is appointed, and group relief, to cover taxable income and gains that will arise in the same period. These possibilities are not available to a liquidator for the reason described in 6.11 above and together support a powerful argument in favour of administration instead of liquidation in appropriate circumstances when tax liabilities are expected to arise on post-appointment disposals. Furthermore, whereas the tax liabilities that would arise after commencement of liquidation will rank as expenses (see 8.37–8.41 below), they will rank as unsecured debts in a liquidation following an administration. This is discussed further in 6.14 below.

Administrator's liability for tax

6.13   When the administration procedure was first used, insolvency practitioners were troubled that the tax liabilities of the company that arose from their transactions could possibly fall to be treated as an administrator's expense within the scope of *IA 1986, s 19(3)*. However, the Inland Revenue has confirmed that in most circumstances tax remains the company's liability (ICAEW TR 799, para 7(a)—see Appendix 2), and does not enjoy any special status as against the administrator. It is not considered that tax liabilities arise "under contracts" within *IA 1986, s 19(4)* unless perhaps the contract is one with the Revenue to pay tax (e.g. a back duty agreement).

6.14   Notwithstanding this, the Inland Revenue have observed (*ibid*) that the administrator can discharge the liability of the company under:

(a)   his general power in *IA 1986, s 14(1)*;

(b)   his specific power in *IA 1986, 1 Sch 13.*

It is unlikely in practice, however, that circumstances will arise in which the administrator will wish to exercise any such powers in this way and unpaid tax liabilities will rank with other unsecured claims against the company.

6.15   There remain certain tax matters which the administrator will have to regard as expenses. These include the following.

(a)   PAYE/NIC on emoluments paid by him as agent of the company to employees. [*ITER 1973, Regs 2(1), 3*]. See 5.22–5.23 above and 10.9–10.12 below for a detailed discussion of the provisions: for the reasons given in 5.22, it is not necessarily correct as a matter of law that PAYE income tax liabilities are an administrator's liability but in practice non-payment would invite an application by the Inland Revenue for an order under *IA 1986, s 27* for the tax to be paid on the basis that they would otherwise be unfairly prejudiced, which order could well be granted.

(b)   Income tax which is required to be deducted at source; for example on annual payments. [*ICTA 1988, ss 348, 349*]. See 5.16–5.20 above for a more detailed discussion of the provisions.

(c)   Schedule A liability on certain rent receipts. [*ICTA 1988, s 23*]. See 5.6–5.8 above for a detailed discussion of the provisions.

6.16   The administrator is also specifically obliged to account for VAT. [*VAT Gen R 1985, Reg 11*]. See 9.5 below for a detailed discussion of the provisions.

Impact of corporation tax liabilities

6.17   An administrative receiver's concern with the tax consequences of his activities will centre on their impact on any tax recoveries (e.g. any repayment claims he can make) and any possible personal liabilities. Otherwise, the tax consequences for the company of his actions will fall to be dealt with by a successor liquidator.

6.18   A liquidator, on the other hand, will be concerned with the tax liability for post-liquidation periods which can rank as a winding up expense (see 8.37–8.41 below for a full discussion), together with the unsecured claims of the Inland Revenue for tax liabilities of pre-liquidation periods.

6.19   Unlike receiverships, in an administration it is the likely return to all and not a special class of creditors that has to be borne in mind when considering strategies for achieving the purposes for which the administration order was made. The eventual return to creditors will be impaired by tax liabilities arising after the administration order. Accordingly, it is usually appropriate to consider tax planning possibilities with the same degree of care as is appropriate to a going concern case.

6.20 In this respect administration is closer to liquidation than administrative receivership as regards the insolvency practitioner's involvement with tax matters, although the process itself resembles administrative receivership at the operating level. This has important practice management consequences, and it is necessary to ensure that staff who are experienced in receivership work are not misled into ignoring tax by the similarity of the day-to-day work involved.

Preferential claims

6.21 It is not part of the administrator's duties to settle the claims of the company's pre-order creditors. Consequently, there are no provisions to order the ranking of such claims in the administration in like manner to administrative receivership or liquidation. If the company returns to solvency, the ranking of liabilities will then be irrelevant. If it does not, a further insolvency process will follow and the claims of creditors will be dealt with then.

6.22 The relevant date for preferential claims is the date of the making of the administration order where:

(a)   a company voluntary arrangement is made while the administration order is in force [*IA 1986, s 387(2)(a)*];

(b)   a compulsory winding up order is made immediately upon the discharge of the administration order [*IA 1986, s 387(3)(a)*].

6.23 If a voluntary liquidation were to follow administration rather than compulsory liquidation, the relevant date is the date of the winding up resolution instead. [*IA 1986, s 387(3)(c)*]. The result is that some claims which would have enjoyed preferential status in a compulsory liquidation will rank instead as unsecured claims. This may cause the court to be reluctant to discharge the administration order without a simultaneous winding up order or otherwise seeing that those who would be preferential creditors in a compulsory winding up are protected.

Outcome of administrations for creditors

6.24 It is important to recognise that there are two decision points concerning administration orders at which tax considerations are relevant and can affect the outcome for creditors.

Entry route considerations

6.25   The first decision point is before the order is made, when it will be relevant to compare the tax consequences that will follow under administration with those of liquidation. Where application is made for an order to achieve 'a more advantageous realisation of the company's assets than would be effected on a winding up' [*IA 1986, s 8(3)(d)*], the independent report made under *Ins R 1986, Rule 2.2* will address the matters referred to at 6.10–6.11 above, and consider whether:

(a)   trading losses are available to shelter any expected capital gains or Schedule D Case III income of the accounting period in which the order is made;

(b)   trading losses are available in subsidiaries to be claimed as group relief against taxable profits of the same period.

Exit route considerations

6.26   The second decision point occurs when it has been concluded that there is an inescapable shortfall for creditors and a further insolvency process has to follow. In a research paper on administration orders made in 1987 published by the ICAEW, the outcome of the administrations included in the survey can be summarised as follows:

			%
(1)	Restoration of the company to solvency	10	8
(2)	Liquidation	17	13
(3)	Voluntary arrangement	102	79
		129	100

(Mark Homan, 'The Result of Administration Orders Made in 1987', p 12)

6.27   The paragraphs below consider the impact on creditors' recoveries of an administration followed by a liquidation and a voluntary arrangement respectively in the following illustrative circumstances:

	£
Net proceeds of asset disposals (anticipated)	100
Tax charge on realisations (estimate)	30
Existing creditors (unsecured)	140

6.28   By way of a benchmark for comparison, note that, if the company were to go into liquidation rather than administration, the asset disposals would be made by the liquidator and tax of £30 would have to be paid as a winding up expense, leaving assets of £70 to meet the claims of the unsecured creditors. Ignoring costs, the creditors would receive a dividend of 50p in the £.

6.29 If the company went into administration first, the tax liability resulting from the disposals made by the administrator would increase the unsecured creditors' claims to £170. They would share the net proceeds of £100 in the subsequent liquidation and their dividend (ignoring costs) would be 59p in the £.

6.30 Voluntary arrangements involve a composition in satisfaction of a company's debts or a scheme of arrangement of its affairs and lead to what is sometimes described as a "cram down" of the claims of creditors. The creditors who are bound by the voluntary arrangement are those who have notice of the meeting of creditors and are entitled to vote at it. [*IA 1986, s 5(2)(b)*]. Where the arrangement follows an administration order, the creditors vote on the basis of their claims at the date of the order. [*Ins R 1986, Rule 1.17(2)*]. The effect of this is that those creditors whose claims have arisen between the date of the administration order and the meeting of creditors cannot be bound by the arrangements. This means that tax liabilities of the company arising in the period of the administration may have to be paid in full in a subsequent voluntary arrangement unless the Inland Revenue can be persuaded to accept a lesser amount (see 7.6 below).

6.31 Using the above figures, the result would be that £30 would be applied in discharging the administration period tax liability, leaving £70 available to meet other creditors' claims of £140, which would have to be abated by 50p in the £. This outcome for creditors is the same as if the company had gone straight into liquidation, and will negate the benefit that could have been obtained by following administration with liquidation.

6.32 Furthermore, there are three further difficulties with voluntary arrangements which could worsen substantially the position of a creditor where administration is followed by a voluntary arrangement rather than liquidation. These are as follows.

(a) *VAT bad debt relief.* Under the VAT bad debt relief regime before *FA 1990, s 11*, no VAT bad debt relief was available for amounts owing by a debtor company subject to a voluntary arrangement. Such relief was available where the debtor was in liquidation. [*VATA 1983, s 22(3)*]. The position is improved after 1 April 1991 in respect of supplies made after 1 April 1989, but is still a relevant factor for creditors where old debts are unpaid. See 12.29–12.38 below for a detailed discussion of the VAT bad debt relief provisions.

(b) *Tax consequences for the debtor company. ICTA 1988, s 94* provides that, where a deduction for tax purposes has been allowed for a debt which is later released, the amount released is treated as a trading receipt in the period in which the release is effected. See further 7.9–7.11 and 8.24 below. The Inland Revenue have stated their view that a compromise in satisfaction of debt under a voluntary arrangement would give rise to a "release" for these purposes (ICAEW TR 799, paras 16(b)–(d)—see Appendix 2). It will, therefore, be necessary to consider what losses, if any, would be available to shelter such a charge. No such charge would arise if the debt simply remained unpaid in a liquidation.

(c) *Tax consequences for the creditor.* These are discussed in detail in Chapter 12 below. One material point, however, is that *ICTA 1988, s 74(j)* allows a corporation tax deduction to be made for debts proved to be bad and for doubtful debts to the extent they are estimated to be bad. In the case of the bankruptcy or "insolvency" of the debtor the amount which may reasonably be expected to be received on such debts is taken as their value. No relief will be available in respect of any part of a debt which is paid under the terms of a voluntary arrangement, and relief will only be available on any amounts "satisfied" by the arrangement if that part of the debt meets the *ICTA 1988, s 74(j)* conditions described above. In practice, this will involve comparing the terms of the arrangement with the expected outcome of a hypothetical liquidation. Creditors who, for commercial reasons, are willing to bear a disproportionate loss in a voluntary arrangement need to take account of this restriction on the amount of relief available, which will be a matter for discussion with their Inspector of Taxes (see the Inland Revenue's statement in ICAEW TR 799, paras 16(e)–(f) discussed in 12.18 below and reproduced in Appendix 2).

Chapter 7

Company Voluntary Arrangements

What is a voluntary arrangement?

7.1   As discussed in 1.4 above, a voluntary arrangement under *IA 1986, Pt I* is a simplified procedure for obtaining the approval of creditors and members to a composition in satisfaction of a company's debts or a scheme of arrangement of its affairs [*IA 1986, s 1(1)*], and then for putting that arrangement into effect. A voluntary arrangement may be proposed by the directors or, where applicable, the administrator or the liquidator. An insolvency practitioner must be proposed as nominee for the arrangement, and unless he is the liquidator or administrator, he must report to the company under *IA 1986, s 2*. Meetings of the members and creditors must approve the arrangement. By *IA 1986, s 5(2)* the approved voluntary arrangement:

'(a)   takes effect as if made by the company at the creditors' meeting, and

(b)   binds every person who in accordance with the [Ins R 1986] had notice of, and was entitled to vote at, that meeting (whether or not he was present or represented at the meeting) as if he were a party to the voluntary arrangement.'

The arrangement is then implemented by a person (usually the nominee) being appointed as supervisor and put in possession of the assets included in the arrangement, under *Ins R 1986, Rule 1.23*, and thereafter carrying out the terms of the arrangement.

Approval of proposed voluntary arrangement

7.2   The Inland Revenue will in many cases be a creditor of the company in respect of tax for periods up to and including the date the arrangement takes effect. Insofar as they are preferential creditors, they must be accorded priority under *IA 1986, s 4(4)*. Insofar as they are unsecured, their debt must be included in the arrangement and they will then be bound by the arrangement like any other creditor. [*IA 1986, s 434(d)*]. The Revenue seek to deal with all voluntary arrangements at a central point and should be notified through the Enforcement Office, Barrington Road, Worthing, West Sussex BN12 4XH. The Revenue have briefly indicated, in their response in June 1990 to the ICAEW's submissions set out in ICAEW TR 799, para 2(a), factors which will be considered in deciding how to vote on a voluntary arrangement proposal. They state:

> 'The Inland Revenue deal with every Administration Order and Voluntary Arrangement on its own individual merits taking into account all known features of the case. When deciding how to vote, the Revenue give consideration to, amongst other things, the way in which the taxpayer has attended to his tax obligations, the level of uncertainty over assets and liabilities and whether a voluntary arrangement is the appropriate course for the Revenue to approve as a creditor. The Revenue are also very much aware of the interests of other parties and of the purpose of the voluntary arrangement procedure.'

The three factors mentioned by the Revenue in this passage indicate, first, that the company's tax-paying history (including its PAYE history) will affect the Revenue's attitude to the arrangement. It is understood that they will be concerned with the prospects of future punctiliousness in payment of tax and are especially sensitive to failure to account for PAYE. They will also be interested (if such a failure has occurred) in knowing whether individuals who have previously been involved in the company's affairs will continue to be involved. The second factor mentioned in the quoted passage also emphasises the importance of ascertaining the amount of the Revenue's claim by attention to overdue tax returns and unsettled computations before the arrangement is finalised.

7.3   In preparing the arrangement for the approval of creditors, it will therefore be necessary for the nominee to be fully informed as to the past tax record of the company. He must also ensure that the information in the proposal concerning the company's financial position does not differ too greatly from the information available to the Revenue, and that the arrangement will require PAYE to be correctly operated during the supervision period. It is possible that the mere fact that the financial return to the Revenue is likely to be greater in a voluntary arrangement than a liquidation will not be the most influential factor in deciding whether to approve the proposal, particularly where past PAYE tax is unpaid. The Revenue's perspective may be wider than that of the insolvency practitioner proposing the arrangement, since they will be concerned with preserving the integrity of the collection system and not merely whether the balance is favourable in a particular case between the arrangement and other possible outcomes of the insolvency (such as liquidation).

The effect of a voluntary arrangement

7.4   The proposal and implementation of a voluntary arrangement does not of itself cause a cessation of any trade carried on by the company, nor affect the company's accounting period nor, indeed, the powers of the Inland Revenue or Customs & Excise to enforce tax liabilities. The question of beneficial ownership of the company's assets after the proposal takes effect is a more difficult one and depends on the terms of the arrangement (see 7.7 below).

Supervisor's liability for tax

7.5   A supervisor of a voluntary arrangement is not constituted an agent of the company by any statutory provision and his capacity to deal with the company's assets will depend on the terms of the arrangement. The tax on any disposals or income will normally be a liability of the company, not of the supervisor, as discussed further below in 7.7. An exception may be the deduction taxes (see 7.8 below).

Tax liabilities in the voluntary arrangement

7.6   Tax liabilities which arise in the course of the arrangement (e.g. tax on interest on cash assets held for the purposes of the arrangement, or tax on chargeable gains made on the disposal of assets) or those which have arisen in the course of an administration immediately preceding (see 6.30 above) cannot *per se* be included in the arrangement itself. *IA 1986* is (at best) unclear whether they may be "crammed down" by virtue of *section 5* even if the Inland Revenue are a creditor at the date the arrangement takes effect. In practice such liabilities may be paid out of the assets held for the purposes of the arrangement, and may indeed be an inducement to the Revenue to agree to the arrangement (rather than contemplate an administration and/or liquidation) by the supervisor using his powers in *Ins R 1986, Rule 1.28(b)*. This rule sets out the fees, costs, charges and expenses which may be incurred for the purposes of the voluntary arrangement as including:

'any fees, costs, charges or expenses which—

(i)   are sanctioned by the terms of the arrangement, or

(ii)   would be payable, or correspond to those which would be payable, in an administration or winding up'.

The expenses which would be payable in a winding up are set out in *Ins R 1986, Rule 4.218*. The expenses payable in an administration are referred to only obliquely in *IA 1986, s 19(4)(5)* but will be those incurred to carry out the powers granted in *IA 1986, 1 Sch*. Based on the comments made in relation to tax on releases (see 7.11 below) it might appear that the Revenue accept that corporation tax liabilities do not fall within *Rule 1.28(b)* but indications have been given to the author that this is not the case and that they regard tax liabilities as falling within the power for a supervisor to pay expenses. This is not, however, a mandatory provision and it may be prudent to provide for these liabilities to be met in full in the same way as (other) expenses, since, apart from the points made elsewhere in this chapter, the liabilities for tax will otherwise remain with the company and if the company is to continue trading after the arrangement has run its course this may be a serious matter.

7.7   In preparing the proposal it is as well to be clear as to who will legally own the funds held for the purposes of the arrangement. There may be significant differences in liability, depending on whether or not the result of the arrangement is that the assets continue to be administered on behalf of the company by the supervisor, for him to apply in repaying the company's debts, so that any tax liabilities in respect of those assets are liabilities of the company. This analysis will normally follow from general principles (see *English Sewing Cotton Co v CIR CA, [1947] 1 All ER 679* and the discussion of the position of assets held by administrative receivers in Chapter 5 above, where similar points arise). It is likely to be the most favourable position in that, for example, the company's losses will be available to offset profits or gains in respect of the assets in the arrangement and, because beneficial ownership of the assets remains unchanged, group relief will be unaffected. There may, however, be situations in which the assets are so alienated that their beneficial ownership is altered by the arrangement and they are held by the supervisor on behalf, not of the company, but of the creditors, in which case there may be a disposal by the company of the assets concerned, group relief will be affected and the supervisor may himself be liable for income tax under *ICTA 1988, s 59* and may consequently have to withhold income tax from distributions to meet such liabilities.

7.8   A supervisor may (depending on the terms of the arrangement) become responsible for deduction taxes. In particular, he may (like an administrative receiver—see 5.16–5.20 above) be a person "through whom" interest is paid, liable to withhold basic rate income tax under *ICTA 1988, s 349*. The Inland Revenue may also hold him responsible for ensuring that PAYE is collected although, in view of the points made in 7.3 above, the extent of his legal liability to do so may be academic.

Releases of debts

General implications

7.9   The taxation issues raised by the release of debts are important in various insolvency contexts but perhaps most important in voluntary arrangements. The issues arising for shareholders are addressed in Chapter 12. The issues for debtor companies are as follows.

(a)   Where the release is of a debt which has previously given rise to a deduction in computing profits under Schedule D Case I, the position was formerly that the release did not give rise to a tax charge in that the accounts for the year in which the deduction was claimed could not be re-opened if the liability was there correctly and definitely stated and the release itself did not give rise to a trading receipt (see *The British Mexican Petroleum Co Ltd v Jackson HL 1932, 16 TC 570*). This was rectified by *FA 1960* which introduced what is now *ICTA 1988, s 94* as follows:

'*Debts deducted and subsequently released*

Where, in computing for tax purposes the profits or gains of a trade, profession or vocation, a deduction has been allowed for any debt incurred for the purposes of the trade, profession or vocation, then, if the whole or any part of the debt is thereafter released, the amount released shall be treated as a receipt of the trade, profession or vocation arising in the period in which the release is effected.'

Section 94 applies to trading debts which have been accrued in the accounts of the debtor company as liabilities but remain unpaid and are then released. It should be noted that the receipt arises in the period of release and is not retrospective and may give rise to a post-cessation receipt. [*ICTA 1988, s 103(4)*]. Where a release occurs then (subject to the rules governing post-cessation receipts discussed in 8.25 below, where applicable) losses may be available to offset any resulting profit, including perhaps a loss reflecting the deduction concerned carried forward from a prior year.

(b) Where the release is of an amount of interest (yearly or short) which has been claimed as a charge on income by being debited in the books of the person to whom it is paid, the release may give rise to a disallowance of the charge as not having been "ultimately borne" by the debtor. [*ICTA 1988, s 338(3)*]. This only applies to interest on an advance from a bank carrying on a *bona fide* banking business in the UK or from a person who is in the Revenue's opinion *bona fide* carrying on business as a member of the London Stock Exchange or as a discount house. [*ICTA 1988, s 338(3)(b)*].

(c) Apart from these situations, the release of a debt will not normally affect the tax position of the debtor. There may, however, be specific grounds for concern in special situations (e.g. in relation to subsidies nullifying the right to capital allowances under *CAA 1990, s 153*).

It is worth emphasising that it is only the limited categories of debt described above which can normally give rise to a tax charge. Thus where the principal amount of a bank loan or debenture incurred on capital account is released there will normally not be a tax charge on the debtor company.

What is a "release"?

7.10 *ICTA 1988, s 94* applies only to a "release". This is a term of art of respectable pedigree and has been defined as 'the giving or discharging of the right or action which a man hath, or may have or claim against another man, or that which is his' (Sheppard, Touchstone of Common Assurance, 8th edition 1826, p 320). This denotes some positive agreement by the creditor which is binding on him (so, for example, under English law it must be under seal or for good consideration). Certain types of agreement which have a similar commercial effect will not amount to a "release" in the technical sense. For example, a set-off is not a release and it is very doubtful whether a covenant not to sue will fall within *section 94*. Nor, it is considered, would there be a release if debts are assigned by the creditors to a friendly third party who decides not to enforce them; or necessarily if the terms of the arrangement are merely that certain assets will be used in payment of certain debts, without anything further; or if the terms of the arrangement do not involve any questions of 'full and final settlement' but merely payments on account until the available funds run out. Where, however, the terms of a company voluntary arrangement are that a stated lesser sum will be accepted in discharge of a debt, all debts included in the arrangement will be released if it is approved under *IA 1986, s 5(2)(b)*, whether or not a particular creditor votes in favour or at all. Notwithstanding the legal and formal distinctions, it appears from the statements regarding voluntary arrangements set out in the following paragraph that the Inland Revenue may give a wider interpretation to the term "release".

Releases in voluntary arrangements

7.11   The Inland Revenue's view appears to be that a voluntary arrangement (and indeed any formal arrangement with creditors) will *per se* constitute a release of the debts comprised in it. This view is expressed as follows:

> '*Tax treatment of the debtor*
>
> . . .
>
> (b)   *Section 94, ICTA 1988*, originated in *Finance Act 1960, section 36*, the aim of which was to rectify an anomaly whereby a trader incurred a debt, obtained a tax deduction for the amount of the debt, and subsequently got his creditor to release him from all or part of the debt. The Courts had held that the amount released could not be taxed even though the trader had obtained a deduction for the debt. The legislation in what is now *section 94* therefore imposes a charge in these circumstances.
>
> (c)   It is a feature of the legislation that it only applies where a debt is formally released by the creditor. Thus the mere failure to pay or even the bankruptcy or liquidation of the debtor will not give rise to a charge under *section 94*.
>
> (d)   There *is* a release where there is a formal arrangement with creditors. The position is similar where there is a scheme approved

by the Court, notwithstanding that there were some creditors who did not want to agree but were obliged to do so because the necessary majority agreed. A compromise in satisfaction of debt under a voluntary arrangement would therefore give rise to a "release" which would be treated as a taxable receipt of the debtor by virtue of *section 94*.

. . .

Status of tax liability (ICTA 1988, s 94)

(g) Both *Rules 1.28(b)* (company voluntary arrangements) and *5.28* (individual voluntary arrangements) provide what "fees, costs, charges and expenses" may be incurred for the purpose of a voluntary arrangement. Apart from those sanctioned by the voluntary arrangement itself, those permitted are defined as those which either would be payable, or would correspond to those which would be payable, (1) in an administration or winding up (companies) or (2) in the debtor's bankruptcy (individuals)—see *Rule 1.28(1)(b)(ii)* and *Rule 5.28(b)(ii)*. The relevant Rules for this purpose are *Rules 4.218* and *6.244*—Order of Payment of Costs, etc., out of Assets. The only relevant provision in *Rule 4.218* is at *Rule 4.218(1)(b)*—"expenses incurred or disbursements made by the Official Receiver or under his authority, including those incurred or made in carrying on the business of the company". Clearly the release of a debt by a creditor giving rise to a taxable receipt under *section 94* cannot be within *Rule 4.218(1)(b)*. The same applies to the corresponding rule for individuals at *Rule 6.224(1)(b)* which is in similar terms. The *section 94* tax liability, therefore, is outside the ambit of the Insolvency Rules.'

(ICAEW TR 799, para 16.)

Arrangements under CA 1985, s 425

7.12 Apart from voluntary arrangements under *IA 1986*, as described above in this chapter, the court may, under *CA 1985, s 425, inter alia* sanction a compromise or arrangement between a company and its creditors or any class of them. *Section 425* is not an insolvency provision as such, although it may be used in an insolvency, and has some advantages over the new procedure in that it does not necessarily require a meeting of shareholders and may be more effective in flushing out unknown creditors. The Inland Revenue evidently regard a court scheme as resulting in a release for the purposes of *ICTA 1988, s 94* (see 7.11 above).

VAT

7.13   It is understood that Customs & Excise do not consider that a supervisor of a company in the course of a voluntary arrangement is under an obligation to account for VAT (though the company remains liable to do so). A voluntary arrangement would not be binding on Customs in respect of VAT arising in the course of the arrangement.

7.14   Prior to 26 July 1990, when *FA 1990, s 11* came into effect, creditors of an insolvent company could not obtain bad debt relief for VAT purposes unless the company was in liquidation, administration or administrative receivership, even where a formal arrangement was made with creditors. A creditor is now entitled to relief in respect of a supply on or after 1 April 1989 if a year has passed since the supply in respect of which the creditor has written off the debt. This improvement upon the bad debt provisions of *VATA 1983, s 22*, which *FA 1990, s 11* replaced, may make voluntary arrangements more popular, and is discussed in 12.29–12.38 below.

Chapter 8

Income and Corporation Tax in Liquidation

The effect of winding up

Accounting periods

8.1 A company resident in the UK for tax purposes, or carrying on business here through a branch or agency, continues to be subject to corporation tax on profits arising in its winding up. [*ICTA 1988, s 8(2)*]. However, on commencement of the winding up the company's corporation tax accounting period ends and a new one begins. For this purpose, a winding up is taken as commencing on the passing by a company of a resolution for its winding up, or on the presentation of a winding up petition if no such resolution has previously been passed and a winding up order is made on the petition. Thereafter an accounting period ends after each twelve months from that date, or on the completion of the winding up. [*ICTA 1988, s 12(7)*]. See 8.30 below for the position where a date is assumed for the completion of the liquidation.

Chargeable gains

8.2 A company's assets are not disposed of (or deemed to be disposed of) for the purposes of corporation tax on chargeable gains when a liquidation begins. Even where they are vested in the liquidator by order of the court under *IA 1986, s 145* (which happens very rarely), it is expressly provided that *CGTA 1979* applies as if the assets were vested in, and the acts of the liquidator in relation to the assets were the acts of, the company. Acquisitions from or disposals to him by the company are disregarded accordingly. [*ICTA 1988, s 345(5)*].

Ownership of assets—voluntary liquidation

8.3 Subject to what is said in 8.2 above, it has been established in a number of cases that, while on a liquidation a company retains legal ownership of its assets, it ceases to be the beneficial owner of them. This is important because beneficial ownership is necessary for certain group relationships to subsist (see 8.31–8.32 below) and for a hive-down to be effective (see 18.10–18.13 below). The distinction has evolved from the law of trusts, on the basis that, like a trust fund, the assets of a company controlled by its liquidator can only be applied for the ·benefit of other persons (in essence, creditors and shareholders), under the statutory scheme. In Lord Diplock's words in *Ayerst v C & K (Construction) Ltd HL 1975, 50 TC 651* at p 670, the company's title to its undertaking no longer carries 'with it the right of the owner to enjoy the fruits of it or dispose of it for his own benefit'. Perhaps the most frequently quoted analysis of the position was in the judgments delivered by the Court of Appeal in Chancery in *Re Oriental Inland Steam Co CA 1874, 9 Ch App 557*. In that case, Mellish LJ said (at p 560):

> 'No doubt winding-up differs from bankruptcy in this respect, that in bankruptcy the whole estate, both legal and beneficial, is taken out of the bankrupt, and is vested in his trustees or assignees, whereas in a winding-up the legal estate still remains in the company. But, in my opinion, the beneficial interest is clearly taken out of the company. What [*section 95* of the *Companies Act 1862*] says . . . is, that from the time of the winding-up order all the powers of the directors of the company to carry on the trade or to deal with the assets of the company shall be wholly determined, and nobody shall have any power to deal with them except the official liquidator, and he is to deal with them for the purpose of collecting the assets and dividing them amongst the creditors. It appears to me that that does, in strictness, constitute a trust for the benefit of all the creditors, and, as far as this Court has jurisdiction, no one creditor can be allowed to have a larger share of the assets than any other creditor.'

See also the judgment of James LJ in the same case, at p 559.

8.4   These judgments were applied in a number of High Court decisions, most notably *CIR v Olive Mill Ltd (in liquidation) Ch D 1963, 41 TC 77*, referred to in the context of investment companies in 8.29 below, and *Pritchard v M H Builders (Wilmslow) Ltd Ch D 1968, 45 TC 360*. They do, however, present a fundamental problem, identified by Cross J in the *M H Builders* case: that of identifying the persons (if any) to whom the assets actually do belong. It is noteworthy that in *English Sewing Cotton Co v CIR CA, [1947] 1 All ER 679*, the first case where the question of beneficial ownership of assets of an insolvent company was considered (albeit as *obiter dicta* in the course of considering tax liabilities associated with mortgaged shares), Lord Greene MR proceeded on the basis that 'if anyone says that the company had lost part of their beneficial interest that proposition can only be established if it can be shown that it has gone somewhere'. This point was, however, pursued directly in the Court of Appeal and the House of Lords in *Ayerst v C & K (Construction) Ltd v CIR HL 1975, 50 TC 651*, which concerned a hive-down carried out following a liquidation, and in particular the requirement under what is now *ICTA 1988, s 343(2)(3)* that the trade be in common direct or indirect beneficial ownership before and after the transfer (see further 18.10–18.13 below). The company argued that the creditors and shareholders of the company as a class continued to own the company's assets beneficially throughout its liquidation, although it had to accept that the individuals constituting that class could fluctuate, depending for example on whether preferential creditors had been paid off or other changes had occurred in the identity of those entitled to prove in the liquidation. The company's logic was not accepted by the Court of Appeal which held that it would make *ICTA 1988, s 343* unworkable. In his judgment, Stamp LJ accepted an analysis of the position given by Cross J in the *M H Builders* case, that once a company is in liquidation the beneficial ownership of its assets is in suspense, and the strict trustee/beneficiary concept would not apply. The speech of Lord Diplock in the House of Lords confirmed that beneficial ownership leaves the company at the commencement of its liquidation, and drew various analogies with other situations where assets are held without an identifiable beneficial owner (such as with a deceased's estate in the course of administration) without, however, explicitly analysing where (if anywhere) beneficial ownership of the assets lies.

8.5 Consequently, although it is clear from these cases that a company in liquidation does not beneficially own its assets, it is not clear who (if anyone) does. The best authority is the analysis of the Court of Appeal in the *C & K (Construction)* case that the beneficial ownership is in suspense, and this is at least consistent with later cases such as *CIR v Ufitec Group Ltd QB, [1977] STC 363*, where the beneficial ownership of assets which were subject to a contract for sale was held to be effectively suspended between vendor and purchaser in that it was held to have passed from the vendor though not yet arrived with the purchaser. The principle now appears a matter of accepted law—see most recently *J Sainsbury plc v O'Connor Ch D, [1990] STC 516* per Millett J at pp 530–531, discussed in 18.11 below. It has to be said that this is not a satisfactory position. The idea of property existing without an "owner" (using the term loosely) is not one which commends itself to common sense, and, as is clear from the decided cases, does not sit easily in the trust law context from which it arose. It does not even accord entirely with tax principles, particularly those of corporation tax on chargeable gains. The point must now (subject to the outcome of the *Sainsbury* case) be regarded as of largely academic interest, but for an interesting account of a case in the East African Court of Appeal where the principles just set out were not followed, see *Rudewa Estates Ltd v Stamp Duties Commission, [1968] BTR 1206*.

8.6 Beneficial ownership may also be lost where there is a binding contract for sale (see 18.10–18.12 below) but not necessarily, it seems, where there is an option to sell or possibly even cross-options (see *J Sainsbury plc v O'Connor Ch D, [1990] STC 516* though the case is to be appealed).

Ownership of assets—compulsory liquidation

8.7 The principle that beneficial ownership is lost on (among other things) commencement of liquidation applies equally to compulsory as to voluntary liquidation, but, in the case of a compulsory liquidation, it may be necessary to consider whether beneficial ownership is lost on the date of the winding up order, or on the date of presentation of the petition on which the order was made. This may be of importance where, for example, a hive-down occurs after presentation of the petition but before the order. It is a difficult point, and there is no authority on it. For the reasons set out in the following paragraphs it is arguable that beneficial ownership is only lost on the making of the order, and is not retrospective, but the safer course is to assume that it is lost on presentation of the petition.

8.8   *IA 1986, s 129(2)* provides that (in the absence of an earlier voluntary winding up) 'the winding up of a company by the court is deemed to commence at the time of the presentation of the petition for winding up'. *IA 1986, s 127* provides for the avoidance of property dispositions, etc. in the interim, but is clearly inapplicable to the actions of a receiver as the disposition relevant to him is the original charge under which he was appointed. The question is how far the principle contained in *IA 1986, s 129(2)* applies for tax purposes. Certainly, it is not applicable for all purposes: see *Re Christonette International Ltd Ch D, [1982] 3 All ER 225*, where it was held that a company is only 'in the course of being wound up' for the purposes of what was *CA 1948, s 94(1)* after the winding up order is made and that the crystallisation of a floating charge does not relate back to the date of presentation of the petition. *IA 1986, s 129(2)* is not applicable automatically for the purposes of *ICTA 1988*; see *ICTA 1988, s 12(7)* discussed in 8.1 above, which says specifically that an accounting period ends on the presentation of a winding up petition if an order is made on the petition. In one tax provision, now repealed, it is the date of the order (not that of the petition) which mattered: see *ICTA 1988, 19 Sch 10(6)*, which applied the old close company apportionment rules. An argument may therefore exist that for tax purposes *IA 1986, s 129(2)* does not automatically apply to determine the date when a winding up is to be taken as having begun, and that an interpretation in line with the rule applicable to floating charges is to be preferred.

8.9   *Ayerst v C & K (Construction) Ltd HL 1975, 50 TC 651* in fact concerned a compulsory liquidation, and is the only relevant reported case to have done so. In it, Lord Diplock said (at p 669) that *'the making of a winding up order* brings into operation a statutory scheme' (emphasis added). Templeman J referred (at p 663) to a company ceasing to be beneficial owner of its assets 'when it goes into compulsory liquidation'; the Court of Appeal used similar words. Unfortunately, none of this is particularly helpful as in that case the hive-down occurred after the winding up order had been made and it could no doubt be said that Lord Diplock was speaking *per incuriam*.

8.10   Another support to the argument given in 8.7 above may be the principle that transactions cannot be retrospectively altered for tax purposes. This principle was confirmed by the Court of Appeal in *Morley-Clarke v Jones CA, [1985] STC 660*, which concerned a retrospective variation by the court of a maintenance order. One reason for rejecting the retrospective effect for tax purposes was that the Inland Revenue were not a party to the order. But speaking generally, Oliver LJ said, at p 669:

> 'It seems to me that when one is examining the fiscal consequences of what has actually been done, one cannot, even by order of the court, retrospectively overturn reality.'

It has to be admitted that the *Morley-Clarke* case is unreliable authority where dealing with an express statutory deeming provision instead of a court order, as are also the various cases (some of which were cited in it) on rescinded contracts (such as *Spence v CIR CS 1941, 24 TC 311*).

Cessation

The effect of cessation

8.11   The date when the trade of a company is to be taken for tax purposes as having ceased is of great importance in determining its tax liability, as this date (and not the date the liquidation commences) is the date when balancing charges on plant and machinery will arise and by reference to which any terminal loss claim must be made. After a cessation, also, the special provisions relating to post-cessation receipts and the availability of loss relief will apply. Where a cessation occurs before a liquidation, the cessation will bring about the end of a corporation tax accounting period. [*ICTA 1988, s 12(3)(c)*]. These points are subject to the application of *ICTA 1988, s 343*. Originally an anti-avoidance provision, this provides that a company is not to be regarded for certain purposes as having ceased its trade where the trade is, within a two-year period, carried on by another company in the same 75% ownership (as defined in *ICTA 1988, s 344*). The effect is that no terminal loss claims can be made and balancing charges will not arise. An accounting period will, however, end. *ICTA 1988, ss 343, 344* are considered in detail in Chapter 18.

The timing of cessation

8.12   A company's trade does not necessarily cease on commencement of its winding up (*CIR v Oban Distillery & Co Ltd CS 1932, 18 TC 33* and *Ayerst v C & K (Construction) Ltd HL 1975, 50 TC 651* per Templeman J, as he then was, at p 658) although the dates may coincide as in *John Mills Productions Ltd v Mathias Ch D 1967, 44 TC 441*. IA 1986, s 87 says that in a voluntary winding up a company 'shall from the commencement of the winding up cease to carry on its business except so far as may be required for its beneficial winding up' and *IA 1986, 4 Sch 5* provides in similar terms for the liquidator's powers in a compulsory liquidation. It is clear from these sections that a company's trade can continue after its liquidation; but they are of no assistance in deciding when the cessation does occur (*Baker v Cook KB 1937, 21 TC 337*). The date of a cessation is thus a matter of fact, to be decided by the Appeal Commissioners, which depends upon the particular circumstances of the company concerned. The courts are generally reluctant to interfere with a finding of fact and will only do so where, broadly, the decision is one at which no reasonable body of Commissioners could have arrived (see *Edwards v Bairstow HL 1955, 36 TC 207*). Decided cases are, nonetheless, of some interest, although for this reason, and for those mentioned in 8.17 below, they must be regarded cautiously.

8.13   In many cases, it will be relatively clear when a cessation occurs: where, for example, there is a formal closure of the business and staff are laid off. In some circumstances, however, it will be less easy to determine the date, particularly where it is necessary to distinguish between a continuation of a trade and the realisation of trading assets (including trading stock). This is illustrated by a number of cases concerned with alcoholic drinks. In the best known of them, *CIR v The 'Old Bushmills' Distillery Co Ltd (in liquidation) KB (NI) 1927, 12 TC 1148*, the liquidator of a Northern Ireland company which owned two whiskey distilleries sold one outright, but was unable to sell the other. He continued to purchase some spirits for blending purposes and disposed of the stock over a period of two years, periodically distributing the proceeds of the sales as dividends in the liquidation. The recorder's finding that the company had not been trading, but merely realising assets, was upheld in the High Court. Similarly, in *CIR v Nelson CS 1939, 22 TC 716* an individual carrying on business as a whisky broker closed his bank account and instructed his accountant to wind down his business, advertising his retirement in the press and by circular letter. The subsequent sale of his stock as part of the business was held to have occurred after cessation of his business.

8.14   These cases may be contrasted with two partnership cases where the Commissioners' findings that realisations of stock were carried out in the course of a trade were both upheld. In *J & R O'Kane & Co v CIR HL 1922, 12 TC 303* wine merchants circularised customers informing them of the dissolution of the partnership, and shortly afterwards issued lists of stock for sale to their customers. They also continued to purchase spirits for sale, under running contracts with suppliers. The House of Lords expressed themselves in complete agreement with the Commissioners' finding that the trade had not ceased. The other case was *Hillerns & Fowler v Murray CA 1932, 17 TC 77* where, on very similar facts, a grain merchants' partnership was held to have continued to trade. As will be appreciated, the dividing line between a realisation of assets and continuation of a trade is extremely thin.

8.15   Where trading operations have continued for the benefit of the liquidator they will be taxed as such even if they were actually carried out by a third party. In *Baker v Cook KB 1937, 21 TC 337* the company in question carried on the business of making and distributing Pathe News films. The liquidator hived off the two activities to separate companies, and it was provided that the new companies would carry out the respective existing contracts, paying 90 per cent of the proceeds to the liquidator. One of the companies also made new contracts to exploit certain film rights which the liquidator retained, paying him 80 per cent of the profits. It was held that the new companies had, in return for commissions, carried on the trade on behalf of the liquidator so that the income he received continued to be assessable as trading income and there was no cessation at that time (as there clearly would have been if the business had been sold lock, stock and barrel).

8.16 Some care must therefore be exercised in drafting contracts to avoid any suggestion that the trade has continued, particularly if the common stamp duty saving device is incorporated whereby contracts are completed and debts collected by the purchaser as agent for the vendor. A vendor was held not to continue trading under an arrangement of a similar kind in *Sethia v John KB 1947, 28 TC 153*. Compare, however, *Parker v Batty KB 1941, 23 TC 739* where the terms of the sale included an arrangement whereby the proceeds of existing hire-purchase contracts were paid to the vendor and it was held that a new trade had begun.

8.17 As each one depends on its own facts, the decided cases must be viewed with caution. A number also relate to the provisions (now repealed) of excess profits duty, and another factor is the introduction of the provisions charging post-cessation receipts in *FA 1960*. It may, however, be useful to set out some of the factors common to the decided cases in which the courts have considered whether a cessation has occurred. These are as follows.

(a)   The size, nature and extent of the sales in relation to previous sales (*CIR v Nelson*, above).

(b)   Existence of working capital (*CIR v The 'Old Bushmills' Distillery Co Ltd*, above).

(c)   Closure of premises (*Aeraspray Associated Ltd v Woods Ch D 1964, 42 TC 207*; *Tryka Ltd v Newall Ch D 1963, 41 TC 146*).

(d)   Advertising and publicity (*J & R O'Kane & Co v CIR*; *Hillerns & Fowler v Murray* and *CIR v Nelson*, above).

(e)   Disposal of a key asset (*CIR v Daniel Beattie & Co CS 1955, 36 TC 379*; *H & G Kinemas Ltd v Cook KB 1933, 18 TC 116*).

(f)   Entering into new contracts (*CIR v The 'Old Bushmills' Distillery Co Ltd*, above).

(g)   Whether the trading name was also sold in circumstances where it could not be used by the vendor (*CIR v Nelson*, above).

Old trade or new?

8.18   Where trading activities do continue, the circumstances may justify an argument that the old trade has ceased and a new one has begun, so avoiding in part the consequences of a cessation mentioned in 8.11 above but not enabling losses of the original trade to be carried forward. As before, this is a matter of fact, and again the dividing line is very thin. Three well-known cases illustrate this. In *J G Ingram & Son Ltd v Callaghan CA 1968, 45 TC 151* a receiver was appointed over a company which manufactured and sold rubber surgical products of various kinds. The receiver sold its factory, and then retired. At about the same time, its shares were sold to a third party purchaser which moved its plant to different premises, and eventually sold it and paid off all the staff except for one representative, starting to produce plastic goods under the company's name. Finally, the shares in the company were sold to a second purchaser, which started manufacture which was exactly the same as the original business of the company, except that the components were plastic instead of rubber. It was held that the company had discontinued its original trade at the time shortly after the first sale when its plant was sold and employees laid off, and had thereafter started a new trade. Similarly, in *Gordon & Blair Ltd v CIR CS 1962, 40 TC 358* a brewing company which also sold beer ceased its brewing operations and thereafter only sold bottled beer produced by someone else. It was held to have started a new trade when the brewing ceased and accordingly the losses of the previous trade were not available to carry forward. On the other hand, in *Robroyston Brickworks Ltd v CIR CS 1976, 51 TC 230* a company which made bricks ceased production, paid off its employees and sold its plant, using the proceeds to pay creditors, but was able to show that this was part of a planned move to the new premises of a competitor which then bought its shares, so that no discontinuance of its trade had occurred, and loss relief was available. These issues also arise in relation to hive-downs and are further discussed in Chapter 18.

Computing tax in the liquidation

Trading and other income

8.19   Generally, trading and other income are computed and taxed in a liquidation under the ordinary rules. So, where a liquidator continues to trade, losses and ACT will continue to be available to set against the company's tax liabilities, subject to the usual restrictions, and any losses which are incurred will be available for relief in the usual ways, apart from group relief (see 8.31–8.33 below). Where the trade ceases, a terminal loss claim may be made under *ICTA 1988, s 394*. Losses, including terminal losses, may be set against franked investment income under *ICTA 1988, ss 242, 243*. An important point to note is that the income chargeable will include receivers' income (see 8.27–8.28 below).

Expenses in the liquidation

8.20 A liquidator's expenses will be allowable in computing profits for tax purposes where deductible under the normal principles for deductions from trading profits. If the company has ceased to trade, and it is possible to show that the company has become an investment company (see 8.29 below), expenses may also be allowable as management expenses. Alternatively, expenses may be deductible if incurred in connection with the disposal of capital assets, when they may be taken into account in computing chargeable gains under *CGTA 1979, s 32*, or in determining the net proceeds of sale in respect of which balancing adjustments on plant and machinery will be made under *CAA 1990, s 26(1)*. Costs of collecting debts may also be taken into account in valuing debts on the cessation of the trade.

Interest

8.21 Strictly, interest paid after cessation would not be allowable as a charge on income by reason of the restriction in *ICTA 1988, s 338(6)*, but it is understood that by concession the Inland Revenue normally allow relief for interest paid after a cessation on a loan incurred before that date for the purposes of the trade. Interest which is allowable as a trading expense may continue to be allowable (see 8.25 below).

Balancing adjustments—plant and machinery

8.22 Where a trade is permanently discontinued, balancing adjustments are made in respect of plant and machinery on the last day of trading. [*CAA 1990, s 24(6)(c)(v)*]. The value to be brought into account is normally in practice the proceeds on eventual sale unless there is no sale, in which case the market value at the time of cessation is taken. [*CAA 1990, s 26(1)(b)(e)*]. Clearly, this creates potential problems if sale is deferred, and there is thus an argument that the market value should be taken in any event. This argument is not accepted by the Revenue, although they have stated that, by concession, where assets are not likely to be sold for a long time, the market value at date of cessation may be taken for capital allowance purposes. See CCAB June 1971, Tolley's Official Tax Statements 1990–91, 10.401.

Balancing adjustments—industrial buildings

8.23 Generally, a balancing adjustment in respect of an industrial building is made at the date of sale of the building, and the date of cessation of the company's trade is not relevant to this. [*CAA 1990, s 4*]. There are special rules in *CAA 1990, s 15*, concerning balancing allowances and balancing charges where a discontinuance follows temporary disuse of the building. By ESC B19, trading losses may be carried forward and set against balancing charges arising after a cessation even though the charge would strictly be assessable under Schedule A or Schedule D Case VI.

Releases of debt

8.24   Where a deduction has been allowed in computing trading profits for tax purposes, then if the whole or any part of the debt is thereafter released (or waived), the amount released (or waived) is treated as a trading receipt arising in the period in which the release (or waiver) is effected. [*ICTA 1988, s 94*]. It may alternatively result in a post-cessation receipt as discussed in the following paragraph. The release of a liability to pay accrued but unpaid interest may also cause a disallowance of a charge on income previously claimed as the interest will then not have been "ultimately borne" by the company. [*ICTA 1988, s 338(5)(a)*]. The question of releases is considered in detail in 7.9–7.11 below.

Post-cessation receipts

8.25   Sums received after cessation of a trade in respect of that trade may (if not already brought into account) be taxed under Schedule D, Case VI as post-cessation receipts under *ICTA 1988, s 103*. The provision also applies to debts released after cessation. [*ICTA 1988, s 103(4)*]. Trading losses of the trade which has ceased may not be set off under *ICTA 1988, s 393(2)(3)* against profits taxed in this way, but losses and expenses which would have been allowable deductions if the trade had not been discontinued may still be set against post-cessation receipts, as may unrelieved capital allowances to which the company was entitled before the cessation. [*ICTA 1988, s 105*]. The relief does not, however, extend to expenses arising directly or indirectly from the discontinuance itself, including liquidator's expenses unless allowable on the bases described in 8.20–8.21 above.

Capital gains in the liquidation

8.26   The company remains liable for corporation tax on capital gains resulting from disposals made after liquidation. The usual rules of computation apply. In suitable cases, a proportion of the expenses of realising the assets may be allowable, including any appropriate element of the liquidator's or receiver's expenses. It should be noted that this liability attaches to gains made by receivers or mortgagees as well as those made on disposals by the liquidator of charged or uncharged assets (see 8.27–8.28 below).

Receivers' and mortgagees' income and gains

8.27   The income of receivers and mortgagees in possession, as well as gains made by them, will be regarded for tax purposes as income or gains of the company itself. Accordingly, the tax computations of the company in liquidation should take these amounts into account and the tax will fall to be discharged as the company's liability. This was common ground so far as capital gains were concerned in *Re Mesco Properties Ltd CA 1979, 54 TC 238*, discussed further in 8.36–8.40 below, and it is generally assumed that the same principles apply to income receipts.

8.28   The rule described in 8.27 above creates a potential problem because the liquidator will have no direct knowledge of the amounts involved to put in his computations. It may well be that the first he will know of the liabilities will be the arrival of assessments as the Inland Revenue will of course have the advantage of (for example) returns of interest from the receiver's bankers under *TMA 1970, s 17*. Much of the necessary information will, however, be evident from the receiver's statutory returns filed with the Registrar of Companies under *IA 1986, ss 46–48*. A liquidator is also entitled to require the production of accounts from a receiver under *IA 1986, s 41(1)(b)*. This information may not initially be sufficient to enable him to complete the tax returns with total accuracy, and may not show, for example, which items of expenditure are allowable for the purposes of corporation tax on chargeable gains. The question is then how far the receiver can be compelled to give further details of his receipts and payments. In *Smiths Ltd v Middleton Ch D 1978, [1979] 3 All ER 842*, the court applied equitable principles to establish that a receiver could be compelled by the company to provide full accounts when required to do so to supplement the statutory abstracts, and it seems that a liquidator, as the company's *alter ego*, would enjoy an equivalent right. The right is, however, subject to the receiver's duty to the debenture-holders where this conflicts (*Gomba Holdings UK Ltd v Homan and Another Ch D, [1986] 3 All ER 94*).

Investment companies

8.29   As noted in 8.20 above, it may in practice be possible to show that a company in liquidation which has ceased to trade should be regarded as an investment company and thus be entitled to claim deductions for management expenses under *ICTA 1988, ss 75, 130*. Strictly, however, this treatment is only arguably correct, and the Inland Revenue's "official" line is that a company cannot be regarded as becoming an investment company simply because it has ceased its former activity and is realising assets pending distribution to creditors. This is presumably because on commencement of a liquidation it is considered that the company ceases to carry on a business which 'consists wholly or mainly in the making of investment and the principal part of whose income is derived therefrom', so that the definition of investment company in *ICTA 1988, s 130* no longer applies. This may follow from the decision in *CIR v Olive Mill Ltd (in liquidation) Ch D 1963, 41 TC 77*. This case concerned a slightly different definition applicable for the purposes of profits tax, contained in *FA 1937, s 19*. A holding company which had gone into liquidation argued that its business still consisted 'wholly or mainly in the *holding* of investments or other property' (emphasis added). Buckley J adopted a test laid down by Lord Reid in a case on the compensation payable to a company in liquidation in respect of the nationalisation of a coal mine, *Henry Briggs, Son & Co Ltd (in liquidation) v CIR HL 1960, 39 TC 410*, to the effect that "holding" in this phrase meant retention of property as an investment, not for realisation. The latter definition does not match the wording in *ICTA 1988, s 130* which refers to "making" of investments, but on the face of it the same argument could be applied, that the company's purpose in liquidation is ultimately to distribute its assets not retain them. The result is that expenses of management would not be available to carry forward after the date of liquidation, although this point is an arguable one and as already mentioned is not consistently taken by the Revenue. It should be noted that the post-cessation receipts provisions do not apply to investment companies, since profits or gains of an investment company do not derive from a trade. [*ICTA 1988, ss 103, 105*]. These principles will, of course, apply equally to a company which was an investment company before liquidation, though it is understood that in such cases the Revenue may accept that investment company status continues for the first accounting period after liquidation begins.

Rates of tax

8.30   Since the rate of corporation tax may be fixed retrospectively, special rules exist to determine the rate of tax applicable in the final year of a winding up, contained in *ICTA 1988, s 342*. Where the rate of tax for the final year is not known, the Inspector of Taxes and the liquidator must concur in fixing an assumed date for the ending of the liquidation. [*ICTA 1988, s 342(5)*]. The Inspector may raise an assessment in respect of the final period before it comes to an end. [*ICTA 1988, s 342(4)*]. The assessment is raised at the rate of corporation tax in the preceding financial year, unless a different rate for the final year has been enacted, or proposed in a Budget resolution, in which case it will be this rate. [*ICTA 1988, s 342(2)(3)*]. Theoretically, this can create a problem if the financial year ends before the Budget resolution but, in practice, this is easily avoided since only a few days are likely to be involved. If the estimate for the ending of the winding up is wrong and the real date is earlier, that date determines the final year. [*ICTA 1988, s 342(6)*]. If the estimated date is earlier, an accounting period will still end on that date and subsequent periods will end on its anniversaries, until completion of the winding up.

Group aspects

Group elections and group relief

8.31   In determining group relationships under *ICTA 1988, s 838* it is expressly provided that references to ownership are to be construed as references to beneficial ownership. [*ICTA 1988, s 838(3)*]. This means that, where this definition is applicable, a parent company which is in liquidation will cease to be a member of the same tax group as its subsidiaries, since it will cease to be the beneficial owner of their shares (see 8.3–8.10 above). The provisions to which this is relevant include *ICTA 1988, s 247* (group income) and *ICTA 1988, ss 402, 413(3)–(6)* (group relief), and reliefs under these provisions will not be available in respect of accounting periods after liquidation. A hive-down will also be ineffective after liquidation (see 18.13 below). The liquidation of a subsidiary will not, however, affect the beneficial ownership by the parent of the subsidiary's shares.

Capital gains

8.32   *ICTA 1988, s 838* is inapplicable to the group capital gains provisions, *ICTA 1970, ss 272–279*. *ICTA 1970, s 272(4)* expressly provides that the winding up of a company is not the occasion of the company, or of any subsidiary of it, ceasing to be a member of a group for the purposes of tax on chargeable gains. Transfers of capital assets between members of the group after liquidation do not therefore of themselves give rise to any chargeable gain on the disposal of the capital assets (though in appropriate cases the possibility of a charge under *ICTA 1970, s 278* may need to be considered). This includes distributions *in specie* (see 12.23 below). *ICTA 1970, s 272(4)* does not, however, result in a company acquired after the commencement of the winding up being treated as part of the group for the purposes of tax on chargeable gains.

Time limits for elections

8.33   The time limits for elections are reviewed in Chapter 17 below.

Income tax deductions

8.34   A company in liquidation will be liable to account for income tax which is required to be deducted from certain payments, including certain payments of annual interest and other annual payments under *ICTA 1988, s 349*. The same applies to payments of emoluments under the PAYE regulations and payments to sub-contractors in the construction industry. It should be noted that the PAYE regulations apply specifically to payments by a liquidator (among others) to a former employee of the company. [*ITER 1973, Reg 16*]. Income tax must accordingly be deducted from payments to employees in satisfaction of their preferential claims for wages, and accounted for as a post-liquidation PAYE liability. On the other hand, as with receivers (for which see 5.24 above) no deduction is required from payments made *to* a liquidator to which the construction industry tax deduction scheme applies (see Inland Revenue booklet 'Construction Industry Tax Deduction Scheme' IR 14/15 (1982), para 155).

Interest on and penalties for unpaid tax

8.35   Interest on and penalties for unpaid tax which arise from post-liquidation liabilities are strictly to be discharged by the company in the same way as other forms of tax arising after the liquidation. See Chapter 16.

Liquidator's liability to pay tax

8.36   The liquidator of the company is its "proper officer" within *TMA 1970, s 108(1)*. However, this provision does not impose any personal liability on him, at least in the case of a liquidator of a UK company. (For the position of liquidators of foreign companies, see Chapter 15). A similar point was decided by the Privy Council in *ITC v Chatani PC, [1983] STC 477*, a case on a provision of the Jamaican tax legislation. The liquidator's obligations are thus confined to fulfilling the formal obligations of the company under the Taxes Acts, such as filing of returns; and service of documents will be properly effected if they are served on him. A liquidator must, however, take care to retain funds to discharge any tax liabilities, or to obtain a clear indemnity, since if he underestimates them and makes a distribution, the amount distributed may be irrecoverable as money paid under a mistake of law, as in *Taylor v Wilson's Trustees CS 1975, [1979] SLT 105*.

Order of priority of tax

The Beni-Felkai case

8.37   There was formerly some uncertainty as to the priority for payment of corporation tax in a liquidation. In *Re Beni-Felkai Mining Co Ltd Ch D 1933, 18 TC 632*, a company went into voluntary liquidation in the course of a reorganisation involving the transfer of its assets to two French companies, in circumstances where it was assumed to be solvent because of the substantial interests it held in Algerian mines and railways. Unfortunately, because of the general strike of 1926, the value of its assets fell, the French companies became insolvent, and the Inland Revenue sought to claim a little under £600 of tax in respect of profits earned after the date of liquidation, which could only be recovered by striking out of the account a part of the liquidator's remuneration. The judge accepted that the liquidator could not be held personally liable for the tax, but after a consideration of the authorities and of the then current Winding Up Rules applicable to a compulsory liquidation, decided that the tax liabilities should be regarded as expenses of the liquidation, to be discharged, like other expenses, in priority to his remuneration. However, a part of the remuneration was still allowed by the court in exercise of its discretion, representing his services in preserving the company's assets.

The Mesco Properties case

8.38   That case was followed in what is now the leading authority in this area, *Re Mesco Properties Ltd CA 1979, 54 TC 238*, which concerned a company in compulsory liquidation. Chargeable gains had been made in respect of assets sold by the liquidator (some of which were charged and others of which were unencumbered) as well as by receivers and mortgagees in possession. It was common ground that no liability to discharge the tax fell on the receivers or mortgagees, and that the liability remained that of the company in each case. However, as in the *Beni-Felkai* case, the company was insolvent, and the liquidator sought directions as to the priority which the tax should have. Argument turned on *CWR 1949, Rule 195(1)* which set out the order of application of the assets of the company in a compulsory liquidation remaining after payment of the fees and expenses properly incurred in preserving, realising or getting in the assets. Under that rule, the "necessary disbursements" of the liquidator incurred in the winding up were to be discharged out of the residue in priority to his remuneration. The questions to be considered were:

(a)   whether the tax was an expense incurred in preserving, realising or getting in the assets; or

(b)   whether it was a necessary disbursement incurred in the winding up; or

(c)   whether the tax liability was postponed to the debts of unsecured creditors.

If (a) or (b) had applied, the tax would have had priority over the liquidator's fees; while if (c) had applied, his fees would have been paid in full.

8.39   The High Court, and then the Court of Appeal, in *Mesco Properties* held that the tax should be regarded as a "necessary disbursement" of the liquidator. Brightman J (as he then was) in the High Court referred to the *obiter dicta* of Maugham J in the *Beni-Felkai* case concerning the procedure in compulsory liquidation. His conclusion was that the tax could not be regarded as an expense of realising the assets as unlike, say, a solicitor's fees, it was not an expense which assisted the sale, or even necessarily resulted from it (since no gain might in fact result). The tax was, however, a necessary disbursement and, as found in *Beni-Felkai*, an expense incurred in the winding up. The Court of Appeal accepted his arguments, remarking that whether or not a disbursement was "necessary" could not depend only on whether the liquidator decided to pay it or not. Buckley LJ advanced a further argument, based as he put it on "common sense and justice". The realisation itself was a necessary step in the winding up and if the result was a tax liability, then it was the liquidator's duty to apply the assets 'for the benefit of all in accordance with their rights', including the Inland Revenue. While this last argument does, perhaps, beg the question of priorities to some extent, the result was that corporation tax on chargeable gains (and by analogy on other profits) arising after commencement of the liquidation fell to be discharged as a disbursement in accordance with *CWR 1949, Rule 195(1)* (or as an expense in a voluntary liquidation) whether or not it resulted from actions of a liquidator or of a receiver or mortgagee. For a similar conclusion in a case on the bankruptcy procedure in Northern Ireland, see *Re McMeekin (a bankrupt) QB(NI) 1973, [1974] STC 429*. It would, however, appear that the position is different in the Irish Republic—see *Revenue Commissioners v Donnelly SCE, [1983] ILRM 329.*

Current provisions

8.40   The narrow point at issue in the *Mesco Properties* case is now expressly provided for by *Ins R 1986, Rule 4.218(1)(p)* which subordinates to (*inter alia*) the liquidator's remuneration up to an amount corresponding to that which would be chargeable under the Official Receiver's scale:

> 'the amount of any corporation tax on chargeable gains occurring on the realisation of any asset of the company (without regard to whether the realisation is effected by the liquidator, a secured creditor, or a receiver or manager appointed to deal with a security)'.

The balance of the liquidator's remuneration is payable next in order.

8.41   This rule does not in terms deal with tax on income (e.g. on interest), and by analogy with *Mesco Properties* this should strictly still be treated as an expense of the liquidation and thus senior to the liquidator's remuneration (as well as other payments). In practice, however, the Inland Revenue do not normally seek any corporation tax in priority to the liquidator's remuneration allowable under *Rule 4.218(1)(p)* though prudence dictates that this should be confirmed in relation to each individual liquidation. This is a point of considerable practical importance given that the assets under a receiver's control may well represent the bulk of the company's assets and the tax liability may be relatively substantial.

8.42   Where there is a receiver appointed under a (crystallised) floating charge which had not crystallised at the time liquidation began (i.e. a receivership commencing after liquidation), assets comprised in the charge may be available to pay the costs of the liquidation under *Ins R 1986, Rule 4.218* including tax (see further 5.14 above).

Chapter 9

VAT in Administrative Receivership, Administration and Liquidation

Administrative receivers and VAT

The Willment case

9.1   The leading case concerning an administrative receiver's obligation to pay VAT is still *Re John Willment (Ashford) Ltd Ch D, [1979] STC 286*. In that case, the company carried on a garage business. On 6 December 1974 a receiver was appointed by its bankers under a fixed and floating charge (i.e. he would now be an administrative receiver). Thereafter, the company's trade was continued, VAT was charged on its supplies, and tax invoices were issued in the usual form in its name. The receiver made returns to Customs & Excise and accounted for the tax due in respect of the first two accounting periods, but having received legal advice did not account for tax in later periods. In due course the receiver took out a summons applying for directions whether he was bound to account for this tax or whether, in view of his duty to the debenture-holder, he should apply the VAT monies collected in settlement of the secured debt and accrued interest. The judge held that the receiver had a discretion how to deal with the funds which came into his hands but, in view of the provisions contained in *FA 1972, s 38(8)*, could only exercise this discretion in favour of Customs since, if he did otherwise, he would be causing the company to commit a criminal offence (and might himself be guilty of aiding and abetting it). *FA 1972, s 38(8)*, which became *VATA 1983, s 39(8)*, was repealed from 30 September 1986 as part of the steps recommended by the Keith Committee to decriminalise VAT offences. With effect from 1 January 1986, the position is now dealt with by specific regulations (see 9.2 below), and the decision is no longer direct authority. It is, however, an instructive case in that the following interesting points were accepted as common ground by the parties.

(a)   *Agency of the receiver.* Despite the appointment of the receiver, the company remained the taxable person for the purposes of what is now *VATA 1983, s 2*. The receiver acted in the capacity of agent for the company so that it was correct to treat supplies after his appointment as continuing to be made by the company and invoices as still being issued by the company. Different considerations would have applied if a receiver were other than an agent of the company, as where he acted after liquidation, or the charge deed so provided, or if he was a fixed charge receiver.

87

(b)   *Application of VAT regulations.* It was accepted that the receiver did not fall within *Value Added Tax (General) Regulations 1975, SI 1975 No 2204, Reg 55A* (as amended), under which certain persons acting in a representative capacity (including receivers) had to comply with certain requirements under these regulations but only if Customs so required. These provisions are now contained in *VAT Gen R 1985, Reg 63.* The parties agreed that Customs had not made any such requirement and, furthermore, it was open to argument whether a receiver appointed by a debenture-holder came within the regulation.

(c)   *Receiver's own liability.* As in the case of corporation tax in a receivership, it was accepted that no personal liability could fall on the receiver under what is now *IA 1986, s 37(1)*, which provides that a receiver of property of a company appointed out of Court is to be personally liable on contracts, but is entitled to an indemnity. It was also accepted that *LPA 1925, s 109(8)*, providing for the discharge of 'rent, taxes, rates and outgoings' affecting the mortgaged property, does not confer on the taxing authority a right to sue in respect of VAT, following *Liverpool Corporation v Hope CA, [1938] 1 All ER 492*, but that it did give the receiver a discretion as to how he could apply the money (including if he wished in payment of VAT). See now also *IA 1986, ss 14, 42, 1 Sch* for powers of administrators and administrative receivers.

(d)   *VAT monies as trust monies.* The VAT monies collected could not be regarded as impressed with a trust in favour of Customs following their collection. This reflects *Attorney General v Jeanne Antoine KB 1949, 31 TC 213*, where it was held that sums deducted by an employer in respect of PAYE income tax, but stolen before payment to the Inland Revenue, were not trust monies.

The present position of administrative receivers

9.2   *VATA 1983, s 31(4)* empowers the Commissioners to make regulations providing for persons who carry on a business of a taxable person who has died or become bankrupt or incapacitated to be treated for a limited time as taxable persons, and for securing continuity in the application of *VATA 1983* in cases where persons are so treated. As will be appreciated, this provision did not, as originally enacted, cover in clear terms the position of a company where a receiver or liquidator was appointed, but *VATA 1983, s 31(5)*, added by *FA 1985, s 31*, now provides that the reference to bankruptcy or incapacity in *VATA 1983, s 31(4)* is to be construed in relation to a company which is a taxable person as a reference to its being in liquidation or receivership or to an administration order being in force in relation to it. This is reflected in *VAT Gen R 1985, Reg 11*, which is as follows:

'(1)   If a taxable person dies or becomes bankrupt or incapacitated, the Commissioners may, from the date on which he died or became bankrupt or incapacitated until some other person is registered in respect of the taxable supplies made or intended to be made by that taxable person in the course or furtherance of his business or the incapacity ceases, as the case may be, treat as a taxable person any person carrying on that business; and the provisions of the Act and of any Regulations made thereunder shall apply to any person so treated as though he were a registered person.

(2) Any person carrying on such business as aforesaid shall, within 21 days of commencing to do so, inform the Commissioners in writing of that fact and of the date of the death or of the nature of the incapacity and the date on which it began.

(3) In relation to a company which is a taxable person, the references in paragraph (1) of this regulation to the taxable person becoming bankrupt or incapacitated shall be construed as references to its going into liquidation or receivership or to an administration order being made in relation to it.'

Thus, the regulation provides that the Commissioners may treat a receiver appointed over a company as a taxable person if he is a person carrying on the business of the company. This would include an administrative receiver under *IA 1986*, but not a receiver appointed under a fixed charge (see for this topic Chapter 13 below). A receiver who is within *Regulation 11* must notify Customs & Excise in writing of his appointment within 21 days, whereupon he may be treated as a taxable person himself and if so treated is then liable (and, in fact, personally liable) for the VAT on supplies made. There are separate requirements relating to the delivery of returns and payment of tax (see 9.11–9.13 below). *Regulation 11* is not, in fact, normally applied but serves as a sanction against administrative receivers who might otherwise be tempted to exercise their discretion not to pay VAT.

9.3   The position described above is confirmed by Customs & Excise in Notice No 700 ('The VAT Guide' (1 October 1987 with amendments)) which states in para 59:

'*Administrative receivers.* Usually an administrative receiver acts as the agent of the company. If this is the case, tax is accounted for in the normal way. If the administrative receiver is not the company's agent the procedure [described in 13.3–13.4 below where goods are sold in satisfaction of a debt] must be used.'

The final sentence is believed to refer to the position where the receiver as appointed is not the company's agent. In practice, if he is an agent when appointed but his agency ceases (e.g. where a liquidation begins) he will continue to make returns in the usual way. If, however, a liquidator has already been appointed and has taken responsibility for the returns, then the receiver will not do so but will use the Form 833 procedure—see 13.3 below.

9.4   *Regulation 11* is unhelpful on what the position of the company will be if a receiver carrying on its business is treated as a taxable person in respect of that business. Generally, the legislation does not embrace the possibility of two persons being registered in respect of the same business although the receiver could well be acting as agent so that strictly supplies continue to be made by the company. Presumably, the company should deregister if it (as opposed to the receiver) has ceased to make taxable supplies (see *VATA 1983, 7 Sch* and 9.17–9.19 below). It should, however, be remembered that the sales of residual assets could be taxable supplies (see 9.7 below).

Administrators and VAT

9.5   An administrator appointed under *IA 1986, s 8* is in a similar position to an administrative receiver for VAT purposes. The administrator is an agent of the company and, therefore, his appointment does not affect the VAT registration of the company which will remain registered for VAT and liable to charge and account for VAT in the normal way. The administrator is not normally personally liable for tax but, as in the case of the receiver, *VAT Gen R 1985, Reg 11* (see 9.2 above) applies so that the Commissioners may treat the administrator as a taxable person if he carries on the business of the company and the provisions of *VATA 1983* and regulations made thereunder will then apply as if the administrator were registered. Alternatively, if an administrator failed to account for VAT which he had collected, Customs could apply for an order for payment of the tax under *IA 1986, s 27* on the basis that they would otherwise be unfairly prejudiced, which order would be likely to be granted.

Liquidators and VAT

9.6   Although the company's assets do not normally vest directly in a liquidator by virtue of his appointment, a liquidator will be responsible for undertaking the company's affairs for the ultimate benefit of creditors and members and will be responsible for its VAT registration. As might be expected, a company's business has been held not to terminate automatically for VAT purposes on its liquidation (*Shire Equip Ltd v C & E Commrs, MAN/83/52 (1464)*). *VAT Gen R 1985, Reg 11* (as amended) gives the Commissioners power to treat a liquidator carrying on the business of a company as a taxable person. A liquidator is also under certain obligations to deliver VAT returns (see 9.11–9.13 below), but in practice a receiver will continue to make the returns, notwithstanding the appointment of a liquidator, where his appointment pre-dated that of the liquidator and he has control of the assets (see 9.2–9.4 above).

Disposing of the assets

Effect of termination of the business

9.7   Notwithstanding the termination of a business, an administrator, receiver or liquidator who disposes of its assets (including capital assets) will still be involved with the making of taxable supplies. This follows from the wording of *VATA 1983, s 2(1)*, as extended by *VATA 1983, s 47(5)*, which provides that anything done in connection with the termination, or intended termination, of a business is treated as being done in the course or furtherance of that business and may as such fall within the scope of VAT. See also *M Wolfe (t/a Arrow Coach Services) v C & E Commrs, LEE/75/ 22 (171)* where, under the more restrictive provisions of *FA 1972, 2 Sch 3* as originally enacted, a sale of a coach after cessation of a business was deemed to be made in the course of a business.

Receivers appointed of particular assets

9.8   It is considered that *VAT Gen R 1985, Reg 11* does not strictly apply to receivers appointed over specific assets (e.g. buildings) or to mortgagees in possession although in practice it is understood that Customs & Excise may sometimes allow this treatment to fixed charge receivers of land. VAT must, however, still be accounted for where appropriate on disposals by such persons and the position is dealt within 13.3–13.4 below.

VAT treatment of certain assets

9.9   A liquidator or an administrative receiver will commonly dispose of assets of a business as a going concern so that the transaction is ignored for VAT purposes, being treated as neither a supply of goods nor a supply of services. This type of disposal is considered in detail in 9.36–9.49 below.

9.10   Where assets are disposed of other than in the course of a transfer as a going concern, the VAT treatment depends on the normal VAT treatment applicable to the type of asset in question (be it stock in trade or capital asset).

The commonest types of assets encountered are as follows.

(a)   *Land and buildings.* The VAT treatment of supplies of property was fundamentally changed by *FA 1989* which amended *VATA 1983, 5 Sch Group 8, 6 Sch Group 1*, as well as introducing a new *Schedule 6A*. Broadly, VAT is not chargeable on land and buildings intended for domestic and some residential and charitable use. Supplies of property for such purposes are either exempt or zero rated. Supplies of land and buildings for other uses are either compulsorily standard rated or exempt subject to the right of the vendor/landlord to elect to waive exemption and charge VAT. The following are the main categories of supplies which are always standard rated.

(i)   The sale of a freehold in an uncompleted building or a building completed or fully occupied, whichever occurred first, less than three years prior to the sale.

(ii)   The sale of a freehold in an uncompleted civil engineering work or a civil engineering work completed or fully used, whichever occurred first, less than three years prior to the sale.

(iii)   Surrenders or assignments to a person to whom a surrender could be made.

(iv)   Under proposals announced by Customs & Excise but not at the time of writing introduced into law, the disposal of any interest in land subject to a developmental lease by a relevant supplier, e.g. the grantor of the lease or his successor.

Most other supplies of property are exempt subject to the election to waive exemption and charge VAT. No procedure is prescribed for making the election but Customs must be notified in writing within 30 days of the election being made. An election, once made, is irrevocable and will bind the administrator, receiver or liquidator. It may not be possible to determine whether the election has been made in relation to a property and Customs should be asked to confirm whether an election has or has not been made if there is any doubt. An election by a member of a VAT group is binding on all other members, including any future members while the property is held by a member of the group, and continues to be binding even on companies which later leave the VAT group.

The election applies to the whole of a person's interest in a building or land including interests acquired after the election was made. For these purposes, "building" includes buildings linked internally or by a covered walkway and parades, precincts and complexes divided into separate units are treated as a single "building". The supply of property which is compulsorily standard rated or the subject of an election to waive exemption may be taken effectively outside the scope of VAT if it is or is part of a transfer of the assets of a business as a going concern (see 9.36–9.49 below). It should be noted that Customs regard a single property let to tenants as a business (or part of one capable of separate operation) and, therefore, the disposal of such a property is potentially subject to the rules relating to transfers of going concerns. The VAT treatment of transfers of going concerns involving property is, however, subject to legislation proposed but not introduced at the time of writing. For a discussion of the rules mentioned, see 9.36 below.

In the case of property acquired or subject to a self-supply on or after 1 April 1990 where VAT was charged and the value of the supply or self-supply exceeded £250,000 (exclusive of VAT), the scheme for capital items will apply (see *VAT Gen R 1985, Regs 37A–37E*). The scheme requires the taxable person to review, at least once a year for a period of up to ten years, the extent to which the property is used for making taxable supplies. If the taxable use changes, the taxable person must make an adjustment to the input tax originally claimed (or foregone) when the item was acquired. An increase in taxable use will allow a claim for a further refund of input tax. A decrease in taxable use will create a liability to repay input tax originally claimed. Unless detailed records have been kept it may be difficult for the administrator, receiver or liquidator to know what the taxable use of the item was during the first interval. Where land is sold, the possibility of an adjustment to the VAT payable under these provisions will need to be borne in mind.

(b)   *Shares, securities and debts.* These are all normally exempt supplies under *VATA 1983, 6 Sch Group 5.* The assignment, by an owner, of goods comprised in a hire-purchase or conditional sale agreement, of his rights and interest therein to a bank or other financial institution is outside the scope of VAT. [*Value Added Tax (Special Provisions) Order 1981, SI 1981 No 1741, Art 12(2)*].

(c)   *Second-hand cars.* VAT will normally only be payable on any excess of consideration received over the price paid, under *Value Added Tax (Cars) Order 1980, SI 1980 No 442, Art 6.* In practice, VAT will hardly ever be paid in relation to a company which is not dealing in cars. This treatment is inapplicable to commercial vehicles, the sale of which may in suitable cases constitute a taxable supply.

(d)   *Ships.* The supply of ships is normally a zero rated supply unless the ship is less than 15 tons gross tonnage or designed or adapted for use for recreation or pleasure, in which case standard rating applies (see *VATA 1983, 5 Sch Group 10 Item 1*). The exception largely consists of pleasure yachts.

(e)   *Aircraft.* As with ships, the supply is normally zero rated unless the aircraft is of less than 8,000 kilogrammes in weight or designed or adapted for use for recreation or pleasure. In the case of both ships and aircraft, special schemes can be operated whereby VAT can be accounted for on the profit element only. See Customs & Excise Notices No 720 ('VAT: Second-hand Boats and Outboard Motors' (1 December 1985)) and No 721 ('VAT: Second-hand Aircraft' (1 December 1985)).

(f)   *Exports.* The general principle is that goods exported may be zero rated subject to the production of evidence appropriate to the type of goods and method of export concerned. See *VAT Gen R 1985, Regs 49–57.* Customs & Excise Notice No 703 ('VAT: Exports' (March 1987 with amendments)) is also helpful.

(g)   *Goodwill.* Supplies of goodwill are considered taxable by Customs (see CEPR No 790, 10 December 1982). In fact, VAT will frequently not be chargeable on goodwill since if sold at all, it will normally be sold as part of the assets of a business sold as a going concern (see paragraphs 9.36–9.49 below). It seems that sales of goodwill not so excluded are correctly treated as taxable supplies for VAT purposes since, under the contract, there is something 'done for a consideration' under *VATA 1983, s 3(2)(b)* (i.e. the assignment), notwithstanding the uncertainty of the legal status of goodwill as property (for which see an article and a letter in Taxation Practitioner for February and May 1984 respectively). Note, however, that it is not necessary for a formal assignment to pass goodwill (see *The Old Red Lion (Restaurant) v C & E Commrs, LON/83/ 28 (1446)* and other cases cited in 9.39 below).

(h) *Plant and equipment.* Though capital assets, the disposal of plant and equipment is still capable of being a taxable supply (see 9.7 above). The area in which problems arise most frequently is fixed plant. Customs regard fixtures as 'flowing with the land' and treat any consideration paid for them for VAT purposes in the same way as the consideration for the supply of the land. The same applies to fittings, provided a separate consideration is not stated. In the case of computer equipment of value of £50,000 or more, acquired on or after 1 April 1990, the scheme for capital items will apply and an adjustment to the input tax originally claimed (or foregone) may have to be made if the equipment is disposed of within up to five years (see (a) above for a brief summary of the scheme as it applies to land).

VAT accounting and payment in administrative receivership, administration and liquidation

9.11 As discussed in 9.2–9.6 above, the VAT registration of the company is normally unaffected by the appointment of a receiver, administrator or liquidator. *VAT Gen R 1985, Reg 58(3)* provides that, where Customs & Excise have made a requirement under *VAT Gen R 1985, Reg 63* (see 9.12 below), the VAT accounting period of the company shall end on the day immediately preceding the date of appointment of the receiver, administrator or liquidator and a VAT return must be furnished in respect of that period no later than the last day of the month next following the end of that period. A new accounting period will start on the day of appointment and end (and all subsequent periods begin and end) on the company's normal return dates as previously determined under *Regulation 58(1)*.

9.12 *VAT Gen R 1985, Reg 63* is as follows:

'Where any person subject to any requirements under this Part of these Regulations dies or becomes incapacitated and control of his assets passes to another person, being a personal representative, trustee in bankruptcy, receiver, liquidator, or person otherwise acting in a representative capacity, that other person shall, if the Commissioners so require and so long as he has such control, comply with those requirements:

provided that any requirement to pay tax shall only apply to that other person to the extent of the assets of the deceased or incapacitated person over which he has control; and save to the extent aforesaid this Part of these Regulations shall apply to such person, so acting, as if he were the deceased or incapacitated person.'

It is not absolutely clear that this regulation applies to receivers or liquidators of insolvent companies since neither receivership nor liquidation are in the strict sense "death or incapacity" of the company. This doubt was recognised in the *Willment* case (see 9.1(b) above) although *Regulation 63* has been amended since then. Administrators are not expressly mentioned at all. In practice, however, at least in administrative receivership and liquidation *Regulation 63* (and *Regulation 58* discussed in the preceding paragraph) are normally accepted as applicable with the result that the appointee will comply with the regulations as regards accounting and payment of tax to the extent of the assets which he controls.

9.13   Under *VATA 1983, 7 Sch 4(4)*, where the receiver, administrator or liquidator has failed to make a return or has made an incomplete or incorrect return the company will be liable to be assessed for any tax due and interest thereon although not, it seems, for any default surcharge or serious misdeclaration which would otherwise arise. Notification of an assessment to a receiver, administrator or liquidator is treated as notification to the company. [*VATA 1983, 7 Sch 4(10)*]. The position regarding interest and penalties is further considered in Chapter 16 below.

Input tax

9.14   *VATA 1983, ss 14, 15* provide that input tax incurred by the company may be credited against output tax due from the company in so far as such input tax is attributable to the following supplies made in course or furtherance of its business:

(a)   taxable supplies;

(b)   supplies outside the UK which would be taxable supplies if made in the UK; and

(c)   supplies of dutiable goods in warehouse which would be taxable supplies if not disregarded for VAT purposes by *VATA 1983, s 35*.

The ability of a taxable person to recover input tax is governed by *VAT Gen R 1985, Pt V. Regulation 30(1)* provides that input tax on importations and supplies wholly used or to be used in making taxable supplies may be recovered while input tax wholly used or to be used in making exempt supplies or carrying on any activity other than making taxable supplies is not recoverable. Any input tax which does not fall into the previous two categories is recoverable only to the extent that the importations and supplies are used or to be used in making taxable supplies expressed as a proportion of the whole use of such importations and supplies. *Regulation 30(2)* allows an alternative method of determining the recoverable proportion of any remaining input tax in proportion to the value of taxable supplies made by the person as against the value of all supplies, disregarding certain matters, made by that person. *Regulation 30(5)* allows Customs & Excise to permit the use of other methods for determining the amount of input tax which is recoverable which is usually known as a 'special method'. *Regulations 31–32* allow recovery of input tax attributable to exempt supplies in special cases or where amounts fall below the *de minimis* limits which are currently:

(a)   £100 per month on average; or

(b)   both £250 per month on average and 50 per cent of all input tax; or

(c)   both £500 per month on average and 25 per cent of all input tax.

Regulation 30B provides that where a self-supply occurs the input tax on the supply deemed to be made to the person cannot be attributed to the supply deemed to be made by the person. Input tax is claimed provisionally on each return and at the end of every twelve months an "annual adjustment" is required based on a revaluation of the figures for the whole year under *Regulation 33*. See also Section IV of Notice No 706 ('Partial Exemption' (April 1990)).

9.15   Customs & Excise have indicated that they apply the above rules to insolvencies as follows.

(a)   Where the company was historically fully taxable from commencement of the insolvency to deregistration, all input tax on the administrative receiver, administrator or liquidator's fees is recoverable but significant sales constituting exempt supplies will normally require the apportionment (and/or disallowance) of other input tax, e.g. on estate agent's or solicitor's fees, even if included in the practitioner's own fees. The normal *de minimis* concessions and disregards apply while the company is registered.

(b)   Where the company was historically partially exempt, Customs expect the "adjustment" required by *VAT Gen R 1985, Reg 33* (see 9.14 above) to be made in the period immediately preceding the "relevant date" and again at deregistration and in any period or periods in which an anniversary of the "relevant date" falls before deregistration. Where "normal trading" continues, the usual partial exemption rules apply to determine recovery of input tax. Where it does not, the practitioner's fees are treated as attributable to taxable supplies (except where third party fees not so attributable are included, though these may fall within *de minimis* provisions). Again, the normal *de minimis* concessions and disregards apply while the company is registered.

(c) Fees attributable to a transfer of a going concern by the transferor are normally recoverable, though they will be treated as "residual input tax" in the case of a partially exempt company.

See 9.19 below for a discussion of deferral of VAT deregistration and 9.21 on the recovery of VAT after deregistration.

9.16 Under *FA 1988, s 21*, an amount due from Customs & Excise under *VATA 1983* or by way of repayment supplement to a person shall be set off against any liability of the person to pay an amount by way of tax, penalty, interest or surcharge and the obligations of both parties are discharged to the extent of the set-off. This provision may allow Customs to set off repayments due during an "out of court" administrative receivership or administration against pre-insolvency tax due, though they no longer regard the section as applicable in liquidations and voluntary arrangements (see CEPR 6 February 1991). In *Re Potco Realisation Ltd Ch D 1988, [1989] STC 429* it was held that *section 21* applies to sums due at the time when the section came into effect on 29 July 1988. Further, the section extends to claims on Form VAT 427 (see para 9.21 below) for repayment of input tax after deregistration. For a further discussion of *section 21*, see 20.9–20.13 below. Customs may also withhold tax repayments from insolvent companies where not all previous returns have been filed under *VATA 1983, s 14(7)*.

Cancellation of VAT registration

Compulsory deregistration

9.17 A natural consequence of disposal of the company's assets is that it ceases to make taxable supplies, so that its registration (and any separate registration of a receiver, administrator or liquidator) must be cancelled. A registered person who ceases to make or have the intention of making taxable supplies must under *VATA 1983, 1 Sch 7* notify Customs & Excise of that fact within 30 days of the date on which he so ceases. Such notification must be in writing and state the date upon which taxable supplies or the intention to make such supplies ceased. [*VAT Gen R 1985, Reg 4(4)*]. In the absence of notification, daily penalties may be incurred under *FA 1985, s 17(1)(a)*. *VATA 1983, 1 Sch 9* states that where Customs are satisfied that a registered person has ceased to be either liable or entitled to be registered they may cancel the registration with effect from the day on which the person ceased to be registrable or such later date as may be agreed.

Discretionary deregistration

9.18   Where cessation of supplies does not occur outright, the position is governed by *VATA 1983, 1 Sch 2*, which provides that a person who makes taxable supplies shall cease to be liable to be registered if Customs & Excise are satisfied that the value of taxable supplies in the period of one year then beginning will not exceed a specified limit (currently from 1 May 1991, £33,600) after disregarding supplies of capital assets other than standard rated supplies of land. A person cannot be deregistered under *VATA 1983, 1 Sch 2* if the reason the value of taxable supplies will fall below the specified limit is that the person will cease to make taxable supplies or will suspend making them for a period of 30 days or more. There is no mandatory notification requirement in the legislation. Deregistration under this category is at the discretion of the trader (see *VAT Gen R 1985, Reg 8A(1)*). Deregistration will take effect on the day on which the person requests deregistration or such later date as may be agreed. Customs provide an application form for cancellation of registration in their Leaflet No 700/11/90 ('Should I Cancel my Registration?' (May 1990 but updated each time limits change)) but its use is not mandatory.

Deferral of deregistration

9.19   Customs & Excise have confirmed that they will in suitable cases allow deregistation to be deferred on the request of the receiver, administrator or liquidator even after taxable supplies have ceased. Deferring deregistration should allow the company which has made exempt supplies to continue to reclaim input tax in respect of invoices received after the date on which it might otherwise have deregistered and to obtain the benefit of the *de minimis* limit for recovery of input tax by partially exempt persons (see 9.14 above). This will, however, involve the company in continuing to charge VAT on its own supplies, a situation which may be unsatisfactory for customers who are not themselves registered. If during the period of deferment a practitioner fails to make a return or pay tax for any period Customs will cancel the registration.

Final return following deregistration

9.20   Following deregistration, unless the VAT registration has been transferred (see 9.45 below), a final return on Form VAT 193 must then be delivered, and tax paid on most goods in stock, and assets (including capital assets) then held for the business, on which VAT has previously been recovered as an input. No tax is payable if the total tax chargeable does not exceed £250. The authority under which Form VAT 193 is issued is *VAT Gen R 1985, Reg 58(4)* as now amended. It might be thought from the wording of this provision that it imposed a direct obligation to notify Customs & Excise that a person had ceased to be liable to register. In fact, it seems clear that it does no such thing and should be construed as merely prescribing the type of return which is to be rendered in these particular circumstances. This is supported by the stated time limit which is 'within 1 month of the effective date for cancellation of [the] registration'. That date cannot normally be known until notification has been given under *VATA 1983, 1 Sch 7 or 7A*, or deregistration has been requested under *VATA 1983, 1 Sch 8A*, or Customs have otherwise acted to cancel the registration.

Recovery of VAT after deregistration

9.21 Where deregistration has been effected, VAT may still be recovered on *services* (not goods) supplied to the company after deregistration, which were attributable to taxable supplies made by the company in the course or furtherance of its business when it was a taxable person, under *VATA 1983, s 14(9)(d)* and *VAT Gen R 1985, Reg 37(5)*, which confer on Customs & Excise a discretionary power to repay input tax in these circumstances on a claim made in a form and with such supporting evidence as they may require. The prescribed form is Form VAT 427 which must, in accordance with paragraph 6 of Leaflet No 700/11/90 ('Should I Cancel my Registration?' (May 1990)) be submitted "as soon as possible" after the cancellation of the registration. Formerly, Customs imposed a limit of six months from deregistration for submitting Form VAT 427 but usually allowed claims made outside that period. The claim must be supported by relevant tax invoices. Customs have indicated that after deregistration in insolvency they accept that practitioners' fees, not including third party charges, are attributable to taxable supplies and therefore recoverable on Form VAT 427 but that third party charges, e.g. fees of professional advisers, will only be recoverable if they are attributable to taxable supplies. Form VAT 427 may also be used to reclaim input tax incurred on goods acquired before cancellation of the registration and not recovered in a previous VAT return provided that invoices are provided confirming that the goods were purchased before cancellation (see paragraph 6 of Leaflet 700/11/90, referred to above). Customs accept that the power to withhold tax under *VATA 1983, s 14(7)* where not all previous VAT returns have been submitted does not apply to claims on Form VAT 427 but do regard the power to set off VAT under *FA 1988, s 21* (which is now much more important) as applicable to such claims (see, for a discussion of *FA 1988, s 21*, 9.16 above and 20.9–20.13 below).

Credit notes

Validity of credit notes

9.22 The *VAT (Accounting and Records) Regulations 1989, SI 1989 No 2248* came into force on 1 January 1990 and require every taxable person to keep specified records for VAT purposes and to give effect to an increase or a decrease in consideration for a supply, evidenced by a credit note, debit note or similar document. *Regulation 7* provides that a taxable person must adjust his VAT account by making a negative entry in the tax payable portion of the account where there is a decrease in the consideration due on a supply made by him after the end of the accounting period in which the supply took place and which is evidenced by a credit note, debit note or any other document having the same effect. The person receiving the supply must adjust his VAT account by making a negative entry in the tax allowable portion of the account. In the case of both the supplier and the recipient of the supply the adjustment is made in that part of the VAT account which relates to the prescribed accounting period in which the increase or decrease is given effect, unless the taxable person is insolvent when the entry must be made in that part of the VAT account 'which relates to the prescribed accounting period in which the supply was made or received'. [*Reg 7(6)*]. For these purposes, a company is insolvent if it is in liquidation or an administrator or administrative receiver has been appointed. [*Reg 1(2)*].

9.23   The extent (if at all) to which the new regulations will allow credit notes to be used in circumstances not previously recognised is, at the time of writing, uncertain. "Credit note" is not defined in the new regulations and, presumably, the old cases concerning credit notes will still apply to determine when a credit note may properly be issued to reduce the consideration for a supply for VAT purposes. The point is that until the *VAT (Accounting and Records) Regulations 1989* came into force the issue of credit notes had no statutory authority (apart from one reference in *VAT Gen R 1985, Reg 14*) and was based on commercial practice and the cases where their use had been sanctioned by the tribunals or courts, although Customs & Excise had recognised the issue of credit notes in the context of reservation of title and hire-purchase repossessions (discussed in 9.28–9.35 below) for some time. Section VII of Notice No 700 ('The VAT Guide' (1 October 1987 with amendments)) sets out when a credit note should be issued.

9.24   The leading case on credit notes for VAT purposes is *British United Shoe Machinery Co Ltd v C & E Commrs, [1977] VATTR 187* in which it was held (at p 192) that credit notes are 'a common and usual commercial method of rectifying an overcharge or giving credit for damaged or returned goods', but such credit notes must be 'issued *bona fide* in order to correct a genuine mistake or overcharge, or to give a proper credit' otherwise they would be for a false purpose and void as being contrary to public policy. Examples of the proper use of credit notes were given in the case of *Castle Associates Ltd v C & E Commrs, MAN/87/448 (3497)* which concerned the issue of credit notes to reduce the debts of a company which had ceased trading. The Tribunal held that whether the credit notes were properly issued depended on the value of the services originally supplied by the appellant and in relation to which it had provided an invoice. The Tribunal said:

'In a case where services are supplied for an as yet unascertained consideration, and the parties are at arm's length, the position usually presents little difficulty; the supplier of the services states his charges, the recipient disputes them if he wishes, and after discussion the amount is agreed. If an invoice stating the supplier's original version of the charges has been issued in the meantime, a credit note is issued, giving credit for the difference between the charges originally stated and the agreed charges, and no doubt such a credit note would be perfectly acceptable for the purposes of value added tax. Again, if the amount has been agreed, and the invoice erroneously states a higher amount, a credit note is the appropriate method of evidencing the correction of the error. In each of those cases, the invoice misstates the transaction as it was agreed between the parties and the credit note evidences the correction of the error. But once the parties have agreed the amount of the charges for the services, and the services have been supplied, the value of the supply is ascertained. If thereafter the supplier unilaterally decides, or both parties contract, that the full amount of the agreed charges is not to be payable, in our judgment the decision or the new contract does not alter the value of the supply for the purposes of value added tax, nor does it make any difference if a credit note is issued to evidence the decision or the new contract.'

9.25   Where an invoice has not been paid it is not open to the supplier to issue a credit note to cancel the invoice (*Temple Gothard and Co v C & E Commrs, LON/78/238 (702)*). Equally, where a supply has in substance taken place, a subsequent agreement between supplier and recipient that a supply either has not occurred or was made for no consideration will not of itself justify the issue of a credit note cancelling the original invoice (*J Rickard v C & E Commrs, LON/88/802 (3711)*).

9.26   Before the *VAT (Accounting and Records) Regulations 1989* came into effect, it was established that a credit note was not valid unless it was seen and accepted by the person to whom it was issued. See *Silvermere Golf and Equestrian Centre Ltd v C & E Commrs, [1981] VATTR 106* and *Mannesmann Demag Hamilton Ltd v C & E Commrs, [1983] VATTR 156*. Under *VAT (Accounting and Records) Regulations 1989, Reg 7(2)*, as discussed in 9.22 above, both the supplier and the recipient are required to adjust their VAT accounts when the consideration due on a supply is increased or decreased by the issue of a credit or debit note, so that it is no longer open to the recipient of a credit note to reject it. Presumably, however, it is still necessary for the credit note to be seen by the customer for it to "evidence" a decrease in the value of the supply to him.

Effect of a credit note on preferential and unsecured claims

9.27   If a credit note is properly issued then *VAT (Accounting and Records) Regulations 1989, Reg 7(2)* imposes an obligation on the company (and thus its administrative receiver, administrator or liquidator as previously discussed) which receives it, to adjust the VAT account accordingly. As mentioned in 9.22 above, *VAT (Accounting and Records) Regulations 1989, Reg 7(6)* requires an insolvent person to make an entry in that part of his VAT account which relates to the accounting period in which the supply was (made or) received. This means, in the author's view, that no liability to account for VAT arises in the insolvency as such, consistent with the treatment before the 1989 Regulations (see *Re Liverpool Commercial Vehicles Ltd Ch D, [1984] BCLC 587*). The unsecured claim (and, where appropriate, the preferential claim) will, however, be increased by the VAT adjustment. It would appear that the VAT may in appropriate cases be "referable to" the preferential period within *IA 1986, 6 Sch 3* even though it was not due at the "relevant date". The last point may, however, be open to argument.

Reservation of title claims, hire-purchase repossessions, etc.

9.28   An area in which difficulties arise very frequently is reservation of title claims. It is common for agreements for the sale of goods to provide that title to the goods will not pass on or before delivery or appropriation (as would otherwise be the case under the sale of goods legislation), but will pass only on payment. Clauses in contracts to this effect are known as "Romalpa" clauses after the case in which they were first considered, *Aluminium Industrie Vaassen BV v Romalpa Aluminium Ltd CA, [1976] 2 All ER 552*. This may be illustrated as follows.

Example

Mr Smith, a VAT registered trader, supplies his customer, Jones Ltd, with goods costing £10,000 (exclusive of VAT) taxable at the standard rate. Under *VATA 1983, s 4(2)*, the time of supply will be the time the goods are removed to Jones Ltd's premises (unless, broadly, a VAT invoice is issued within 14 days, when the time of the issue of the invoice will be the time of supply under *VATA 1983, s 5(2)*). Mr Smith will account for £1,750 tax on the supply at the end of the accounting period in which the supply occurs. When Mr Smith accounts for the tax he has not been paid by Jones Ltd which subsequently becomes insolvent. The sale contract with Jones Ltd incorporated a Romalpa clause and, although Mr Smith parted with possession of his goods at the time of sale (and accounted for £1,750 of VAT), on Jones Ltd going into receivership he could repossess them. If he then sold them to a third party for, say, £5,000 (plus VAT of £875), he would still have paid out overall £2,625 of VAT, but the only income received would be the reduced amount of £5,875.

9.29   The transactions just described raise a number of issues. One is whether the sale by Mr Smith to Jones Ltd really is a taxable supply.

Another is how the repossession affects the preferential claim of Customs & Excise, since if the first supply was a taxable supply, Jones Ltd will have claimed input tax during the relevant quarter. Depending on how the supply and repossession are treated a double tax charge could result as Mr Smith would have to account for VAT twice on the sale of the same goods. It will be appreciated that these questions affect the receiver, administrator or liquidator as well as Mr Smith because if the original sale was not a supply, or is cancelled, the preferential claim of Customs could be greater; while if the repossession could be treated as itself a supply, the receiver, etc. might have to account for VAT himself. Almost identical points arise in the context of hire-purchase, conditional sale and other repossessions, and it is not proposed to consider these separately.

9.30   The analysis of the original transaction (the sale by Mr Smith to Jones Ltd) raises intriguing questions on the interaction between contractual principles and VAT law. Following the *Romalpa* case, the contractual position (where there is a retention of title clause) is clearly that title to the goods has not passed at the time of the contract. There is therefore an argument that no "supply" can have taken place, because although possession of the goods has passed to Jones Ltd they are still the property of Mr Smith. A transfer of possession would arguably not, of itself, constitute a supply. The difficulty with this argument is that the term "supply" is not usefully defined in the VAT legislation, the only definition being the circular statement in *VATA 1983, s 3* that '"supply" in this Act includes all forms of supply'. Further, the courts have traditionally displayed great reluctance to follow principles of contract law or sale of goods law in interpreting VAT legislation. A case in point is *C&E Commrs v Oliver QB 1979, [1980] STC 73* where it was held that a supply (in that case, of stolen goods) had occurred even though title never rested in the vendor, the proper test being whether possession had passed, by which was meant 'control . . . in the sense of having the immediate facility for their use.' See also *Tas–Stage Ltd v C & E Commrs QB, [1988] STC 436.*

The "conditional supply" argument

9.31   The reluctance mentioned in 9.30 was demonstrated in the first case where Romalpa clauses were considered, *Vernitron Ltd v C & E Commrs, [1978] VATTR 157.* The case concerned the sale of hi-fi equipment by Vernitron Ltd under a contract incorporating a Romalpa clause. Vernitron put forward the arguments mentioned above, claiming that what occurred at the time of sale was a supply made 'conditionally, and . . . not effectively made until payment had been made in full'. Consequently, as payment was never made by the customer in that case, no supply ever occurred. The Tribunal rejected this argument. They observed that the customer was entitled, under the terms of the contract, to sell the goods to a third party as a consequence of which (under *Sale of Goods Act 1893, s 25*) title would pass. They interpreted "supply" in terms of the description of time of supply in what is now *VATA 1983, s 4(2)(a)*. Thus, since the goods were removed at the time of contract, a supply had taken place. They also rejected the argument raised by Vernitron, that *VATA 1983, s 4(2)(c)* should govern the time of supply. This provides that where goods are 'sent or taken on approval or sale or return or similar terms' the supply occurs 'when it becomes certain that the supply has taken place', because a supply under reservation of title could not, in the Tribunal's view, be regarded as a similar one to a sale on approval, or a contract for 'sale or return' since its purpose was an onward sale.

9.32   The "conditional supply" argument was raised subsequently, but by Customs & Excise, in *Re Liverpool Commercial Vehicles Ltd Ch D, [1984] BCLC 587*. The company (LCV) had bought some vans from a supplier, Iveco Ltd. It had claimed the VAT as an input which reduced the VAT claimed by Customs as a preferential claim when LCV went into receivership a few months later. In the course of the argument, Customs argued (at p 591e) that:

> 'the supply was only a conditional supply, and as regards LCV until it actually paid for the vehicles it was only contingently entitled to a credit for the corresponding input tax, the contingency being the passing of the property in the vehicles on payment of the purchase price in full or a sub-sale by LCV. . . . Until the contingency was satisfied, LCV's VAT return for the relevant prescribed period was subject to subsequent revision . . .'.

The judge was not at all impressed with this argument, which he said (at p 591h) was 'wholly at variance with the structure of the legislation'. He considered that the delivery of the goods pursuant to the contract was 'a supply on which the VAT has become due within the clear terms of the legislation'. The *Vernitron* case was not cited, but the judge reached the same result, finding that the time of supply occurred at the latest when the invoice was issued. The *Vernitron* case was cited and followed in the *Mannesmann* case (see 9.26 above and 9.33 below).

The issue of credit notes in respect of repossessed, etc. goods

9.33   The practice which has developed to rectify this has been for the supplier to issue a credit note to the customer at the time of repossession with a view to cancelling his own taxable supply. He thus claims a credit for the cancelled output tax in his next return. This procedure has been long sanctioned by Customs & Excise and included as A3 in Notice No 748 ('Extra-statutory concessions' (1 October 1989)) although in at least one decided case a Tribunal has in fact rejected as invalid the use of a credit note on the repossession of goods under a Romalpa clause. This was in *Mannesmann Demag Hamilton Ltd v C & E Commrs, [1983] VATTR 156*, where a credit note issued (without the agreement of the receiver of the customer) in respect of goods which had been repossessed was held to have been issued '*bona fide* but mistakenly' and the tribunal said that the credit note was 'not in reality a credit note' because a valid supply had taken place and there had been no overcharge or damaged goods or return by the customer as contemplated in the *British United Shoe Machinery* case (see 9.24 above). Counsel for the taxpayer raised an alternative argument, based on *EC Sixth Directive, Art 11.C(1)*. This says:

> 'In the case of cancellation, refusal or total or partial non-payment . . . the taxable amount shall be reduced accordingly under conditions which shall be determined by the Member States'.

This argument also failed because the EC provision is in discretionary (not mandatory) form, i.e. it is effectively but not directly applicable.

Current practice regarding credit notes in respect of repossessed, etc. goods

9.34   Leaflet No 700/5/85 ('Hire Purchase and Conditional Sale: Repossessions and Transfers of Agreements' (1 January 1985)) sets out the current view of Customs & Excise of the law applicable to the repossession of goods. The leaflet states the concession subject to certain conditions. The conditions are (in the case of VAT registered customers) that:

(a)   the supplier has repossessed the goods, or the customer has returned them to him under the terms of a hire-purchase or conditional sale (including reservation of title) agreement (so if the supplier is unable to repossess the goods, for example because they have been lost, he cannot meet this condition);

(b)   the supplier has issued a credit note to the customer to cover the full amount of the unpaid instalments;

(c)   a record is kept of the credit which has been allowed;

(d)   there are unpaid instalments due from the customer for which the supplier is making no claim;

(e)   the resale of the goods would be a taxable supply; and

(f)   the supplier holds satisfactory documentary evidence from the customer to show that he has accepted the credit note.

In the case of customers not registered for VAT, conditions (a), (d) and (e) apply, and in addition documentary evidence must be kept to show the nature of the adjustment and reason for it. This leaflet has not been updated since the 1989 Regulations but is believed still to represent Customs' view.

Conclusion on credit notes in respect of repossessed, etc. goods

9.35 Despite the introduction of the *VAT (Accounting and Records) Regulations 1989* which give recognition and effect to credit notes the circumstances in which a credit note may be properly issued are not set out and the only guidance available is that given by the VAT Tribunals and High Court in the decided cases. The 1989 Regulations contemplate a credit note being issued where there has been a decrease in consideration due on a supply, and it is to be hoped that the VAT Tribunal will interpret this to allow the use of credit notes where there has been total or partial non-payment in relation to a supply as part of a settlement between the parties. Such an interpretation would give some effect to *EC Sixth Directive, Art 11.C(1)* set out in 9.33 above. If the use of credit notes is permitted in the circumstances outlined in *Article 11.C(1)* then the 1989 Regulations will be a significant relief and may go some way to forestall criticism of the delay inherent in the VAT bad debt relief scheme introduced by *FA 1990* (see 12.29–12.38 below).

Transfer of a business as a going concern

Basic conditions

9.36 An area causing particular difficulties in insolvencies is the provisions, contained in *Value Added Tax (Special Provisions) Order 1981, SI 1981 No 1741, Art 12(1)*, which result in the transfer of a business or part of a business as a going concern being treated as neither a supply of goods nor a supply of services so that it is effectively outside the scope of VAT. Customs & Excise have indicated that these provisions are under review and are likely to be changed in the near future, but the results of this review are not known at the time of writing except that it is now clear that the relief will be restricted where the transfer includes property the supply of which would (apart from *Article 12*) be a taxable supply (see 9.10 above). The conditions for *Article 12(1)* to apply are as follows.

(a)   The supply is of a business or part of a business.

(b)   If it is of part of a business, that part is capable of separate operation.

(c)   It is transferred as a going concern.

(d)   The assets are to be used by the transferee in carrying on the same kind of business, whether or not as part of any existing business, as that carried on by the transferor.

(e)   If the transferor is a taxable person, the transferee must already be, or immediately become as a result of the transfer, a taxable person.

As will be appreciated, the application of these conditions presents special problems in insolvency. For example, all or part of a business may already have been closed down, or may be expected to be closed down by the purchaser. Key assets may be retained by the receiver, administrator or liquidator, or may be subject to separate charges, or even be transferred separately to the same purchaser (perhaps following a hive-down). Also, as a practical matter the purchaser may well be a shell company having no assets other than a business which was, in the pre-insolvency period, far from profitable, so that any provisions incorporated in a contract enabling the receiver, administrator or liquidator to recover any undercharged VAT will be of doubtful value.

9.37   If the above conditions are not met VAT must be charged and accounted for by the vendors. Unless the contract specifically provides otherwise, the consideration for the transfer will normally be inclusive of any VAT which is chargeable (see *VATA 1983, s 10(2)*). The failure to charge VAT may give rise to a liability on the vendor to pay interest and/or a penalty in relation to VAT not accounted for on the VAT return for the period in which the transfer took place. *Article 12(1)* presents problems for the purchaser as much as for the vendor because Customs & Excise may seek to disallow input tax credit for any VAT incorrectly charged. A recent case where this was considered was *Croft Service Station Ltd v C & E Commrs, MAN/88/508 (3512)*, where it was stated to be the practice of Customs to enforce only one liability and that where a transferor has correctly accounted for VAT, even though incorrectly charged, Customs will not seek to disallow the transferee's claim for input tax. This practice is not, however, always followed by Local VAT Offices in the author's experience (and as the cases indicate). Where the vendor is a company which becomes insolvent still owing VAT, the transaction will be certain to come under particular scrutiny by Customs. Tribunals have no power to relieve the purchaser where the transaction has been wrongly treated and if an appeal is made solely to provide conclusive evidence in proceedings against a third party, an award of costs against the appellant is likely to follow (*Advanced Business Technology Ltd v C & E Commrs, LON/83/195 (1488)*).

9.38   The test adopted by the Tribunals in numerous cases on *Article 12* in fact derives from an employment law case, *Kenmir Ltd v Frizzell QB, [1968] 1 All ER 414*, where it was propounded by Widgery J (as he then was) at p 418:

'In deciding whether a transaction amounted to the transfer of a business, regard must be had to its substance rather than its form, and consideration must be given to the whole of the circumstances, weighing the factors which point in one direction against those which point in another. In the end, the vital consideration is whether the effect of the transaction was to put the transferee in possession of a going concern, the activities of which he could carry on without interruption. Many factors may be relevant to this decision though few will be conclusive in themselves. Thus, if the new employer carries on business in the same manner as before, this will point to the existence of a transfer, but the converse is not necessarily true, because a transfer may be complete even though the transferee does not choose to avail himself of all the rights which he acquires thereunder. Similarly, an express assignment of goodwill is strong evidence of a transfer of the business, but the absence of such an assignment is not conclusive if the transferee has effectively deprived himself of the power to compete. The absence of an assignment of premises, stock in trade or outstanding contracts will likewise not be conclusive, if the particular circumstances of the transferee nevertheless enable him to carry on substantially the same business as before.'

In *Cedac Structures Ltd v C & E Commrs, LON/88/522 (3307)* the Tribunal held that it is implicit in *Article 12* that the supply of assets and the transfer of the business should be interrelated and that the interrelationship must be that the supply of assets is a part, or the entirety, of a transaction or series of transactions comprising the transfer of a business. In deciding whether the transaction formed part of a series of transactions that included the transfer of the business the Tribunal looked at the intention of the transferor at the time the assets were supplied.

Transfer of goodwill

9.39   The test in *Kenmir Ltd v Frizzell*, set out above, raises a number of issues resulting from the requirement that the business be transferred as a going concern. The most obvious relates to goodwill. In *Aries Metal Treatments Ltd v C & E Commrs, MAN/83/310 (1680)*, for example, the fact that goodwill had expressly been assigned, together with the trading name and a lease (with fixtures and fittings attached to the property) was regarded as a strong indication that the business had passed as a going concern. It makes no difference if a contract to assign goodwill is never completed as in *Bawtry Enterprises Ltd v C & E Commrs, MAN/83/332 (1677)*. A case in which a Tribunal found that goodwill passed without formal assignment was *The Old Red Lion (Restaurant) v C & E Commrs, LON/83/28 (1446)*, which concerned a restaurant business which continued in the same premises after the sale (see *Hivemead Ltd v C & E Commrs, MAN/83/311 (1632)*, for a case where a manufacturing business was carried on in the same premises). The Tribunal will be particularly likely to hold that goodwill has passed automatically when the transferee takes on senior employees of the transferor having a knowledge of its business contracts, as in *Shire Equip Ltd v C & E Commrs, MAN/83/52 (1464)*. See also *Eric Ladbrook (Holbeach) Ltd v C & E Commrs, LON/83/184 (1557)*. Apart from goodwill, other items transferred must be consistent with the transfer of a business on an ongoing basis, for example, stock, work in progress and customer lists, although the transfer of such items may not be conclusive in itself.

Relevance of intention

9.40   Another relevant factor is the intention of the parties, particularly where this is evidenced by advertisement or in the contract. As the Tribunal put it in *Caunt (t/a Edward James Confectionery) v C & E Commrs, MAN/83/160 (1561)*:

> 'For the transfer of a business as a going concern, there must, in our judgement, be a consensus between the vendor and the purchaser. The commonest example is where a business is advertised by a vendor for sale as a going concern. In such a case we think that the vendor is impliedly undertaking with a prospective purchaser that until completion the business will be kept open instead of being closed down.'

This view was expressed by the same Tribunal in *Westpark Interiors Ltd v C & E Commrs, [1983] VATTR 289* at p 295, in almost identical words. In another case a purchaser showed from the evidence of the contract and negotiations that he had no intention of purchasing goodwill or any continuing business, and his only interest was in certain vehicles, although other assets including the benefit of contracts and a restrictive covenant were in fact included in the sale (*Euromove International Movers Ltd v C & E Commrs, LON/84/153 (1710)*). A statement in the contract that the business is transferred as a going concern can, therefore, be of great importance if it is to be claimed that *Article 12(1)* applies. To take an example of the Tribunal's likely approach, in *Staimer Productions Ltd v C & E Commrs, EDN/83/68 (1605)* it said:

> 'It is true that some stock and some work in progress were transferred to the appellants, but the appellants did not rely on these items to enable them to continue the business as a going concern. In short, the effect of the transaction was not necessarily to put the transferee in possession of a going concern whose activities he could carry on without interruption, although in the event he was able to do so. This construction of the contract in the circumstances surrounding its making squares with the declared intention of the parties in Clause 7 (of the Transfer Agreement) that the offer was to be for a purchase of assets only and not of the business of (the vendor).'

An intention to carry on a different kind of business in the future does not prevent a transfer from being a transfer of a going concern if the purchaser is able to, intends to and does carry on the same kind of business at least for a time. In *C & E Commrs v Dearwood Ltd QB, [1986] STC 327* the appellant company purchased the stock, fixtures, lease and goodwill of an insolvent company which had carried on trading in reproduction furniture. VAT was charged on the transaction. The purchaser did not intend to carry on the trade in reproduction furniture but intended to sell bedroom and kitchen furniture which it eventually did. However, for at least six months after the sale the purchaser sold off the stock of the insolvent company from its premises and using its name. Customs & Excise refused to allow the purchaser credit for the VAT on the purchase on the ground that the sale was a transfer of a business as a going concern. On appeal, the VAT Tribunal held that the transaction had not put the purchaser in possession of a going concern whose activities "would" be carried on without interruption and, therefore, VAT was chargeable on the supply of the assets. Customs appealed against the decision of the VAT Tribunal to the High Court which allowed the appeal. McCowan J held that the correct test of whether a business is transferred as a going concern is whether it "could" be, not whether it "would" be, carried on without interruption after the transfer and the fact that the purchaser intends to change the kind of business carried on in the future is irrelevant.

What is a going concern?

9.41   Problems are presented when the business is, or has been, run down. Clearly, a business can continue as a going concern notwithstanding the insolvency of the company concerned (see *Shire Equip Ltd*, 9.39 above, and *Dearwood Ltd*, 9.40 above where this was expressly stated). But as the judgment in *Kenmir Ltd v Frizzell* (see 9.38 above) illustrates, it is important to maintain continuity of the business. In the *Old Red Lion (Restaurant)* case (see 9.39 above), the premises were shut for a week for redecoration, an interval which the Tribunal held was insignificant in the circumstances: 'the concern may have been purposely run down, but it was still running'. In *Montrose DIY Ltd v C & E Commrs, EDN/87/98 (2652)*, the Tribunal held that the cessation of business due to the insolvency of the company, in closure of its shop premises for two months, did not prevent the sale of the business from being a transfer of a going concern. See also *ECSG Ltd v C & E Commrs, LON/88/580 (5204)*. Customs & Excise indicate in Leaflet No 700/9/87 ('Selling or transferring a business as a going concern' (1 November 1987)) that 'a short period of closure which does not significantly disrupt the existing trading pattern, e.g. "for redecoration", will not prevent a business from being transferred as a going concern'.

9.42   This merges with the requirement that the transferred assets must be used in carrying on the same kind of business, whether or not as part of any existing business, as that carried on by the transferor. As stated in 9.40 above, it was held in the *Dearwood* case that the correct test of whether a business is transferred as a going concern is whether the effect of the transaction is to put the transferee in possession of a going concern, the activities of which he *could* carry on without interruption whether or not the activities *would* be carried on without interruption. So, in *Caunt (t/a Edward James Confectionery)* (see 9.40 above), the taxpayer managed to show that he had changed direction completely by changing the outlets of the confectionery business whose stock he acquired (in fact, a company he controlled) and changing his suppliers. By contrast, in

Cosalt Coolair Ltd v C & E Commrs, MAN/85/38 (1908), a useful case in which a number of the issues were discussed, a company acquired a branch of a catering equipment business which it integrated into its own air conditioning operations, but was still held to qualify under *Article 12(1)(b)(ii)*. As the Tribunal put it, this test involves 'looking into the corporate mind ... to derive its intentions in respect of the assets acquired'. It should be borne in mind that actions of the purchaser may involve running down the business, but *Article 12(1)* is likely to apply if he continues its operations even for the briefest passage of time (see *Dearwood Ltd*, 9.40 above), and possibly even if he does not if he could have done.

Transfer of part of a business

9.43   It is especially difficult to tell whether a part of a business is transferred which is capable of separate operation. Here, the test used in another employment law case has been applied by Tribunals. Lord Fraser of Tullybelton said in *Melon and others v Hector Powe Ltd HL, [1981] 1 All ER 313*:

> 'A change in the ownership of a part of a business will, I think, seldom occur except when that part is to some extent separate and severable from the rest of the business, either geographically or by reference to the products, or in some other way. In the present case, if the factory at Blantyre had been solely devoted in making suits for Willerbys, and if it had been transferred to Executex [the purchasers] with a view to their continuing the same work, that might well have been a transfer of part of the [vendors'] business, especially if the transfer had been accompanied by an undertaking by the appellants not to compete with them for Willerbys' work.'

This passage was applied in the *Cosalt Coolair* case (see 9.42 above) where it was argued that the branch in question was not fully independent and needed the administrative support of the purchaser's group. The Tribunal said:

> 'The fact that a business can only run if integrated into another business which has the facilities necessary to support it does not, in the judgement of the Tribunal, necessarily mean that it is incapable of separate operation. The matter can be tested by supposing the case of a sole proprietor who owns and manages four retail shops. If he sells one of these it could not be said to have become incapable of separate operation merely because the guiding hand of the proprietor has been removed. It would immediately become replaced by the guiding hand of the new owner and would continue operating as a going concern as before.'

In the *Cosalt Coolair* case, the argument failed as a very similar argument had done earlier in *Quadrant Stationers Ltd v C & E Commrs, LON/83/32 (1599)*. In *Conard Systems and Engineering Ltd v C & E Commrs, MAN/89/23*

(4193) the Tribunal held that the transfer of two substantial contracts with equipment, components and materials for carrying out the work was the transfer of part of a business capable of separate operation as a going concern but the Tribunal also pointed out that:

> 'It should not be assumed . . . that every case in which the benefit of contracts is transferred will amount to the transfer of a business. We can well imagine cases in which a large and prosperous company, which has more work than it can deal with, arranges with its customer as a temporary expedient for a small job to be carried out by another. In such cases, no doubt, no part of the company's business would be held to have been transferred.'

Registration requirements after transfer

9.44   The final requirement is for the transferee to be or become a taxable person as a result of the transfer. A taxable person is defined in *VATA 1983, s 2(2)* as a person who makes or intends to make taxable supplies while he is or is required to be registered for VAT. *VATA 1983, s 33(1)* provides that for the purposes of the registration limits the transferee of a business as a going concern is to be treated as having carried on the business before as well as after the transfer. In *Acrefirst Ltd v C & E Commrs, [1985] VATTR 133 (1857)* the Tribunal held that *VATA 1983, s 33* applied equally where any part of the business was transferred, using the turnover estimate provided by the purchaser on the application submitted for a VAT registration to take effect from the day after the transfer. In the case of *Patricia McMichael v C & E Commrs, LON/88/968 (4369)* it was held that *VATA 1983, s 33* did not cause a transferee of a business which made taxable supplies before the transfer to be liable to be registered where the transferee does not make any taxable supplies after the transfer. However, since the introduction of a new *VATA 1983, 1 Sch 1(2)* by *FA 1990* this is no longer correct and the transferee will become liable to be registered if the value of the taxable supplies made by the business in a period of one year ending at the time of the transfer exceeded £35,000 (the current figure from 19 March 1991) or there are reasonable grounds for believing that the value of taxable supplies in the period of 30 days beginning at the time of the transfer will exceed £35,000 and the transferee will be registered with effect from the time of the transfer.

Transfer of VAT registration

9.45   Where a business is transferred as a going concern, a joint election may be made by the transferor and transferee (on Form VAT 68) for the transfer of the VAT registration under *VAT Gen R 1985, Reg 4(5)*. As a result, any liability of the transferor to pay tax or furnish returns will become the liability of the transferee. In *Ponsonby v C & E Commrs, QB 1987, [1988] STC 28* this was held to include a liability to be assessed for failure to make returns and pay tax. In addition, on transfer of the VAT registration, any entitlement of the transferor to input tax credit (whether or not existing at the date of the transfer) will also be transferred to the transferee [*Reg 4(7)*] although it should be noted that the right of the transferor or the transferee to a repayment, whether or not existing at the time of the transfer, may be satisfied by payment to either of them and provision should be made in any sale contract accordingly. Any return furnished, or payment of tax, or claim for input tax credit is also treated as having been made by the transferee where the registration of the transferee in substitution for the transferor took place after the date of the transfer and with effect from the date of the transfer. [*Reg 4(8)*]. In the *Ponsonby* case (see above) it was held that *Regulation 4(8)* is designed to deal with the period of interregnum in circumstances where the transfer of the business and the substitution of the transferee for the transferor as registered taxpayer do not occur simultaneously and is limited to things done during that interregnum. This procedure may be tempting for receivers and liquidators in as much as a certain amount of paperwork can be avoided, but should be approached cautiously for at least two reasons. Any purchaser is likely to be reluctant to take on an old VAT registration because of undisclosed irregularities which may give rise to a liability to pay tax, interest and serious misdeclaration penalty (though not, it seems, default surcharge) and a receiver or liquidator will be unlikely to provide warranties in respect of the company's pre-insolvency VAT position; while the transfer of the registration may prejudice input tax recovery which would otherwise be achieved, because *VATA 1983, s 14(7)* will continue to apply if there have been earlier failures to submit VAT returns.

Conclusions on transfer of a business as a going concern

9.46 There will inevitably be occasions when it is not clear whether the relief applies. One possibility in such circumstances is an application to Customs & Excise for a ruling. However, there is no formal clearance procedure and there may well be difficulty in obtaining a ruling in the time available. Indeed, Customs have been known to be reluctant to give firm rulings in this area, arguing, among other things, that the VAT treatment is a matter for the vendor and his advisers to decide! An alternative may be a joint deposit account between the parties' solicitors pending resolution of the question. In any event, in cases of doubt the agreement may state that VAT (if applicable) is additional to the price and that both parties will refer to Customs after the sale. A purchaser who has paid any part of the VAT outright would also do well to secure a professional undertaking that he will be notified if Customs reply to the vendors before they reply to him.

Further consequences of a transfer of a business as a going concern

Records

9.47 Where a business is transferred as a going concern *VATA 1983, s 33(1)(b)* transfers the obligation to preserve the VAT records specified in

VAT (Accounting and Records) Regulations 1989, SI 1989 No 2248, Reg 2 relating to the business for periods prior to the transfer for six years from the transferor to the transferee except where Customs & Excise, at the request of the the transferor, otherwise direct. In practice, the transferor may be unwilling to hand over the records, especially where only part of a business is being transferred. This requirement is often overlooked and express provision should be made in any sale agreements for such records to be transferred or for the transferor to obtain written permission from Customs before the transfer takes place that the records may be retained. Where records are handed over on the transfer of the business the transferor should retain the right to have access to the records and take copies of them if necessary.

Capital items adjustments

9.48   A further consequence of the transfer of a business as a going concern is that the transferee takes over responsibility for continuing to make adjustments under the scheme for capital items in *VAT Gen R 1985, Regs 37A–37E* for remaining adjustment intervals (if any) in relation to any capital items included in the assets transferred. The scheme is described in relation to land in 9.10(a) above. Where the transferee takes on the VAT registration of the transferor, the adjustment interval applying to the capital item does not end on the day of the transfer but continues, and ends on the last day of the tax year following the day of the transfer (or the last day of a longer period if one applies) and the last day of every period of twelve months thereafter until the adjustment period ends. In either case, it will be essential for the transferee to know the date of acquisition of the capital item; the total input tax incurred on the capital item; the percentage of that input tax which was claimed on the item in the first interval; and the number of remaining intervals in the adjustment period. The disposal of a capital item as part of a transfer of a business as a going concern is not a supply and, therefore, the transferor does not make any adjustment for any remaining intervals occurring after the transfer. In the case of an exempt or partially exempt business, the disposal of a capital item as part of a transfer of a business as a going concern may create a significant disadvantage, as the taxable supply of such capital items would allow the business to recover further input tax which was not recoverable when the item was originally acquired. An exempt or partially exempt transferee who acquires capital items should be aware that he may be required to repay input tax originally claimed by the transferor to Customs & Excise if he uses the capital item to make exempt supplies to a greater extent than the transferor. Conversely, if a transferee makes greater use of a capital item for making taxable supplies than the transferor then the transferee may be able to recover further input tax not recovered by the transferor.

Transfers of going concerns to partially exempt groups

9.49   *VATA 1983, s 29A* was inserted by *FA 1987* to prevent exempt or partially exempt persons, registered for VAT as a group, acquiring assets as part of a transfer of a business as a going concern, thus avoiding VAT which would be irrecoverable in whole or in part. Under *section 29A(4)*, a representative member of a group of companies which acquires assets as part of the transfer of a business as a going concern, is deemed both to make and receive a supply of certain of those assets ("chargeable assets"). Chargeable assets are any assets which would be liable to VAT at a positive rate if supplied in the UK by a taxable person in the course or furtherance of his business. Assets, the supply of which would be exempt or zero rated, are not chargeable assets. The value of the deemed supply made to and by the representative member is the open market value of the chargeable assets. [*s 29A(6)*]. The representative member must account for output tax on the deemed supply by it but that supply is disregarded when determining any entitlement to recover input tax incurred and the effect is that input tax on the deemed supply to the representative member is only recoverable as residual input tax under the partial exemption rules and the representative member must account to Customs & Excise for the difference between the recoverable input tax and the output tax. It follows that *section 29A(4)* does not apply where the representative member of the group is entitled to credit for the whole of the input tax incurred by the group during the prescribed accounting period (or a longer period under the partial exemption rules if applicable) during which the assets are transferred. Relief from the deemed supply is given in certain circumstances, namely: no deemed supply occurs if Customs are satisfied that the chargeable assets were acquired by the transferor more than three years before they are transferred; no deemed supply takes place to the extent that the chargeable assets consist of land, buildings or computer equipment subject to the scheme for capital items adjustment (see 9.10(a) above); and where Customs are satisfied that the transferor has not received credit for the full amount of input tax arising on the acquisition by him of the chargeable assets they may reduce the VAT chargeable by reason of the deemed supply. [*s 29A(8)*].

Chapter 10

National Insurance Contributions

General

10.1   Class 1 primary and secondary NIC payable by a company are collected for the DSS by the Collector of Taxes through the PAYE mechanism. The obligations of liquidators, administrators, supervisors of voluntary arrangements and administrative receivers are very similar in practice for both PAYE and NIC, though the governing law differs in many respects.

10.2   Liability for making the employer's Class 1 secondary contributions and, in the first instance, the employee's primary contributions, is imposed in *SSA 1975, s 4(3), 1 Sch 3* on the "secondary contributor". The mechanics of deduction of primary contributions and of payment of both primary and secondary contributions are contained in *SSCR 1979, Reg 46, 1 Sch*, reflecting a modified and much shorter form of the *ITER 1973*. The *SSCR 1979* do not strictly impose any additional liability although the term "employer" is defined in the same way as in the PAYE regulations, as 'any person paying emoluments.' [*SSCR 1979, 1 Sch 2*].

10.3   "Secondary contributor" is defined in *SSA 1975, s 4(4)(5)* as:

(a)   in the case of an "employed earner" employed under a contract of service, his employer (this term is not defined in the statute) [*SSA 1975, s 4(4)(a)*];

(b)   in the case of an "employed earner" employed in an office with emoluments, either such person as is prescribed in relation to that office or the government department, public authority or body of persons responsible for paying the emoluments of the office [*SSA 1975, s 4(4)(b)*];

(c)   in the case of "employed earners" paid earnings in a tax week by more than one person in respect of different employments or who work under the general control or management of a person other than their immediate employer, a person prescribed by regulations. [*SSA 1975, s 4(5)*].

"Employed earner" means a person 'gainfully employed in Great Britain either under a contract of service or in an office (including elective office) with emoluments chargeable for income tax under Schedule E'. [*SSA 1975, s 2(1)(a)*].

10.4   *SSCR 1979, 1 Sch 3* deals with the second part of category (c) above, by incorporating the corresponding regulations of the PAYE regulations. It provides that:

> 'where an employee works under the general control and management of a person who is not his immediate employer, that person (referred to in this Regulation as "the principal employer") shall be deemed to be the employer for the purpose of these Regulations, and the immediate employer shall furnish the principal employer with such particulars of the employee's emoluments as may be necessary to enable the principal employer to comply with the provisions of these Regulations'.

Prior to the taking effect of the *IA 1986*, the Revenue were known to take the view that this provision potentially applied to receivers.

Liquidation

10.5   Apart from *SSCR 1979, 1 Sch 3*, only one categorisation regulation has been made for an insolvency situation. By *Social Security (Categorisation of Earners) Regulations 1978, SI 1978 No 1689, Reg 5, 3 Sch 4*, where an earner is employed by a company within the meaning of *CA 1985* which is in voluntary liquidation, the person who is the liquidator at the time of the employment is to be treated as the secondary contributor. It is possible that this category was introduced following a decision by the Minister of National Insurance reported in 1953 (at M30 of the Selected Decisions of the Minister on Questions of Classification and Insurability) that a contract of employment with a company did not terminate on appointment of a receiver under the terms of a debenture making the receiver an agent of the company. It would appear that it was felt necessary to introduce a regulation imposing liability on a liquidator in a voluntary winding up carrying on the company's business but not upon a receiver. See Tolley's National Insurance Contributions 1990–91, 14.15.

10.6   Thus, where a liquidator in a voluntary liquidation continues the business of the company to effect a more efficient winding up, he will be treated as a secondary contributor, and should make and account for deductions of primary contributions and account for secondary contributions in respect of payments to earners during the winding up. Since the liability is the liquidator's and not the company's, it would seem that such contributions would be 'necessary disbursements by the liquidator in the course of his administration' within *Ins R 1986, Rule 4.218(m)*, and thus payable in priority to his remuneration which is listed as *Rule 4.218(o)*. This is in contrast to the normal treatment of liquidators in respect of corporation tax (see Chapter 8 above).

10.7   In a *compulsory* liquidation, the winding up order automatically discharges all contracts of employment (*Chapman's Case (1866), LR 1 Eq 346*) unless the liquidator clearly waives the discharge to continue employment while the company's business continues (see *Re English Joint Stock Bank, ex parte Harding (1867), LR 3 Eq 341* and *MacDowall's Case (1886), 32 Ch D 366*). The liquidator can only continue the business of the company with the sanction of the court or the liquidation committee. [*IA 1986, s 167(1)(a), 4 Sch 5*]. Any continuation of the employment contract by the liquidator will be as agent of the company, and the liquidator will be regarded in a similar light to an administrator or administrative receiver by the Collector and the DSS. He will therefore be obliged to deduct and account for primary Class 1 NIC and to account for secondary Class 1 NIC in respect of any payments to continuing employees. Any such payments should be regarded as liabilities incurred in the course of carrying on the business and thus ranking in priority to the company's general debts and liabilities (*Re S Davis and Co Ltd, [1945] Ch 402*). In the order of priority in *Ins R 1986, Rule 4.218*, such payments should rank as *paragraph (m)* 'necessary disbursements by the liquidator in the course of his administration.'

10.8   It should be noted that there is no specific equivalent to *ITER 1973, Reg 16* in the NIC legislation for deduction from payments to a former employee by, *inter alia*, a liquidator. The DSS does not have a preferential claim for NIC in respect of payments accrued but unpaid at the relevant date, because the liability for NIC does not exist until earnings are actually paid. The payment of accrued earnings by a liquidator should be regarded as a distribution of assets in the insolvency and not a payment in the course of administering the liquidation, because it is an obligation imposed on the liquidator, the accrued earnings being a preferential debt. [*IA 1986, 6 Sch 9*]. The DSS have indicated that if the liquidator were to make a payment of accrued earnings, they consider that NIC would be due on the full amount. In practice, however, liquidators would not usually pay accrued earnings, these being met by the Department of Employment through payments made under the *Employment Protection (Consolidation) Act 1978* which are then recovered as a preferential debt. The DSS have also indicated that the earnings are paid to the employee net of the employee's NIC liability, with special arrangements between the two Departments to allocate the NIC to the individual's account, and that no employer's secondary liability is paid.

Administration

10.9   By *IA 1986, s 14(5)* an administrator is deemed to act as the company's agent in exercising his powers, which include his general powers in *section 14(1)* and the specific power in *IA 1986, 1 Sch 13* to make any payment which is necessary or incidental to the performance of his functions. An administrator is not personally liable on any contract unless expressly agreed. By *IA 1986, s 19(6)* he is not deemed to adopt any contract of employment in the first 14 days after his appointment, and he is generally advised not to do so in order to ensure that the contracts continue with the company for redundancy payment purposes. The priority of payments would also encourage an administrator not to adopt employment contracts: by *IA 1986, s 19(4)* an administrator's remuneration and expenses are charged on and paid out of the property of the company under his control in priority to any floating charge; but by *IA 1986, s 19(5)* any sums payable in respect of debts and liabilities incurred under contracts entered into or contracts of employment adopted by him (even without personal liability) take priority to the charge for his remuneration.

10.10   Despite this, the Inland Revenue take the view that, as the agent of the company, an administrator who pays emoluments thus becomes an "employer" under *ITER 1973, Reg 2*. The response to the ICAEW indicates that they regard NIC in the same way as PAYE (ICAEW TR 799, para 7(c)—see Appendix 2). The Revenue's position on this point is, it is considered, doubtful given that the administrator is not an "employer" under general law and the regulations do not impose any substantive liability. The Revenue also refer, in the response, to *ITER 1973, Reg 3* (see *SSCR 1979, 1 Sch 3*) but, as the administrator is only the agent of the "immediate employer", again the argument is considered doubtful.

10.11   An administrator may also be at risk under *SSA 1986, s 57*, which imposes a criminal liability if a company has committed an offence which is proved to have been committed 'with the consent or connivance of, or to be attributable to any neglect on the part of a director, manager, secretary or other similar officer of the body corporate, or any person purporting to act in any such capacity'. The offence by the company would be, under *SSA 1975, s 146(1)*, the failure to meet its contribution liabilities. It is doubtful whether an administrator should be regarded as 'a similar officer' to a director, and in any event current DSS practice is only to prosecute very exceptionally. It is no longer possible for the DSS to recover contributions in a civil action against directors, etc., since the repeal of *SSA 1975, s 152(4)*.

10.12   In practice, therefore, an administrator should make and account for deductions of primary contributions and should account for secondary contributions in respect of payments of emoluments to earners during the administration period.

Company voluntary arrangement

10.13   Where the voluntary arrangement is implemented while an administration order is in force or while the company is being wound up, the NIC will continue to be the responsibility of the administrator or liquidator. In other circumstances, the directors are likely to continue to be responsible for paying employees and making the contributions.

10.14   If the DSS is one of the creditors it will be necessary for the supervisor of the voluntary arrangement to consider the continuing obligations of the company to make contributions, whilst compromising existing debts.

Administrative receivership

10.15   Although deemed by *IA 1986, s 44(1)(a)* to be an agent of the company unless and until it goes into liquidation, an administrative receiver differs from an administrator in that his duty does not extend to continuing the company's business to the detriment of the person appointing him. However, by *IA 1986, s 44(1)(b)* he is made personally liable on contracts entered into by him, unless specifically excluded, and on contracts of employment adopted by him (again unlike an administrator).

10.16   Even though the contract of employment with the company does not terminate on appointment of a receiver, as acknowledged by the Minister in his Decision M30 referred to at 10.5 above and as held in *Griffiths v Secretary of State for Social Services QB, [1973] 3 All ER 1184*, and there is no categorisation of administrative receivers as "secondary contributors", the Inland Revenue do link NIC with PAYE, apparently on the grounds that he is an "employer" within *SSCR 1979, 1 Sch 2* or a "principal employer" within *1 Sch 3*. Thus an administrative receiver will be required to operate the PAYE mechanism where he makes arrangements for employees to continue to be paid, though the justification for the Revenue's view is doubtful for the reasons given in 10.10 above.

10.17   Payments of contributions by the administrative receiver should be treated as expenses properly incurred by him within *IA 1986, s 45(3)(a)*, and, if he adopts the contracts of employment, taking on personal liability, the indemnity for that liability granted by *IA 1986, s 44(1)(c)* will be within *IA 1986, s 45(3)(b)*. Both expenses and the indemnity are charged on and paid out of the company's property under his control in priority to the charge under which he was appointed. [*IA 1986, s 45(3)*]. Thus in any subsequent insolvency proceeding, the administrative receiver may claim priority to his own secured creditor and to unsecured creditors for reimbursement of any contributions he may have paid.

10.18   It is understood that the DSS accept that no NIC should be paid by a receiver in respect of earnings accrued but unpaid at the relevant date for preferential debts in a receivership. This is on the same grounds as that set out for a liquidator at 10.8 above.

Chapter 11

Stamp Duty and Stamp Duty Reserve Tax

General

11.1   Stamp duty is charged on documents which effect the various matters listed under the heads of *SA 1891, 1 Sch* and in certain other cases provided for by subsequent Finance Acts. There are numerous heads of charge, of which perhaps the most important is the *ad valorem* duty, currently of £1 per £100 or part thereof (i.e. about 1 per cent) of chargeable consideration, charged under the head 'Conveyance or transfer on sale, of any property' reduced to 50p per £100 or part thereof (i.e. about 0.5 per cent) of chargeable consideration for transfers of stock and marketable securities on or after 27 October 1986. This head is of some relevance in insolvency, as are certain of the fixed duties. Set out in this chapter are some salient points of importance to the insolvency practitioner. Stamp duty on all transactions other than land and buildings is expected to be abolished (as currently proposed) on 11 May 1992 (see 11.29 below).

11.2   For stamp duty purposes chargeable consideration can be summarised as consideration in the form of cash (including foreign currency), stock, marketable securities, the assumption of liabilities and the discharge of liabilities. Duty is charged on the VAT inclusive amount of consideration.

11.3   SDRT is charged on agreements to transfer chargeable securities. It applies whether or not the agreement is in writing. It is also charged in respect of certain depositary receipt and clearance service arrangements which are outside the scope of this book. The charge is 50p per £100 or part thereof (i.e. about 0.5 per cent) of the consideration in money or money's worth under the agreement. [*FA 1986, s 87*]. As SDRT was introduced not to duplicate stamp duty but to levy a charge in certain cases where stamp duty did not apply, the two taxes interact in various respects and in particular the SDRT charge is cancelled if a transfer which fulfills certain conditions implementing the agreement is executed and duly stamped—see 11.8 below.

11.4   For SDRT purposes chargeable securities are stocks, shares and loan capital; interests in dividends or other rights arising out of stock, shares or loan capital; rights to allotments, or to subscribe for, or options to acquire stocks, shares or loan capital; and units under a unit trust scheme. [*FA 1986, s 99(3)*]. Agreements relating to shares of a non-UK incorporated company kept on an overseas register [*FA 1986, s 99(4)(a)*] and securities the transfer of which is exempt from all stamp duties [*FA 1986, s 99(5)*], are among the types of transactions which are exempt from SDRT. There is no SDRT equivalent to relief under *FA 1930, s 42* (discussed in 11.22–11.25 below) for intra-group transfers.

11.5 For liquidators and receivers SDRT is generally only a problem in respect of uncompleted agreements to purchase chargeable securities as rarely will they be in a position to acquire chargeable securities themselves. SDRT is not a problem for vendors unless they are market makers, brokers and dealers or qualified dealers. It may be of more relevance to an administrator. SDRT is to be abolished at the same time as stamp duty on transactions other than land and buildings, (as currently proposed) on 11 May 1992.

Enforcement and penalties

Stamp duty

11.6 There is generally no direct obligation to stamp a document. The sanction for failing to stamp a document is, in most cases, that the document cannot be produced in evidence (including proceedings before arbitrators, referees and tax commissioners) except in criminal proceedings. [*SA 1891, s 14*]. A person whose office is to enrol or register an instrument chargeable with duty (such as a company secretary or registrar) also incurs a penalty if he enrols or registers a document which is not duly stamped. [*SA 1891, s 17*]. The Land Registrar may refuse to register a document which has not been duly stamped, under *Land Registration Act 1925, s 14(3)* and in practice normally does so refuse. Where there is doubt as to the stamp duty payable on the document, there is a procedure for adjudication of the document by the Stamp Duty Office, which is conclusive as against third parties although the taxpayer has a right of appeal. [*SA 1891, ss 12, 13*]. Documents must be stamped or submitted for adjudication within 30 days of execution (or, if executed abroad, within 30 days of being brought into the UK), failing which penalties and interest may be charged. [*SA 1891, s 15*].

11.7 Generally the stamp duty legislation does not impose a legal obligation to stamp or specify who is to bear the stamp duty, but *SA 1891, ss 15(2), 59* specify that certain penalties are to be borne by the transferee and the liability for stamp duty on agreements to transfer is borne by the transferee. It is, however, unclear how these obligations could be enforced as there is no provision enabling the Stamp Duty Office to collect such duty forcibly from the transferee if the transferor presents the documents for stamping.

SDRT

11.8   In most cases the charge to SDRT arises two months after the agreement is entered into or, in the case of a conditional agreement, the date the condition is satisfied, unless within that time there is an actual transfer of the chargeable securities to the purchaser or his nominee *and* that transfer is duly stamped. [*FA 1986, s 87*]. Even after that time if within six years of the agreement such a transfer is executed pursuant to the agreement and duly stamped, the charge is cancelled and if SDRT has been paid it is repaid with interest. [*FA 1986, s 92*]. Any SDRT due is payable by the accountable person on or before the last day of the month after the month in which it arises. The accountable person will generally be the purchaser, unless a market maker, broker and dealer or qualified dealer is involved.

11.9   Unlike stamp duty, SDRT is directly enforceable and there is an obligation on the "accountable person" (i.e. normally the transferee) to report that a liability to SDRT has arisen and to pay it. [*Stamp Duty Reserve Tax Regulations 1986, SI 1986 No 1711, Reg 4*].

11.10   Failure to give the required notice of the liability to an SDRT charge by an accountable person results in a liability to pay a penalty of £50 plus a further £10 a day after declaration of default by the court or Special Commissioners. This increases to £50 plus the amount of the tax after one year has elapsed since the notice should have been given. [*TMA 1970, s 93*]. For a negligently incorrect notice the penalty is £50 plus the amount of underpaid tax, while for a fraudulently incorrect notice the penalty is £50 plus twice the amount of underpaid tax. [*TMA 1970, s 95*]. Interest is payable on late paid tax at the rates set monthly under *FA 1989, s 178* and the *Taxes (Interest Rate) Regulations 1989, SI 1989 No 1297*. In general, the position of any claim for unpaid SDRT is the same as for any other non-preferential tax debt, including as regards the Revenue's power of distress—see Chapter 4 above.

Conveyance on sale duty

11.11   Duty under the head 'Conveyance or transfer on sale, of any property' is currently chargeable at a rate of £1 per £100 or part thereof of the chargeable consideration paid on the sale of property (such as debts or land) and 50p per £100 or part thereof of the chargeable consideration for transfers of stock and marketable securities on or after 27 October 1986. In the case of certain property (notably land, intellectual property rights and debts but not shares), where the amount or value of the consideration passing under the transaction (taken as a whole) does not exceed £30,000, and a certificate of value in the appropriate form is included on the document, stamp duty is not chargeable. [*FA 1963, s 55* as amended by *FA 1984, s 109*]. Generally, the duty only applies to documents of transfer (e.g. conveyances of land or stock transfer forms). In some cases, however, contracts may be charged as conveyances on sale. The contracts in question include those for the sale of equitable interests, or for the sale of any interest in debts, goodwill and the benefit of contracts. [*SA 1891, s 59(1)*]. Contracts are, however, only stampable to the extent that an actual conveyance of the property would be. Thus, a contract to sell chattels (which pass by delivery) is not required to be stamped as such.

11.12   Stamp duty under this head is often, in practice, the responsibility of the transferee, as he is the person who will need to obtain registration of any change of ownership in respect of land, shares or certain intellectual property rights. He is also most likely to be the person who will wish to sue for the breach of any agreement and therefore need to rely on the document in civil proceedings.

11.13   A receiver or liquidator is unlikely to be concerned directly with the payment of stamp duty under this head, but he is likely to be asked to co-operate in ensuring that transactions are carried out in such a way that stamp duty is reduced or eliminated. In this connection, it should be noted that *SA 1891, s 5* requires the facts and circumstances affecting the liability of any instrument to duty or the amount of duty with which any instrument is chargeable to be set out in the instrument and provides that a fine is incurred by any person who, with intent to defraud the Crown, executes any instrument in which all the facts and circumstances are not truly set forth, or being employed or concerned in or about the preparation of any instrument, neglects or omits to set them out. It is also professional misconduct for solicitors to be involved in the preparation of an instrument in breach of *SA 1891, s 5* and it is not impossible that the parties and their advisers may be guilty of the common law offence of cheating the public revenue.

11.14   Where assets of a company are transferred to creditors in satisfaction of a debt (or part of a debt) owed by the company to such creditors and any instrument of transfer needs to be stamped, then by virtue of *SA 1891, s 57 ad valorem* stamp duty will be calculated by reference to the face value of the indebtedness discharged without regard to its market value or the badness of the debt. However, *FA 1980, s 102* restricts the charge to the value of the property where the property is conveyed to a creditor and the value of property is less than the amount of the debt discharged. If the assets transferred are chargeable securities, then if there is no duly stamped instrument of transfer within the relevant time limit SDRT is payable, but the amount of SDRT payable will be based on the market value of the debt and not on its nominal amount.

Hive-downs

11.15   The other area where stamp duty may be relevant to receivers and liquidators is where transfers of assets are made between group companies, most frequently on a hive-down. In such cases, relief may be available under *FA 1930, s 42* provided that the necessary group relationship is established and is not broken by, for example, liquidation or arrangements to sell the shares in the hive-down company (see 18.10–18.13 below). In practice, stamp duty on a hive-down agreement is likely to be small as goodwill and the benefit of contracts are normally the only dutiable items and the consideration paid for them is nominal (stock and plant which is severed from the land, i.e. not fixed plant, pass by delivery). Any apportionment must be *bona fide* (see 18.24 below). Stamp duty will, however, create a problem if a hive-down is effected in exchange for an issue of shares. This would require a return of allotments to the Registrar of Companies which must, under *CA 1985, s 88(2)(b)*, be duly stamped. The inevitable result would be adjudication and attendant delays. However, even if *FA 1930, s 42* relief is unavailable, relief under *FA 1986, s 76* may be available to halve the rate of duty payable (see 11.27 below). Prior to 22 March 1988 the return would also have been stampable with an additional 1 per cent of capital duty, but this was abolished by *FA 1988, s 141*.

Fixed duties

Transfers by liquidator to members

11.16   The transfer by a liquidator of assets of the company to its members is not a conveyance or transfer on sale and is, accordingly, only subject to fixed duty of 50p under the head 'Conveyance or transfer of any kind not hereinbefore described' in *SA 1891, 1 Sch*. This was upheld in *Henty & Constable (Brewers) Ltd v CIR CA, [1961] 3 All ER 1146*, where a liquidator distributed assets to an unregistered shareholder who had apparently failed to stamp the instrument of transfer of the shares to him. The Inland Revenue's claim that the liquidator's transfer should be subject to *ad valorem* duty was rejected and the fixed duty held to apply. However, under the *Stamp Duty (Exempt Instruments) Regulations 1987, SI 1987 No 516*, provided a certificate in the appropriate form is included in, attached to or endorsed upon the instrument of transfer and signed by the transferor or his solicitor or the transferor's duly authorised agent, no duty need be paid and the document need not be produced to the Stamp Duty Office.

11.17   Where a distribution of surplus assets is in consideration of an indemnity given by the shareholders to the liquidator in respect of outstanding specific liabilities or the property concerned is subject to a mortgage which is assumed by the shareholders, then the effect of *SA 1891, s 57* is that the distribution is treated as a sale for a consideration equal to the amount of the liabilities taken over by the members. If there is merely an indemnity against unknown liabilities there is no stamp duty payable, however, as there is no ascertainable figure for the duty to be charged on, though if this indemnity is capped by a maximum then *prima facie* stamp duty will be payable on the basis of the cap.

Appointment of receiver

11.18   It was formerly customary to stamp the document appointing a receiver under a charge with fixed duty of 50p, on the basis that such appointments incorporate a power of attorney by reference to the charge instrument. The head 'Letter or power of attorney' was, however, abolished by *FA 1985, s 85, 24 Sch*, for instruments executed on or after 26 March 1985, or those executed on or after 19 March 1985 which were not stamped before 26 March 1985.

Exemptions and reliefs

Charges and secured debts

11.19   Until 1971, transfers of mortgages were subject to stamp duty under the head 'Mortgage, bond, debenture, covenant' in *SA 1891, 1 Sch*. This included (under *paragraph 4*) the 'transfer, assignment, disposition or assignation of any mortgage, bond, debenture or covenant (except a marketable security), or of any money or stock secured by any such instrument'. The head was abolished by *FA 1971, s 64* so that the transfer of a charge or of a debt secured by a charge (other than a marketable security) is no longer subject to stamp duty.

Unsecured debts

11.20   A transfer of a debt, other than a secured debt, is subject to stamp duty under the head 'Conveyance or transfer on sale, of any property' in *SA 1891, 1 Sch* subject only to the exemption for transfers up to £30,000 referred to in 11.11 above. The same applies to a contract for the transfer or assignment of a debt. [*SA 1891, s 59(1)*]. Statutory exemptions include *FA 1967, s 30* (for bearer instruments relating to stock in foreign currencies), *FA 1971, s 64* (for transfer of debentures other than marketable securities) and *FA 1986, s 79(4)* (for transfers of loan capital). By virtue of *FA 1986, s 99(5)* the above exemptions also apply to prevent a charge to SDRT arising on agreements to transfer such securities. Alternatively the relief for intra-group transfers under *FA 1930, s 42* may apply for stamp duty purposes, but not for SDRT.

11.21   It is proposed that stamp duty on all transactions other than land and buildings will be abolished on the introduction of the London Stock Exchange's Taurus system (see 11.29 below), currently proposed to occur on 11 May 1992.

Intra-group transfers

11.22   *FA 1930, s 42* exempts certain transfers between "associated companies" from stamp duty. Companies are associated for this purpose if one is the beneficial owner of not less than 90 per cent of the issued share capital of the other, or a third such body is the beneficial owner of not less than 90 per cent of the issued share capital of each. The 90 per cent relationship is calculated by nominal value rather than by reference to economic value, voting rights, rights on a liquidation or rights to dividends. Ownership may be determined through indirect holdings. The relief is given on submission of the executed transfer document for adjudication, accompanied by a statutory declaration containing certain prescribed details and the required supporting documentation.

11.23   One difficulty in a liquidation is to know which companies are associated, in view of the beneficial ownership requirement. The question of beneficial ownership is considered in detail in 8.3–8.10 above and 18.10–18.14 below. It is only necessary to note here that, on liquidation of a company, it ceases to be the beneficial owner of its assets so that a transfer to a subsidiary or between direct subsidiaries would not be exempt under this provision. See *Ayerst v C & K (Construction) Ltd HL 1975, 50 TC 651*. The other circumstance in which beneficial ownership is lost in this context is where a binding contract for sale has been entered into (see 18.10–18.12 below), but this is largely irrelevant in the stamp duty context because of the provisions in *FA 1967* mentioned in the next paragraph.

11.24   Relief under *FA 1930, s 42* is further restricted by *FA 1967, s 27(3)*, which provides that the exemption does not apply if the instrument in question was executed in pursuance of or in connection with an arrangement whereunder:

(a)   the consideration, or any part of the consideration was to be provided or received, directly or indirectly, by a person other than an associated company of the transferor or transferee;

(b)   the interest transferred was previously conveyed or transferred, directly or indirectly, by such a person; or

(c)   the transferor and transferee were to cease to be associated because of a change in the percentage shareholding of the transferee in the beneficial ownership of the transferor or a third company.

An arrangement is to be treated as falling within paragraph (a) if it is one under which the transferor or transferee or an associated company of either of them was to be enabled to provide any of the consideration, or to part with any of it, by or in consequence of a transaction or transactions involving a payment or other disposition by a person other than a body corporate.

11.25   These provisions have complex ramifications which are outside the scope of this book. The requirement in (c) above can cause particular problems in a hive-down where, as is usual in insolvency, it is intended that the hive-down company will be sold to a third party. In such cases, it may be difficult to make the necessary statutory declaration. Note, however, that there is some authority that the "arrangement" referred to must be a specific arrangement (see *William Cory & Son Ltd v CIR HL, [1965] 1 All ER 917*) although relief may be unavailable even if all steps in the "arrangement" are not contractually pre-arranged. See, *inter alia, Shop and Store Developments Ltd v CIR HL 1966, [1967] 1 All ER 42* and *Ingram v CIR Ch D, [1985] STC 835.* For a further discussion of stamp duty on hive-downs, see 11.15 above. The relief should be available if the hive-down takes place before the receiver (or administrator) has started negotiating with a potential purchaser.

Reorganisations

11.26   A number of special reliefs used to apply where a liquidation occurred in connection with a company reorganisation. These were *FA 1927, s 55* (reconstructions); *FA 1985, s 78* (takeovers); and *FA 1985, ss 79, 80* which provided relief where there was an arrangement under *IA 1986, s 110.* These reliefs were abolished by *FA 1986.*

11.27   Reliefs are given for some reorganisations by *FA 1986, ss 75, 76. Section 76* particularly (acquisition of undertakings) may (depending on the structure used) reduce the duty payable on a hive-down from £1 per £100 or part thereof to 50p per £100 or part thereof when the consideration is wholly in the form of shares or the assumption of liabilities. It must be emphasised that this relief merely reduces the rate of duty payable and does not alter the chargeable consideration. The relief is given on submission of the executed transfer for adjudication, accompanied by a letter containing prescribed information and copies of the relevant documentation.

Exemptions under IA 1986

11.28   Certain documents relating to a compulsory winding up or a creditor's voluntary liquidation are exempt from stamp duty under *IA 1986, s 190.* These include proxies and powers of attorney relating to the property of the company or to any proceedings (e.g. proxies for creditors' meetings); and any assurance (including a deed, conveyance, assignment or surrender) relating solely to freehold or leasehold property or to any estate, right or interest in any real or personal property which forms part of the company's assets and which, after execution of the assurance, remains part of those assets at law or in equity. It is not immediately obvious what the latter relief applies to.

Proposed abolition of SDRT and of certain stamp duties, etc.

11.29   In the 1990 Budget it was proposed that when the new Stock Exchange system of paperless trading (Taurus) is introduced, currently proposed to be 11 May 1992, then (i) SDRT will be abolished and (ii) stamp duty will be abolished in respect of transfers of shares, units in a unit trust, marketable securities, stock, bearer instruments, loan stock etc. [*FA 1990, ss 107–111*]. In the 1991 Budget this was extended to stamp duty on all property other than land and buildings. Abolition will not have the effect of removing the liability to stamp duty or SDRT on pre-abolition agreements or transfers executed in accordance with pre-abolition agreements.

Chapter 12

Taxation of Shareholders and Creditors

Relief for capital losses

Shareholders

Relief against capital gains

12.1   The commencement of the formal insolvency of a company does not give rise to disposals by its shareholders of their shares, although there would be a deemed disposal of the shares when the company is dissolved under *CGTA 1979, s 22(1)*, which provides that the occasion of the entire loss, destruction, dissipation or extinction of an asset is to be treated as a disposal of that asset whether or not any capital sum is received. An allowable loss will normally be claimed before dissolution under *CGTA 1979, s 22(2)* on the basis that the value of the shares has become negligible. For the loss to be allowable, a claim must be made to the Inspector of Taxes whereupon *CGTA 1979* has effect as if the claimant had sold, and immediately reacquired, the shares for a consideration of an amount equal to the value specified in the claim. Strictly, the notional disposal is to be treated as occurring when the claim is made (*Williams v Bullivant Ch D 1982, 56 TC 159* and *Larner v Warrington Ch D, [1985] STC 442*). In practice, however, the Inland Revenue will allow a claim to be made retrospectively not later than two years after the end of the tax year (or accounting period in the case of the company) in which the date of notional disposal fell, provided that the asset is of negligible value when the claim is made and was on the date of notional disposal (whether or not it had first become of negligible value before that date) (see ESC D 28).

12.2   The relief under *CGTA 1979, s 22* is given against capital gains of the same accounting period or year of assessment or, subject to *ICTA 1988, s 345* (in the case of a company) or *CGTA 1979, s 4(1)(b)* (in the case of an individual) those unutilised in subsequent such years or periods. Where a disposal occurs under *CGTA 1979, s 22*, however, or on a distribution in the course of dissolving or winding up the insolvent company, relief may also be available to the shareholder against income under *ICTA 1988, ss 573–576*, where certain conditions are satisfied.

Relief for capital losses of shareholders against income

12.3   In the case of a shareholder which is a company the conditions mentioned in 12.2 above may be broadly summarised as follows.

(a)   The company must have subscribed for the shares [*ICTA 1988, s 573(1)*], i.e. they must have been issued in money or money's worth. [*ICTA 1988, s 573(7)*]. (*ICTA 1988, s 576(1)* provides identification rules in the case of a mixed holding of shares where some were subscribed and some were not).

(b)   The shareholder must be an investment company on the date of the disposal and for a continuous period of six years ending on that date. Alternatively, it will still be eligible for relief if it was an investment company for a shorter continuous period provided it was not before the beginning of that period a trading company or an "excluded company". [*ICTA 1988, s 573(1)(a)*].

(c)   The shares must be in a "qualifying trading company" [*ICTA 1988, s 573(1)*], i.e. broadly one which is UK resident, whose shares have not been quoted on a recognised stock exchange, and which is a trading company on the date of disposal or ceased to be so not more than three years previously and has not since been an "excluded company" or an investment company. [*ICTA 1988, s 576(4)*]. "Trading company" for this purpose includes a holding company of a trading group, as defined in *ICTA 1988, s 576(4)*.

(d)   The company claiming the relief must not be associated with, or be a member of the same 51 per cent group as, the qualifying trading company at any time in the period from the date it subscribed for the shares to the date of disposal. [*ICTA 1988, s 573(1)(b)*].

For the purposes of the definitions in (b) and (c) above, "excluded company" means broadly a company trading in securities, land, futures, or having a trade not carried on on a commercial basis in such a way that profits can reasonably be expected, or the holding company of a group other than a trading group, or a building society or registered industrial or provident society. [*ICTA 1988, s 576(5)*]. Relief is available by setting the loss against income of the accounting period in which it was incurred or carrying it back proportionately to a preceding accounting period ending in the twelve months preceding that accounting period provided that the claimant was then an investment company. [*ICTA 1988, s 573(3)*].

12.4   In the case of an individual shareholder, the conditions set out in 12.3(c) above also apply, and relief is given on a similar basis against income of the year of assessment in which the loss is incurred and, depending on whether or not such a claim is made, any unrelieved loss remaining or the whole of the loss can then be set against income of the following year (in which case such a claim takes precedence over any current year loss claim relating to another loss). [*ICTA 1988, s 574(1)(2)*].

Relief is also available to a spouse in respect of shares subscribed for by the other spouse and transferred *inter vivos*. The position regarding BES companies is dealt with separately in Chapter 14.

12.5   In the case of an investment company, the relief must be claimed within two years after the end of the accounting period in which the loss was incurred. In the case of an individual, it must be claimed within two years after the end of the year of assessment *for* which loss set-off is claimed. ESC D 28 also applies to these provisions, as described in 12.1 above and 12.8 below.

Creditors

General rule

12.6   *CGTA 1979, s 134(1)* lays down a general rule that the disposal of a debt does not give rise to a chargeable gain or, in the usual case where the debtor is insolvent, an allowable loss. [*CGTA 1979, s 29(2)*]. The satisfaction of a debt in whole or in part, unless in the course of certain types of conversion or exchange of securities or certain company reconstructions and amalgamations, is treated as a disposal or part disposal of the debt. [*CGTA 1979, s 134(2)*]. The general rule is, however, subject to a number of exceptions, where an allowable loss or chargeable gain can arise, which are as follows.

(a)   A disposal of a loan where the creditor is not the original creditor in respect of the loan or his personal representatives or legatee (i.e. where the creditor has acquired the loan directly or indirectly from the person who originally made it). [*CGTA 1979, s 134(1)*]. Even then, relief for an allowable loss on a loan which is not repaid will not be available either if the creditor acquired the loan from a "connected person" as defined [*CGTA 1979, ss 63, 134(4)*]; or if the disposal is of a "qualifying corporate bond" unless the disposal is eligible for relief under *CGTA 1979, s 136A* (see further 12.11 below).

(b)   Where the loan is a "debt on a security", subject to the same point as in (a) in relation to disposals of "qualifying corporate bonds" not eligible for relief. See further 12.7 below.

(c)   Where relief is available under *CGTA 1979, s 136*. See further 12.8 below.

(d)   Where relief is available under the special rules relating to "qualifying corporate bonds", described in 12.9–12.11 below.

Debt on a security

12.7   Relief will in many cases be available for capital losses which arise as a result of the failure to repay a "debt on a security" whether the holder is the original creditor or not, unless the loan is a "qualifying corporate bond" as described in 12.10 below. The phrase "debt on a security" is not defined in the legislation though the definition of security in *CGTA 1979, s 82(3)(b)* applies which is that:

> '"security" includes any loan stock or similar security whether of the Government of the United Kingdom or of any other government, or of any public or local authority in the United Kingdom or elsewhere, or of any company, and whether secured or unsecured'.

This is not an enormously helpful definition though it makes clear that relief may be available for debts of foreign as well as UK companies and whether or not they are secured debts. The Revenue stated in 1970 that the definition is regarded as exhaustive and that loan stock 'implies in general a class of debt the holdings in which are transferable by purchase and sale' (IRPR 11 June 1970, Tolley's Official Tax Statements 1990–91, 109.203). Since then, the meaning of the expression "debt on a security" has been considered in a number of cases, notably *Cleveleys Investment Trust Co v CIR CS 1971, 47 TC 300, Aberdeen Construction Group Ltd v CIR HL 1978, 52 TC 281* and most recently *W T Ramsay Ltd v CIR HL 1981, 54 TC 101*. These cases confirm that the phrase does not mean 'a secured loan'. Otherwise, the result of these (occasionally contradictory) decisions is somewhat inconclusive. As a practical matter, a useful indication of the Inland Revenue's approach following the *Ramsay* case was given in a "Point of Practice" contributed to Tolley's Practical Tax, 20 July 1983 by BDO Binder Hamlyn, which was as follows:

'*Debt on a security*

Our Wolverhampton Office has successfully concluded negotiations with HM Inspector of Taxes on whether a certain debt qualified as a debt on a security for which a capital loss could be claimed. During the course of the correspondence the Inspector set out the Board's instructions as to the characteristics which must be satisfied before a debt can qualify as a debt on security, following the decision in *W T Ramsay Ltd v CIR* [see above]. The six characteristics are as follows.

(a)   The debtor should be a government, a public or local authority or a company.

(b)   The debt should be capable of being marketed, sold or assigned.

(c)   Interest should be payable to the lender (or at least the terms of the debt must be such that it is capable of being held as an investment; for example, it would be so capable if it were issued at a discount or repayable at a premium).

(d)   There should be stated terms for repayment of the debt.

(e)   The debt should be for a specified amount and for a defined term (normally for a period of years rather than months or days).

(f)   The debt should be capable of being issued or subscribed for (even if the procedure involved is simple, and if only one lender is involved).

In addition, the existence of a document constituting or evidencing the debt or loan points in the direction of it being a "debt on a security", without being an essential feature.'

Relief for "qualifying loans"

12.8   Where the loan is not a "debt on a security", and was made after 11 April 1978, relief may be available under *CGTA 1979, s 136*. The section applies to a "qualifying loan", that is, a loan made to a UK resident borrower where the money lent is used wholly for the purposes of a trade carried on by the borrower or by another trading company in the same group (to which the money is lent), not being a trade which consists of or includes the lending of money. [*CGTA 1979, s 136(1)(2)*]. This includes money used for setting up a trade which is subsequently carried on by the borrower (or other group company as above). Further conditions include: that an outstanding amount of the loan has become irrecoverable; that the claimant has not assigned his right to recover that amount; and that the claimant and borrower were not each other's spouses or companies in the same group at the time the loan was made or at any subsequent time. [*CGTA 1979, s 136(3)*]. A group for this purpose is a 75 per cent group within *ICTA 1970, s 272*. [*CGTA 1979, s 136(10)*]. There is a provision for clawback of relief where an amount in respect of which relief has been claimed by the company or another company in the group is subsequently recovered. [*CGTA 1979, s 136(5)(5B)*]. The loss strictly arises at the date of the claim but by concession the Revenue will treat the loss as arising in an earlier year of assessment (or accounting period in the case of a creditor which is a company) providing that:

(a)   the claim is made not later than two years after the end of that year (or period);

(b)   all the conditions for relief are satisfied at the date of claim; and

(c)   the relief would have been available at the end of the year (or period) for which the relief is claimed.

(ESC D 28).

Qualifying corporate bonds

12.9   Allowable losses (and chargeable gains) cannot normally arise in respect of disposals of securities which are "qualifying corporate bonds" within the definition in *FA 1984, s 64*. [*CGTA 1979, s 67(1)*]. In respect of such securities issued on or after 15 March 1989, however, or held on that date by the person who made the loan, relief is available in certain specified circumstances set out in *CGTA 1979, s 136A*.

12.10 The definition of "qualifying corporate bond" in *FA 1984, s 64* requires, first, that the debt is a "security" (this term is not expressly defined) [*FA 1984, s 64(1)*]; secondly, that it is a "normal commercial loan" within *ICTA 1988, 18 Sch 1(5)* [*FA 1984, s 64(2)(b)*]; and thirdly, that it is expressed in sterling and no provision is made for its conversion into, or redemption in, a currency other than sterling [*FA 1984, s 62(2)(c)*], including for this purpose sterling amounts defined by reference to the value of another currency or asset, and disregarding provisions for redemption in a foreign currency by reference to the exchange rate prevailing at redemption. [*FA 1984, s 64(3)*]. The definition of "normal commercial loan" excludes, among other things, certain convertible securities and certain loans on which interest depends on the results of the issuer's business or exceeds a commercial return [*ICTA 1988, 18 Sch 1(5)(a)(b)*] but certain deep gain securities within the provisions of *FA 1989, 11 Sch* are included expressly by *FA 1984, s 64(3A)–(3D)*. See further the Finance Bill published on 17 April 1991 and IRPR 15 February 1991. A security issued on or before 13 March 1984 will only be a qualifying corporate bond if it has been acquired after that date by the holder, otherwise than on an "excluded" transaction (principally, certain types of reorganisation). It should be noted that there is no longer any requirement that a security must be quoted to be a qualifying corporate bond—accordingly, a sterling security issued by a private company on unremarkable terms as to interest, etc. is likely to qualify so that if the company becomes insolvent a capital loss can only be realised under *CGTA 1979, s 136A*, as described in the following paragraph.

12.11 *CGTA 1979, s 136A* gives relief in three specific circumstances where a qualifying corporate bond becomes worthless or is not redeemed. The relief is available in respect of a qualifying corporate bond which would, but for the fact that it is a debt on a security (see 12.7 above), be a "qualifying loan" for the purposes of *CGTA 1979, s 136*. Thus, as with *section 136* (see 12.8 above), the money lent must be used for the purposes of a trade carried on by the borrower or a member of its group to which it is on-lent; and the borrower must be UK resident. Also, the claimant must not have assigned the right to recover any outstanding amount of the principal of the loan, and the claimant and borrower must not have been companies in the same group (as defined in *ICTA 1970, s 272*) at any time after the loan is made. [*CGTA 1979, s 136(3)(b)(c)*]. Where the relief is available, the person eligible for relief (called "the claimant") must make a claim whereupon he is treated as if an allowable loss had accrued to him when the claim was made. [*CGTA 1979, s 136A(2)*]. The three circumstances where relief is available are as follows.

(a)   Where the value of the security has become negligible. [*CGTA 1979, s 136A(3)*]. In this case, the allowable loss is the lower of the outstanding amount of the principal of the loan, and the security's acquisition cost (less amounts already recovered). [*CGTA 1979, s 136A(6)*]. The Inland Revenue accept that relief may be claimed under this condition where the security has ceased to have any value because it was redeemed early (SP 8/90).

(b) Where the security's redemption date has passed and *all* the outstanding principal was irrecoverable (taking the facts existing at that date) or proved to be irrecoverable (taking the facts existing on a later date). [*CGTA 1979, s 136A(4)*]. In this case, the amount of the allowable loss is the same as in (a) above. [*CGTA 1979, s 136A(6)*].

(c) Where the security's redemption date has passed and *part* of the principal loan was irrecoverable or proved to be so as in (b) above. In this case, the amount of the loss depends on whether the security's acquisition cost exceeds the "relevant amount". [*CGTA 1979, s 136A(7)*]. If it does, the allowable loss is the excess. If it does not, there is no allowable loss. The "relevant amount" is what has already been recovered of the principal, plus what is in the Inspector's opinion recoverable at the time the claim is made. [*CGTA 1979, s 136A(8)*]. Clearly, where the claimant is the original creditor, he may be eligible for relief up to the full amount of the loan (assuming this is his base cost—see 12.13 below).

There are provisions for a clawback of relief where an amount thought to be irrecoverable is recovered. [*CGTA 1979, s 136A(10)(11)*]. The ESC D 28, described in 12.1 and 12.8 above, also applies to claims under *CGTA 1979, s 136A*—see IRPR 6 December 1990.

12.12 One situation in which a charge to tax *can* arise when a qualifying corporate bond is disposed of, though not in respect of that disposal, is where it has previously been acquired on a reorganisation within *FA 1984, s 64(7)* and *13 Sch Part II*, in which case the gain previously held over will be crystallised without any relief for a recognition of any failure to repay the principal amount of the bond. The severity of these provisions is partly mitigated in relation to securities which become qualifying corporate bonds by virtue of the *FA 1989* amendments—see IRPR 15 February 1991.

Base cost for capital gains purposes

12.13 The base cost of shares for capital gains purposes will generally be the amount paid or subscribed for them plus other items of eligible expenditure, and similarly for loan stock and other debts. A detailed discussion of this topic is outside the scope of this book. It should, however, be noted that *CGTA 1979, s 29A(1)* requires the substitution of market value for the price paid in certain circumstances, in particular where the shares or loan notes are acquired otherwise than by way of a bargain made at arm's length. This provision would apply automatically where the person acquiring the notes is connected with the company as this would be deemed to be an acquisition otherwise than at arm's length under *CGTA 1979, s 62*. *CGTA 1979, s 29A(1)* does not apply to the acquisition of an asset if there is no corresponding disposal of it (as it is considered there would not be on a subscription for shares, see *Harrison v Nairn Williamson Ltd CA 1977, 51 TC 135*) and where there is no consideration in money or money's worth for the acquisition, or the consideration is of an amount or value lower than the market value of the asset. [*CGTA 1979, s 29A(2)*]. There is a provision of similar effect to those just noted in relation to company reorganisation in the second proviso to *CGTA 1979, s 79(1)*. A scheme to transform a non-allowable capital loss into an allowable loss was rejected in *CIR v Burmah Oil Co Ltd HL 1981, 54 TC 200*, and that case and the more recent judgments following *W T Ramsay Ltd v CIR HL 1981, 54 TC 101* must now be considered in this context.

Guarantees and guarantors

12.14   Where a payment is received under a guarantee provided by a third party, one issue which may arise is whether the payment has the same nature for tax purposes as the original payment would have done. This may be important both for the payer (who may, for example, have to deduct tax from the payment) and for the payee (who may be taxed differently on the receipt, or even taxed on the receipt where he would not have been subject to tax on the original payment, for example in the case of a guarantor of preference share dividends). In *CIR v Sir H C Holder, Bart and J A Holder HL 1932, 16 TC 540* the House of Lords considered the position of a guarantor who paid the accrued interest on an overdraft. The guarantor was held ineligible for relief on the interest under the provisions then in force. This case does not, however, give clear authority that payments under a guarantee have a different nature from the nature of the original payments since (as the speeches of Lords Atkin and Macmillan make clear) the point at issue was whether the payer was eligible for relief, which, perhaps unsurprisingly, he was not. The *Holder* case was distinguished by Lord Denning MR in *Westminster Bank Executor and Trustee Co (Channel Islands) Ltd v National Bank of Greece HL 1970, 46 TC 472* (the point was not addressed substantively in the speeches in the House of Lords on appeal) which concerned the obligation of a guarantor to withhold income tax from a payment of interest under a guarantee under what is now *ICTA 1988, s 349*. Lord Denning held that the payment was one of interest. His conclusion was followed in a very convincing judgment by Megarry J (as he then was) in *Re Hawkins (deceased), Hawkins v Hawkins and another Ch D, [1972] 3 All ER 386* where the question was how a payment by a guarantor should be treated for the purposes of administering an insolvent estate. As Megarry J put it:

'What matters is the nature or quality of the thing paid and not the source of the obligation to pay it. Rent is rent, a fine is a fine, a debt is a debt, and interest is interest, whoever pays it.'

12.15   A person making a payment under a guarantee will not generally be entitled to claim a capital loss to set against tax on chargeable gains. A limited relief is, however, available under *CGTA 1979, s 136(4)* where a payment is made under a guarantee given since 11 April 1978. The relief is available where an outstanding amount of principal of, or of interest in respect of, a "qualifying loan" (see 12.8 above) has become irrecoverable from the borrower and the claimant has made a payment under the guarantee (whether to the lender or a co-guarantor) in respect of that amount. [*CGTA 1979, s 136(4)*]. Similar restrictions on assignment and regarding connected persons apply as to the relief to lenders under *CGTA 1979, s 136(3)* (see 12.8 above). There is also a clawback of relief where all or part of a debt in respect of which relief is given is subsequently recovered by the guarantor or another company in its group. [*CGTA 1979, s 136(5)*]. Relief for traders is considered in the following paragraphs.

Relief for traders

Creditors and guarantors

12.16   Where in carrying on his trade a taxpayer becomes a creditor of a company which proves insolvent or pays up under a guarantee, he will normally be eligible for relief for the bad or doubtful debt recognised in his accounts, provided various hurdles can be overcome. It is, however, essential that the debt should arise not merely in the course of but also for the purposes of the trade since otherwise a deduction will be precluded by either *ICTA 1988, s 74(a)*, which precludes deductions for expenses not 'wholly or exclusively laid out or expended for the purposes of the trade . . .,' or *ICTA 1988, s 74(e)*, which prohibits the deduction of 'any loss not connected with or arising out of the trade, profession or vocation,' or possibly *ICTA 1988, s 74(f)* prohibiting the deduction of 'any capital withdrawn from, or any sum employed or intended to be employed as capital in, the trade . . .'. This is a matter of fact, as is illustrated by a number of cases concerning advances by traders, of which the leading case is *Reid's Brewery Co Ltd v Male QB 1891, 3 TC 279* where a brewing company carried on a money-lending business as an "essentially necessary" adjunct to its brewery business and was held eligible to deduct losses incurred in its money-lending business from the profits of its trade. This case was distinguished in *CIR v Hagart & Burn-Murdoch HL 1929, 14 TC 433* where a firm of Scottish solicitors which lent money to clients "in the course of" its legal business was not eligible to deduct the losses it incurred since the money-lending business was held to be too far removed from the practice as solicitors to be regarded as one of the purposes of the business, or "essential and necessary" to it. The latter case was followed in *Bury & Walkers v Phillips Ch D 1951, 32 TC 198* but distinguished in a third case about solicitors who gave a guarantee of a client's indebtedness, on the grounds, first, that there was no separate consideration for the guarantee which was therefore incapable of constituting a separate venture and secondly, and perhaps more convincingly, because the Commissioners had found as a matter of fact that at least some solicitors made a practice of giving guarantees (*Jennings v Barfield Ch D 1962, 40 TC 365*). Factors which are likely to prove important in showing whether a guarantee is given in the "ordinary course" will include the frequency with which guarantees have been given by the trader, the nature of his business and whether a market fee has been charged.

12.17 Where a deduction is not precluded by the provisions just mentioned, then a provision for bad or doubtful debts properly made in accordance with commercial (i.e. accounting) practice in the trader's accounts will be deductible, provided it does not offend the further prohibition in *ICTA 1988, s 74(j)* for deductions in respect of:

'debts except bad debts proved to be such, and doubtful debts to the extent they are respectively estimated to be bad, and in the case of the bankruptcy or insolvency of a debtor the amount which may reasonably be expected to be received on any such debt shall be deemed to be the value thereof'.

As is implicit in the wording of *ICTA 1988, s 74(j)*, there is no overriding principle that the debtor company must be formally insolvent before a provision for a bad or doubtful debt can be made (*Dinshaw v Bombay Commissioner of Income Tax PC 1934, 50 TLR 527*). What is required is a *bona fide* estimate of the value of the debt in the year in question—as Rowlatt J put it in *Anderton and Halstead Ltd v Birrell KB 1931, 16 TC 200* at p 209:

'What the statute requires, therefore, is an estimate to what extent a debt is bad, and this is for the purpose of a profit and loss account. Such an estimate is not a prophecy to be judged as to its truth by after events, but a valuation of an asset *de praesenti* upon an uncertain future to be judged as to its soundness as an estimate upon the then facts and probabilities.'

In that case, the Inland Revenue's attempt to raise an assessment disallowing relief on a "discovery" under what is now *TMA 1970, s 29(3)* based on the fact that subsequent advances were made to the debtor was rejected. The basis of the valuation of doubtful debts was further considered in *Absalom v Talbot HL 1944, 26 TC 166* where (by a majority) the House of Lords held that a speculative builder who sold houses on the basis that part of the purchase price was left outstanding, secured on a second mortgage, should bring into account not the full face value of the debt, but its actual value 'calculated according to the experience of the business' (per Lord Atkin at p 193). If the debtor is bankrupt or insolvent (which it appears means any type of formal insolvency, including administration, receivership or liquidation) then it is the amount reasonably expected to be recovered which must be taken into account. Where the estimate proves to be too low, however, subsequent receipts which exceed the estimate must be brought into account as trading profits in the year of receipt (*Bristow v William Dickinson & Co Ltd CA 1946, 27 TC 157*). It should be borne in mind that (under English law) a guarantor who makes a payment under a guarantee is normally subrogated to the claim of the original creditor in which case the guarantor's ability to claim relief for a loss will depend on the debtor's ability to pay in respect of that claim. Relief available under *ICTA 1988, s 74(j)* is further restricted in the case of certain loans owed or guaranteed by overseas governments, etc. [*ICTA 1988, ss 88A–88C*].

12.18 The Inland Revenue have stated in the context of company voluntary arrangements that they will not necessarily allow relief where a debt is released by a creditor under the terms of an arrangement if this would result in a deduction in excess of the amount permitted by *ICTA 1988, s 74(j)*. This stance will not always be justifiable in the light of the cases just described. The full text of the Revenue's response is as follows:

'The creditor will not be entitled to relief in respect of any part of a debt which is to be paid to him under the terms of an arrangement. But the release of a debt (or part of a debt) by virtue of a voluntary arrangement may not necessarily entitle the creditor to a deduction. In particular, a deduction may only be allowed by virtue of *section 74(j)* for bad debts proved to be such and doubtful debts to the extent that they are respectively estimated to be bad. A release in excess of an amount arrived at on that basis is unlikely to be an allowable deduction.

Inspectors will usually need to consider all the facts of a particular case before deciding whether a deduction is due in respect of any part of a debt which has been released.' (ICAEW TR 799, para 16(e)).

Shareholders

12.19 A shareholder holding shares as trading stock is not affected by the restrictions in *ICTA 1988, s 74(j)*. Relief will normally be available for losses when the value of the shares is written down, or off, in the trader's accounts. The position of guarantors follows that of creditors in that the payment must be made in the course of and for the purposes of the trade if it is to be deductible. See *Jennings v Barfield*, cited in 12.16 above, and *Morley v Lawford & Co CA 1928, 14 TC 229*.

Reconstructions and debt for equity swaps

12.20 In the course of restructuring the indebtedness of a company which is in administration, for example, or where formal insolvency would otherwise be imminent, a creditor may agree to waive his debt or for it to be restructured as equity in the insolvent company. The tax consequences for a creditor of these transactions will depend on a number of factors including whether he is an investor (so that the debt is a capital item in his hands) or a financial trader (e.g. a bank). The following points may be among those requiring to be considered.

(a) If the debt is simply released, this will be a disposal for the purposes of tax on chargeable gains, and may give rise to an allowable loss if the loan is a "debt on a security" (as it normally will be—see 12.7 above) provided it is not a "qualifying corporate bond" unless relief is available on one of the bases described in 12.10–12.11 above.

(b) If shares are subscribed for cash which is used to repay the loan, no tax loss will be crystallised in respect of the loan (even though it is a "debt on a security" not being a "qualifying corporate bond") and the base cost of the new shares is likely to be nil (under *CGTA 1979, s 29A(2)*). The reconstruction will not normally be a reorganisation within *CGTA 1979, Pt IV Ch 2* unless a "scheme of reconstruction or amalgamation" is involved within *CGTA 1979, s 86*.

(c) Where the debt is released in consideration of an issue of shares, however, relying on *CA 1985, s 738(2)* which will deem the shares to be paid up, it should be possible to make a claim under *CGTA 1979, s 136A(3)* on the basis that the value of the debt has become negligible. SP 8/90 may also assist in this situation (see 12.11(a) above). The base cost of the shares will be equal to their market value at the date of issue under *CGTA 1979, s 29A(2)*.

(d) Where interest has accrued, but is unpaid, the release may give rise to an adjustment in the computation of the chargeable gain or loss under *CGTA 1979, s 33A*, depending on whether the loan is waived with or without the right to the accrued interest (because the disposal will fall within *CGTA 1979, s 33A(7)*).

(e) In some cases, it may be appropriate to consider whether a waiver of the interest could give rise to a charge under Schedule D Case VI under *ICTA 1988, s 786(5)*.

(f) The provisions in *ICTA 1988, s 582* must also be borne in mind if interest is to be satisfied by the issue of (among other things) shares or loan stock i.e. "funding bonds". This transaction would not, absent a statutory provision, amount to a payment or receipt of the interest (*Cross v London and Provincial Trust, Ltd CA 1938, 21 TC 705*) but under *section 582* will be so treated and may mean (in the case of interest payable otherwise than on an advance from a bank within *ICTA 1988, s 349(3)(a)*) that funding bonds with a value equal to income tax at the basic rate deductible from the interest must be offered to the Inland Revenue.

(g) For a creditor which is a trader, the waiver or swap of the debt should generally, depending on the accounting treatment adopted, result in a loss being realised, subject to the availability of bad debt relief (see 12.16–12.18 above). Where there is a scheme of reconstruction within *CGTA 1979, s 86*, however, relief will be precluded by *ICTA 1988, s 473*.

(h) The release of a debt is a supply for VAT purposes: whether it is taxable depends on the circumstances.

The consequences for the debtor company must also be considered, since a release may give rise to a taxable receipt or loss relief previously claimed for charges on income. This is considered in 7.9 above.

Distributions

Distributions to shareholders

12.21   Distributions to members of a company are by definition unlikely to arise in an insolvent liquidation but the subject is important enough to deserve a brief mention. It is expressly provided that distributions made in respect of share capital in a winding up will not be treated as income distributions for tax purposes. [*ICTA 1970, s 209(1)*]. This includes arrears of dividends payable in respect of preference shares—see *Re Dominion Tar and Chemical Co Ltd, [1929] 2 Ch 387* which concerned the old income tax deduction rules. The exception afforded by the proviso to *ICTA 1988, s 209(1)* (i.e. that amounts which would otherwise be distributions of income may be treated as capital distributions) also applies as a concession (ESC C 16) where a company is dissolved under *CA 1985, s 652* by being removed from the register without a formal liquidation, and assets are transferred to its members after creditors have been paid off.

12.22   Distributions on a liquidation are treated as capital distributions under *CGTA 1979, s 72*. Where several distributions are made in different years, each amount distributed may be deducted from the base cost of the shares where it is small as compared with the value of the shares. [*CGTA 1979, s 72(2)*]. For this purpose, "small" normally means five per cent or less. Where the amount of the distribution exceeds this, the shareholder will be treated as having made a part disposal of his shares and the normal rules of computation for part disposals contained in *CGTA 1979, s 35* will apply. To avoid the necessity of valuing the shareholder's residual rights in the shares, it is open to a shareholder to adopt the simplified procedure set out in SP D3 (Tolley's Official Tax Statements 1990–91, 124.201). The text of this statement is as follows:

> '1.   During the liquidation of a company the shareholders often receive more than one distribution. For capital gains tax each distribution, other than the final one, is a part disposal of his shares by the shareholder, and the residual value of the shares has to be ascertained in order to attribute a proportion of the cost of the shares to the distribution (unless the Inspector of Taxes accepts that the distribution is "small" and can therefore be deducted from cost). It has been represented to the Board of Inland Revenue that the making and formal agreement of these valuations is holding up the agreement of liabilities and that little if any change in the total tax is involved in the majority of cases.
>
> 2.   Where the shares of a company are unquoted at the date of the first or later interim distribution, therefore, the Board are

prepared to authorise Inspectors of Taxes to accept any valuation by the taxpayer or his agent of the residual value of the shares at the date of the distribution, if the valuation appears reasonable and if the liquidation is expected to be completed within 2 years of the first distribution (and does not in fact extend much beyond that period). The valuation need not include a discount for deferment; and if the distributions are complete before the capital gains tax assessment is made, the Revenue will accept that the residual value of the shares in relation to a particular distribution is equal to the actual amount of the subsequent distributions. In the normal way the Revenue will not raise the question of capital gains tax on an interim distribution until after 2 years from the commencement of the liquidation unless the distribution, together with any previous distributions, exceeds the total cost of the shares.

3.   Where time apportionment (shares acquired before 6 April 1965) applies to a case within the scope of this practice, the Board are prepared to calculate the gain on each distribution by applying the time apportionment fraction as at the date of the first distribution without further adjustment under [*CGTA 1979, 5 Sch 11(8)*].

4.   Strict valuations will continue to be necessary for all other estate duty, stamp duty and capital gains tax purposes.'

12.23   Where a distribution is made of an asset, rather than cash (i.e. a distribution *in specie*), there will be two disposals to be taken into account. First, the company may be subject to tax on chargeable gains in respect of its disposal of the asset, which will be deemed for this purpose to take place at market value. [*CGTA 1979, s 29A(1)(a)*]. Secondly, the shareholder will be deemed to acquire the asset at the same value, which will be taken into account for the purposes of computing his own gain. In *Innocent v Whaddon Estates Ltd Ch D 1981, 55 TC 476* the application of *ICTA 1970, s 273* (as it now is) to a distribution *in specie* by a 75 per cent subsidiary in liquidation to its parent was considered. The judge held that the first disposal (that by the subsidiary) should be ignored; but that by virtue of the proviso to *ICTA 1970, s 273(2)* the second disposal (of the shares in the subsidiary by the parent when the distribution is made) could not be ignored. This was consistent with the Revenue practice confirmed, after the facts giving rise to the case but before the decision, to the ICAEW in 1975 (CCAB TR 172 June 1975, Tolley's Official Tax Statements 1990–91, 36.403).

Distributions to creditors

12.24   Where tax on capital gains is to be considered, the position on full or partial repayment of the loan is similar to a shareholder's position on a distribution, as described in paragraphs 12.21–12.23 above, although repayment of a loan will only in exceptional cases, such as a loan in a foreign currency, give rise to a capital gain. Subject to the special rules for conversions and reconstructions, satisfaction of a debt is treated as a disposal or part disposal made at the time when the debt, or part of it, is satisfied. [*CGTA 1979, s 134(2)*]. Where the debt (or part of it) is satisfied by the transfer of property, then, apart from the exceptional cases just mentioned, the transfer will be treated as taking place at no greater than market value at the time of acquisition, unless the creditor is the original creditor and the debt is not a debt on a security, in which case his base cost on a subsequent disposal will be reduced to the amount of the debt. [*CGTA 1979, s 134(3)*].

Indemnities

12.25   Where a shareholder or creditor gives an indemnity to the liquidator in respect of all or part of the amount distributed to him, it should be borne in mind that any payment made under the indemnity will not operate to reduce retrospectively the amount originally distributed and which will have been taken into account in determining the shareholder's or creditor's capital loss or gain. It will therefore be more tax efficient in many cases for the liquidator to defer a final distribution, or make alternative arrangements such as procuring a bank guarantee or insurance.

Recovery of tax from shareholders and group members

12.26   A number of provisions of the Taxes Acts entitle the Inland Revenue to seek to recover unpaid tax liabilities from a company's shareholders and group members. One important one is *ICTA 1988, s 346* which applies where a person connected with a company within the definition contained in *ICTA 1988, s 839* receives or becomes entitled to receive a capital distribution in respect of shares (other than a capital distribution representing a reduction of capital). If the capital distributed derives from the disposal of assets in respect of which a chargeable gain accrued to the company, or the distribution is itself a disposal of assets giving rise to a chargeable gain, and the tax assessed on the company in respect of the chargeable gain is not paid within six months from the date when it becomes payable, the recipient of the capital distribution may himself be assessed and charged in the name of the company to an amount of that corporation tax. This amount is a proportion equal to the share of the capital distribution which he has received. Another is *ICTA 1988, s 347* which provides that the principal company of a 75 per cent group at the time when a chargeable gain accrued to a member of that group may, in some circumstances, be assessed and charged with the tax in respect of that gain if the subsidiary company fails to pay. This section may also apply to any other company which has owned the asset or been interested in it and was a member of the same group during the preceding two years.

A further provision imposing a charge upon the principal company of a 75 per cent group may arise out of the emigration of a subsidiary. The chargeable gain arising out of the deemed disposal under *FA 1988, s 105* may be postponed upon election by the principal and the subsidiary under *FA 1988, s 107*. The postponed gain will then accrue on the occasion of the principal disposing of its shares in the subsidiary or the company ceasing to be such a subsidiary, even if these events are caused by a winding up. [*FA 1988, s 107(4)*]. This is unlike the provisions in *ICTA 1970, s 278*, dealing with group chargeable gains when a company ceases to be a group member, which do not apply on a winding up or dissolution. Any disposal by the subsidiary company which has emigrated, of assets taken into account in calculating the postponed gain, will also cause the postponed gain to accrue to the principal company. [*FA 1988, s 107(3)*]. By *FA 1989, s 134* unpaid corporation tax arising out of chargeable gains accruing to a non-resident company trading in the UK through a branch or agency may also be collected from another company in the same 51 per cent group or from a controlling director, as defined in *FA 1989, s 134(7)*.

Recovery of tax from other third parties

12.27 Apart from its shareholders and other members of the insolvent company's group, unpaid tax may be recovered directly or indirectly from other third parties in certain circumstances. This may be possible under specific provisions in the tax legislation but the remedies given by *IA 1986* should not be overlooked, either. In particular, the court may set aside a transaction preferring another creditor over the Inland Revenue or Customs & Excise on an application by a liquidator or administrator under *IA 1986, s 239*, may set aside transactions at an undervalue under *IA 1986, s 238* or may make a direction for directors (and where *IA 1986, s 213* applies, others) to contribute to a company's assets where there has been fraudulent or wrongful trading under *IA 1986, s 213* or *IA 1986, s 214*. Moreover, a failure to pay PAYE or VAT may be regarded as grounds for a disqualification order against a responsible director in which context it is referred to by one judge as "conduct contrary to commercial morality" (see *Re Ipcon Fashions Ltd Ch D, (1989) 5 BCC 773* per Hoffman J and *Re T & D Services (Timber Preservation & Damp Proofing Contractors) Ltd Ch D, [1990] BCC 592* though the cases are inconsistent).

12.28 Other provisions enabling the recovery of tax from third parties include the following.

(a) *ITER 1973, Reg 26(3)*. If the Collector of Taxes is satisfied that the employer took reasonable care to comply with the *ITER 1973* and that an under-deduction of PAYE was due to an error made in good faith, he may direct recovery from the employee.

(b) *ITER 1973, Reg 26(4)*. If the Inland Revenue are of the opinion that an employee has received his emoluments knowing that the employer has wilfully failed to deduct the relevant tax, they may direct recovery from the employee.

(c) *ITER 1973, Reg 29(4)*. If tax has not been paid after a formal determination under *Regulation 29(1)*, the Revenue may in the circumstances set out in *Regulation 26(4)* direct the tax to be recovered from the employee together with interest from the reckonable date until payment in accordance with *Regulation 29A* (there is no equivalent to this regulation, nor to the *ITER 1973, Reg 26(3)(4)* in the regulations for sub-contractors in the construction industry).

(d) *SSCR 1979, Reg 50(1)*. Where there has been a failure by the employer to pay any primary NIC due to an act or default of the employee and not to any negligence on the part of the employer, the provisions of *SSA 1975, 1 Sch 3(1)*, which otherwise impose liability on the employer to the exclusion of the employee, do not apply so that liability for the primary NIC remains with the employee (there is no equivalent to *ITER 1973, Regs 26(3)(4), 29(4)* in *SSCR 1979*).

(e) *SSA 1986, s 57*. If an offence under any of the "benefit Acts" has been committed by a company and is proved to have been committed with the consent or connivance of, or to be attributable to any neglect on the part of, a director, manager, secretary, other similar officer, any person purporting to act in such capacity, or any member exercising a management function, such person shall be liable to be proceeded against in addition to the company.

(f) *FA 1986, s 14*. Where a company is liable to a penalty under *FA 1985, s 13* for dishonestly evading VAT, and the company's conduct appears to Customs & Excise to be wholly or partly attributable to the dishonesty of a director, manager, secretary, similar officer, person purporting to act in such capacity, or any member exercising a management function, such person may have a portion (or the whole) of the penalty recovered from him by an assessment.

(g) *Inheritance Tax Act 1984, s 94*. Where a close company makes a transfer of value, inheritance tax is charged on individual participators on amounts apportioned to them, calculated in accordance with *Pt IV* of the Act.

(h) *Inheritance Tax Act 1984, s 237*. Where tax charged on a transfer of value is for the time being unpaid, a charge is imposed in favour of the Revenue on property to the value of which the value transferred is wholly or partly attributable.

VAT relief for bad debts

General

12.29 On 26 July 1990, *FA 1990* introduced important changes in the way that the VAT component of bad debts may be recovered by creditors. Before 27 July 1990, relief from VAT on a bad debt was available under *VATA 1983, s 22* only where a debtor company went into liquidation or an administrator or administrative receiver certified that, in a liquidation, the company's assets would be insufficient to cover the payment of a dividend to the ordinary unsecured creditors. *FA 1990, s 11* replaced the previous provisions for relief from VAT on bad debts with a new scheme under which a VAT registered person was to be entitled to a refund of VAT on any debt which was two years old and which had been written off in that person's accounts. The two-year period has been reduced to one year by the Finance Bill published on 17 April 1991. Relief from VAT on bad debts is no longer dependent on the formal insolvency of the debtor but it should be noted that even if the debtor is insolvent the refund cannot be claimed until a year has elapsed. Under the new scheme, the refund or part of it must be repaid to Customs & Excise where the debt is subsequently paid in whole or in part.

The new scheme

12.30   *FA 1990, s 11* (as amended) provides that where:

(a)   a person has supplied goods or services on or after 1 April 1989 for a consideration in money and has accounted for and paid VAT on the supply; and

(b)   the person has written off in his accounts the whole or part of the consideration for the supply; and

(c)   a period of one year has elapsed from the time of the supply;

the person is entitled to claim a refund of the VAT chargeable by reference to the outstanding amount less any payment received by way of consideration for the supply. In *English Film Co Ltd v C & E Commrs, LON/82/134 (1357)* the Tribunal held that, in order to meet the requirement (under the old rules which has been preserved in the new scheme) that he has accounted for and paid tax on a supply, the person must have acknowledged his liability for output tax on the relevant supply and have paid all the tax payable by him in respect of the accounting period during which the supply was made, without any deduction or retention in respect of that supply. Notwithstanding that the above conditions are met, *FA 1990, s 11(4)* provides that a person is not entitled to a refund of VAT if the value of the supply is greater than its open market value or, in the case of a supply of goods, the property in the goods has not passed to the person to whom they were supplied or another person deriving title from that person. In relation to the previous bad debt relief, which contained the same requirement, Customs & Excise regarded the latter condition as being met if title had passed at the time that the claim for relief was made and regarded title as having passed if it was formally transferred to a liquidator as agent of the debtor (CCAB TR 388, 7 May 1980). The detailed provisions relating to the new scheme are contained in the *Value Added Tax (Refunds for Bad Debts) Regulations 1991, SI*

1991 No 371 which came into force on 1 April 1991. These regulations are referred to without further citation in the remaining paragraphs of this chapter.

Which scheme applies?

12.31   The new scheme is operative from 27 July 1990 but the one-year qualifying period runs from 1 April 1990 to allow the first claims for relief under the new scheme to be made from 1 April 1991. No claim for relief under *VATA 1983, s 22* may be made after 26 July 1990. Which scheme applies is determined by the time of the supply in relation to which the bad debt has arisen. Thus:

(a)   in relation to any supply made before 1 April 1989, relief from VAT on bad debts may only be claimed under the old scheme whenever the claim is made;

(b)   in relation to any supply made after 26 July 1990, relief from VAT on bad debts may only be claimed under the new scheme (by concession, however, a supply which takes place after 26 July 1990 only by virtue of *VATA 1983, s 5*, i.e. because a tax invoice is issued after 26 July 1990 in respect of a supply which would otherwise have been treated as taking place on or before that date, can be the subject of relief under the old scheme—see CEPR 1 May 1991); and

(c)   in relation to any supply made between 1 April 1989 and 26 July 1990, the claimant may choose either scheme (but not both) for claiming relief from VAT on bad debts provided it meets the relevant criteria.

Making a claim

12.32   Under *Regulation 3* a person may claim relief from VAT on a bad debt by including the amount of VAT to be refunded in box 2 of the VAT return. The regulation provides that if the claimant is no longer required to furnish returns, i.e. he is no longer registered for VAT, he shall make a claim in such form and manner as Customs & Excise may direct.

Writing off debts

12.33   *Regulation 9* states that the whole or part of the consideration for a supply is taken to have been written off as a bad debt when the creditor makes an entry in relation to that supply in his "refunds for bad debts" account (see 12.35 below). The entry has effect whether or not a claim for a refund can be made at the time. Where the creditor owes money to the debtor which can be set off against the bad debt the consideration written off in the accounts must be reduced by the amount so owed. Similarly, where the creditor holds an enforceable security in relation to the debtor the consideration written off in the accounts must be reduced by the value of the security. "Security" is defined in *Regulation 2* as (in relation to England, Wales and Northern Ireland) 'any mortgage, charge, lien or other security'. A separate definition applies for Scotland.

Evidence required in support of a claim

12.34 *Regulation 4* provides that, before making a claim, the claimant must hold, in relation to each supply in respect of which a refund is claimed, the following evidence:

(a)   a copy of the tax invoice issued by the claimant in respect of the supply (or, where a tax invoice was not required to be issued, a document which shows the time, nature and value of the supply);

(b)   records or any other documents showing that the claimant has accounted for and paid VAT on the supply; and

(c)   records or any other documents showing that the consideration for the supply has been written off as a bad debt in the claimant's accounts (see 12.33 above).

Records to be kept by the claimant

12.35 *Regulation 5* requires the claimant to keep a record of any claim made. The record must, save as Customs & Excise may otherwise allow, contain the following information:

(a)   in respect of each relevant supply for that claim:

    (i)   the amount of VAT chargeable on the supply;

    (ii)   the VAT accounting period in which the VAT chargeable was accounted for and paid to Customs;

    (iii)   the date and number of the VAT invoice issued in relation to the supply (or, where there is no such invoice, such information as is necessary to identify the time, nature and purchaser of the supply); and

    (iv)   any payment received in relation to the supply;

(b)   the outstanding amount to which the claim relates;

(c)   the amount of the claim; and

(d)   the VAT accounting period in which the claim was made.

The records relating to claims for refunds of VAT on bad debts must be kept in a single account to be known as the "refunds for bad debts account". *Regulation 6* requires the claimant to preserve the records contained in the "refunds for bad debts account" for a period of six years from the making of a claim and that such records must be produced to Customs upon demand.

Attribution of payments

12.36 Where a claimant has made more than one supply to a debtor and a payment is received in relation to those supplies, the payment must be attributed to the supply which is the earliest in time and, if not wholly attributed to that supply, to supplies in the order of the dates on which they were made. Where more than one supply to which a payment could be attributed occurred on the same day, the payment must be attributed to those supplies by, for each supply, multiplying the payment received by a fraction of which the numerator is the outstanding consideration for the supply and the denominator is the total outstanding consideration for the supplies. A payment must not be attributed to supplies in the way just described if the payment is allocated to a particular supply by the purchaser at the time of payment and the consideration for that supply was paid in full.

Repayment of refund

12.37 *Regulation 8* requires a claimant who has received a refund of VAT on a bad debt and who subsequently receives a payment, in whole or in part, in relation to the supply in respect of which the refund was claimed, to repay to Customs & Excise the same proportion of the refund, or remaining balance of the refund, as the payment received bears to the outstanding consideration for the supply. The repayment is made by including the amount in box 1 of the VAT return for the accounting period in which the payment is received. If the claimant fails to comply with any requirement contained in the 1991 Regulations as to evidence, records and attribution of payments, then that person must, save as Customs may otherwise allow, repay any refund obtained by the claim to which the failure to comply relates.

12.38 A case decided in relation to the former provisions for bad debt relief, but which may still be relevant to the new scheme, is *CBS United Kingdom Limited v C & E Commrs, [1987] VATTR 93*. In that case CBS entered into agreements with companies ("the Reproduction Companies") which owned the right to distribute video cassettes. Under the agreements, CBS distributed the video cassettes to retailers in return for a distribution charge paid by the Reproduction Companies. The Reproduction Companies were paid a fixed amount by CBS in respect of each video cassette distributed, which amounts CBS recovered from the retailers. The agreement between CBS and the Reproduction Companies provided that the Reproduction Companies would be responsible for any bad debts arising out of non-payment by the retailers to CBS. In the event that any bad debts were subsequently recovered by CBS, then such amounts (less costs and expenses) would be paid to the Reproduction Companies. During the period under consideration bad debts arose in relation to various retailers and CBS claimed bad debt relief, under *VATA 1983, s 22* in respect of such debts. CBS also claimed and received payments from the Reproduction Companies of the VAT exclusive amounts owed by the retailers. Customs & Excise contended that the amounts received by CBS from the Reproduction Companies should be treated as part of the consideration payable to CBS for supplies made to the retailers. The Tribunal held that CBS had correctly accounted for and paid VAT chargeable on the supplies to the retailers and, therefore, no further liability to pay VAT arose in relation to those supplies. In respect of the payments made by the Reproduction Companies, the Tribunal held that a payment by a third party to a creditor could not affect the outstanding amount of consideration for a supply unless it was made on an express or implied term that the debt relating to that supply was extinguished. The Tribunal also held that Customs were not entitled to recover bad debt relief from a creditor if the creditor, at a later date, obtained payment, in whole or in part, of the balance of the outstanding amount of the consideration. It appears that the last point is no longer the law as *Regulation 8* requires a claimant to repay a refund where 'a payment for the relevant supply is subsequently received'. In relation to the effect of a payment by a third party the position is less clear. *Regulation 8* does not apply only to payments made by the debtor but "payment" is defined in *Regulation 2* as 'any payment or part payment which is made by any person to the claimant by way of consideration for a supply regardless of whether such payment extinguishes the purchaser's debt to the claimant or not'. It is arguable that the payment by the Reproduction Companies in the CBS case was not "for" the supply as no supply was made to the Reproduction Companies. Equally, *Regulation 9(4)*, which provides that the consideration written off in the accounts of the claimant must be reduced by the value of any security held by the claimant in relation to the purchaser, would not, it appears, assist Customs because the agreement between CBS and the Reproduction Companies was not a "security" as defined in *Regulation 2*.

Chapter 13

Other Insolvency Procedures

General

13.1 This chapter deals with the income, corporation tax and VAT considerations applicable to receivers appointed over particular assets or classes of assets (book debts, land), court receivers and mortgagees in possession.

Receivers appointed over particular assets

Income and corporation tax

13.2 The income and corporation tax treatment of a receiver appointed over a particular asset or assets of a UK resident company under a fixed charge is essentially the same as that of an administrative receiver, discussed in Chapter 5 above, save that there can be no question of recourse to the assets secured by a fixed charge to pay preferential claims or post-liquidation tax liabilities (*Re Regent's Canal Ironworks Company, ex parte Grissell CA 1875, 3 Ch D 411*). That is to say, income and corporation tax liabilities resulting from the activities of the receiver (e.g. in selling the asset) or relating to income he receives (e.g. bank interest or rents subject to the special charging provisions discussed in 5.6–5.8 above) normally rest with the company and are not recoverable from the receiver. These liabilities will fall to be discharged either as unsecured claims (if relating to pre-liquidation periods) or under *Ins R 1986, Rule 4.218*. This point was not disputed in *Re Mesco Properties Ltd CA 1979, 54 TC 238*, where some of the gains concerned were made by receivers. See further 8.37–8.42 above. A receiver may have to account for income tax on interest which he pays (see 5.16–5.20 above).

VAT

13.3 The VAT position of a receiver appointed over a particular asset under a fixed charge is covered by *VATA 1983, 2 Sch 6*. This says:

'Where in the case of a business carried on by a taxable person, goods forming part of the assets of the business are, under any power exercisable by another person, sold by the other in or towards satisfaction of a debt owed by the taxable person, they shall be deemed to be supplied by the taxable person in the course or furtherance of his business.'

This paragraph is supplemented by *VAT Gen R 1985, Reg 59*, which says that the person selling the goods (the auctioneer, if the sale is by auction) must within 21 days of the sale furnish a statement to Customs & Excise, pay the tax due, and send the person whose goods were sold a copy of the statement. That person must exclude from his own return the tax chargeable on the supply. The statement sent to him by the receiver (or auctioneer) is made on Form VAT 833, as appears from Customs & Excise Notice No 700 ('The VAT Guide' (revised 1 October 1987)), para 59(a). The receiver or auctioneer must also provide the buyer with a document containing details of the tax chargeable and other information normally found on a VAT invoice under *VAT Gen R 1985, Reg 12(2)*— though technically the document is not itself a VAT invoice, only treated as such.

13.4   One difficulty with *VATA 1983, 2 Sch 6* is in determining who is entitled to recover input tax on the sale. It appears that Customs & Excise have no fixed practice on this point and have been known to allow a deduction on the Form 833 and even to allow fixed charge receivers to register under *VAT Gen R 1985, Reg 11* on the basis that they "carry on" the business of the mortgagor. See 9.2 and 9.8 above. It may, however, be more correct for the receiver to arrange for the tax to be recovered and repaid to him by the company or its liquidator. Customs have published this view in the context of land transactions (see 13.12 below). This is an unsatisfactory state of affairs, however, in that the receiver cannot compel the liquidator to co-operate, and any tax which is recovered (after Customs have exercised their rights under *FA 1988, s 21* and *VATA 1983, s 14(7)*—see 20.9–20.13 below) may accrue to creditors under the floating charge or fixed charge on book debts.

Receivers of book debts

13.5   A standard form fixed and floating charge often also contains a fixed charge on book and other debts, expressed to include both those in existence at the time the charge is created and those which subsequently come into existence. Such debts may in theory be charged separately and occasionally a receiver is appointed over book debts alone. The priority of the fixed charge on book debts over claims of government departments arising after the date of registration of the charge is generally acknowledged. In the case of VAT, however, this is in the view of Customs & Excise subject to *FA 1988, s 21* discussed further in 20.9–20.13 below.

Is a tax claim a book debt?

13.6   A point which does sometimes arise is the extent to which a right to a tax refund is a "book or other debt", caught by the charge. The classic definition of a debt is that given by Lindley LJ in *Webb v Stenton CA 1883, 11 QBD 518* at p 527 where he said:

> 'a debt is a sum of money which is now payable or will become payable in the future by reason of a present obligation, *debitum in presenti, solvendum in futuro*'.

In principle, a right to a tax refund is a debt as the cases on Crown set-off indicate (see Chapter 3 above). This will normally be clear—for example, excess input VAT for an accounting period becomes a debt due to the taxpayer under *VATA 1983, s 14(5)* as soon as the return for the relevant period is made showing the amount due (see *Betterware Products Ltd v C & E Commrs QB, [1985] STC 648* and *C & E Commrs v Fine Art Developments plc HL, [1989] STC 85*). The point is complicated slightly by the decision in *R v C & E Commrs, ex parte Strangewood Ltd QB, [1987] STC 502* where it was held that the Commissioners are entitled not to make repayments of input tax until they have verified the return, but it is not considered that this upsets the underlying obligations of the Commissioners to make the payment—indeed it would be surprising if they were not allowed to check before making a payment.

13.7   The point is, however, less clear where there is something yet to be done to bring a debt into existence. The answer to this will depend partly on the terms of the statutory provision under which the right to repayment arises. It is immaterial that the amount of the tax repayment is unquantified (see *O'Driscoll v Manchester Insurance Committee, [1915] 3 KB 499*) provided it is an absolute right and not, for example, dependent on the exercise of a discretion. Thus, for example, a claim for ACT to be set against corporation tax in an earlier year under *ICTA 1988, s 239(3)*, or to set losses against ACT under *ICTA 1988, s 242*, will, it is considered, create a debt caught by the charge. It can also be argued that a claim under certain provisions which impose on the Crown an obligation to make a repayment, subject to determining what amount is just and reasonable, also creates a debt (e.g. *TMA 1970, s 33*).

13.8   One question to some extent begged by the previous discussion is whether there is a debt *before* a claim is made. There can, it is considered, be no debt where the circumstances do not yet exist for the claim to be made (e.g. potential claim for terminal loss relief under *ICTA 1988, s 394*, before the trade has ceased) but whether the claim is a prerequisite for the debt to come into existence, or whether it is merely a formality, may depend on the statutory provisions in question. It can, for example, conceivably be argued that VAT input tax repayments are a right which does not require a claim, particularly given the mandatory requirement to render the return. Any difficulty is in practice normally capable of remedy by the making of the claim though a receiver will need to consider carefully whether his charge gives him power to do this or whether he should act through the company and (in the case of corporation and income tax) its "proper officer" within *TMA 1970, s 108.*

VAT

13.9 The realisation of book debts by a receiver appointed only over them will not give rise to any taxable supplies by the company and consequently any VAT on related expenses will be irrecoverable by the company.

Receivers of land

Income and corporation tax

13.10 The points arising in relation to fixed charge receivers appointed over land have been covered elsewhere in this book but it may be convenient to draw them together in one place as follows.

(a)   The receiver is not liable to income or corporation tax arising on the disposal of the land (see 5.3 above). This falls to be paid as a disbursement by the liquidator (see 8.36–8.40 above) if the disposal occurs after liquidation has begun; otherwise it is an unsecured claim.

(b)   He is not normally liable to tax on interest on funds on deposit (which is treated as in (a) above) but may have to account for tax on rents if a notice is served on him under the special collection provisions discussed in 5.7–5.8 above.

(c)   If the company is not UK resident he may also have to account for income tax or CGT in certain circumstances—see Chapter 15 below.

VAT

13.11 In cases where the supply is a taxable supply, VAT will be payable by the receiver and returns, etc. required as explained in 13.3 above, under *VATA 1983, 2 Sch 6.* However, the case of *Ashgrove Estates Ltd (In Liquidation) v C & E Commrs, EDN/89/40 (3932)* where the Edinburgh VAT Tribunal held that *2 Sch 6* cannot apply to any supply of land in Scotland is, it is submitted, inapplicable in England and Wales (and possibly wrongly decided).

13.12 The VAT implications of a sale of land by a fixed charge receiver are discussed in some detail in 9.10(a) above. A receiver will be bound by an election to waive VAT exemption made by the company before (and possibly after) his appointment, as the company remains the taxable person. Customs & Excise will accept an election made by the receiver as valid. It will frequently be advantageous for the election to be made since this will enable recovery of associated input VAT on the costs of sale (e.g. on solicitors' and estate agents' fees). Customs state in paragraph 17 of Notice No 742B ('Property Ownership' (January 1990)) that the input tax is recoverable by the company, but it may in practice be possible to arrange for the VAT to be recovered by the receiver (see 13.4 above). Before electing, a receiver should carefully consider the effect on the price which he can get for the land as he must then charge VAT on the sale proceeds and any rents, not only because it may affect his own recoveries but also because of the position of junior mortgagees and the mortgagor.

Court receivers

Income and corporation tax

13.13   Court receivership is not an insolvency procedure as such but it is nonetheless appropriate to mention it briefly. *TMA 1970, s 75* provides that:

> '(1)   A receiver appointed by any court in the United Kingdom which has the direction and control of any property in respect of which income tax is charged in accordance with the provisions of the Income Tax Acts shall be assessable and chargeable with the tax in like manner and to the like amount as would be assessed and charged if the property were not under the direction and control of the court.'

This provision applies to income tax, and thus to non-resident companies (see further Chapter 15), but does not apply to corporation tax. Its wording is ambiguous in that it is unclear whether court receivers are to be treated like other receivers or whether the receiver's appointment is to be disregarded altogether. It is understood that the Inland Revenue take the former view. Accordingly, the Revenue consider that tax on the assets held by the receiver will normally fall to be discharged by the company or a liquidator if one is appointed (see Chapter 8 above); but where the company is (or before the appointment, was) non-UK resident for tax purposes, and does not become so in the course of the receivership, the receiver may be assessable under *TMA 1970, s 78(1)*—see 15.25–15.26 below. Whether the appointment of the receiver by a UK court will of itself make the company become UK resident will depend on the facts of the case and the degree of supervision and control he has of the company's assets—but this appears unlikely.

VAT

13.14   Customs & Excise take the view that the services of a court receiver are supplied to the court which appoints him and under whose supervision he works. Whether this view is correct in all cases may be doubted, but it is the most convenient solution since the beneficiary of the appointment (be it the company whose assets he secures or the plaintiff in the action) may not be known until the proceedings are nearly at an end. The consequences of Customs' view are that VAT on the appointee's fees (which will normally be treated as made in the course of his partnership business as a chartered accountant or insolvency practitioner under *VATA 1983, s 47(4)*) will be chargeable against the assets he controls if the court so directs and will not be recoverable. VAT on disbursements will be chargeable similarly either as part of the appointee's fees or (if they are agency disbursements and bear VAT) separately. The reverse charge will apply to the normal types of expenses incurred abroad (e.g. foreign lawyers' fees). [*VATA 1983, s 7, 3 Sch*]. If the court which appoints the receiver is not a UK court, then in appropriate cases the appointee may zero rate his fee.

Mortgagees in possession

Income and corporation tax

13.15   A mortgagee which takes possession of charged property under the common law power recognised in *LPA 1925, s 95(4)*, or a power expressly given in the charge document, does not thereby become the beneficial owner of the assets. This situation is not discussed specifically in *English Sewing Cotton Co Ltd v CIR CA, [1947] 1 All ER 679* but the conclusion follows from that case. Thus, it is the company which remains liable to tax in respect of income derived from the property or capital gains made on the disposal of the property, as is the case with sales by receivers and others. Some of the gains at issue in *Re Mesco Properties Ltd CA 1979, 54 TC 238* were made by mortgagees and the point was not disputed (see 8.38–8.39 above).

VAT

13.16   The sale by a mortgagee in possession will (if a taxable supply) give rise to an obligation to account for VAT as described in 13.3 above.

Chapter 14

Close and Business Expansion Scheme Companies

Close company aspects

14.1   In the 1989 Budget the Chancellor proposed the abolition of close company apportionment and this was carried into effect by *FA 1989, s 103* for accounting periods beginning after 31 March 1989. Special apportionment rules had applied on the liquidation of a close company or the cessation of its trade or of its investment business under *ICTA 1988, 19 Sch 10* (previously *FA 1972, 16 Sch 13*), but these provisions no longer apply where the liquidation or cessation occurs in an accounting period commencing after 31 March 1989.

14.2   In the same Budget the Chancellor also introduced provisions to prevent the avoidance of income tax by individuals using closely held investment companies, by excluding "close investment-holding companies" from the small companies' rate of corporation tax and by restricting the payment of the tax credit under *ICTA 1988, s 231(3)* where this otherwise obtains a tax advantage. *ICTA 1988, s 13A* defines a "close investment-holding company" as a close company which in any accounting period does not comply with *ICTA 1988, s 13A(2)*. The definition excludes *inter alia* companies which exist wholly or mainly to trade on a commercial basis, or to invest in land let or intended to be let other than to connected persons or their relatives, or to hold shares or securities in or to make loans to or to administer companies under the same control. *ICTA 1988, s 13A(4)* prevents the cessation of trade on a liquidation from automatically causing a close company to become a close investment-holding company by providing:

> 'Where a company is wound up, it shall not be treated as failing to comply with subsection (2) above in the accounting period that (by virtue of subsection (7) of section 12) begins with the time which is for the purposes of that subsection the commencement of the winding up, if it complied with subsection (2) above in the accounting period that ends with that time.'

This protection will not apply if the company has ceased to comply with *section 13A(2)* before the winding up has commenced. This may occur where the trade has diminished to such an extent that it is regarded as having ceased and the company's accounting period is treated by *ICTA*

1988, s 12(3)(c) as having ended, some time before the decision to wind up the company is taken.

14.3   The liquidation of a close company may also require consideration of the treatment of loans to participators falling within *ICTA 1988, s 419*. For a general explanation of the position of participators in close companies, see Tolley's Corporation Tax.

14.4   A tax liability arises under *ICTA 1988, s 419* where a loan is made by a close company to a participator or an associate of a participator. This is extended by *ICTA 1988, s 422* to loans by companies controlled by close companies. These provisions are now encountered less frequently following the restrictions upon loans to directors in what are now *CA 1985, ss 330–344*. However, *ICTA 1988, s 419* remains of significance since it is frequently used by the Inland Revenue as the basis of charge where those concerned with the company have been implicated in back duty enquiries.

14.5   The effect, if *ICTA 1988, s 419* applies, is that an amount of tax becomes chargeable on the company equal to a proportion of the loan corresponding to the rate of ACT. On repayment of the loan, this tax is repayable to the company. The potential importance of this in a liquidation is that it may provide a possible source of recovery of tax where, for example, the amount of the loan is set off against a distribution to the member concerned. It should be noted that there is no provision for recovery of tax where the loan itself has become irrecoverable.

Business Expansion Scheme companies

General

14.6   Under the BES legislation, tax relief is available where a "qualifying individual" (determined by *ICTA 1988, s 291*) subscribes "eligible shares" (as defined in *ICTA 1988, s 289(4)*) in a "qualifying company" (determined by *ICTA 1988, ss 293–296*) carrying on a "qualifying trade" (determined by *ICTA 1988, ss 297, 298*). The relief may be given first upon investment and secondly upon disposal of the shares.

14.7   Where an individual makes a BES investment, under *ICTA 1988, s 289* the amount subscribed for those shares is available as a deduction from his total income for the year of assessment in which the shares are issued up to a maximum relief of £40,000. Additionally, where the shares are issued before 6 October in a year of assessment, one half of the relief available in respect of those shares (to a maximum of £5,000) may be carried back to the preceding year of assessment.

14.8   Relief from capital gains tax was introduced in *FA 1986* for shares issued after 18 March 1986. Under *CGTA 1979, s 149C(2)*, a gain accruing on the disposal of the shares in respect of which relief has been given (and not withdrawn) is not a chargeable gain for the purpose of capital gains tax. This exemption does not apply to disposals of shares issued before 19 March 1986. Instead, by *CGTA 1979, s 149C(3)* if relief has not been withdrawn it is disregarded in calculating the capital gain. The position where a loss is made on a disposal of the shares is discussed at 14.18–14.21 below, and varies depending on whether the date of issue of the shares was before 19 March 1986 or not.

14.9 Depending on the circumstances, relief under the BES may be withdrawn on the liquidation of a BES company. [*ICTA 1988, s 293(5)*]. See 14.13–14.15 below.

Withdrawal of relief

14.10 Relief under the BES will be withdrawn if during the "relevant period" (see 14.11 below) any of the individual, the company or the trade cease to qualify for the purposes of *ICTA 1988, ss 291–298*; or the shares are disposed of [*ICTA 1988, s 299*]; or value is received from the company by the individual [*ICTA 1988, s 300*] or by another member of the company. [*ICTA 1988, s 303*].

14.11 "Relevant period" is defined in *ICTA 1988, s 289(12)*. For the purposes of determining whether an individual qualifies, when the shares may have been disposed of, or whether value has been received, it will be the period starting on incorporation of the company (or if the company was incorporated more than two years before the date on which the shares were issued, the start of that period of two years) and ending five years after the issue of the shares. For the purposes of determining whether the company or its trade qualifies, the relevant period will be the period commencing on the date the shares were issued and ending three years after that date (or the date it began to carry on the trade, where the shares in the company were issued for the purpose of raising money for that qualifying trade which the company intends to carry on).

14.12 If relief is withdrawn, income tax will be charged under *ICTA 1988, s 307(1)* by an assessment to tax under Schedule D Case VI for the year of assessment in which the relief was originally given. Additionally, *CGTA 1979, s 149C* will not apply, causing any gain or loss accruing on the disposal of the shares by the individual to become a chargeable gain or allowable loss.

Liquidation

14.13 Where a BES company is insolvent, and even where it goes into liquidation, this factor will not of itself necessarily prevent a company from continuing to qualify. *ICTA 1988, s 293(2)* sets out the definition of what constitutes a "qualifying company". *ICTA 1988, s 293(5)* states that a company ceases to comply with *section 293(2)* if, before the end of the "relevant period", a resolution is passed, or an order is made, for the winding up of the company (or in the case of a winding up otherwise than under *IA 1986*, any other act is done for the like purpose) or the company is dissolved without winding up.

14.14 However, *ICTA 1988, s 293(5)* is subject to *section 293(6)*, which states that a company is not to be regarded as ceasing to be a qualifying company if:

(a) it does so by reason of being wound up or dissolved without winding up and it is shown that the winding up or dissolution is for *bona fide* commercial reasons and not part of a scheme or arrangement the main purpose (or one of the main purposes) of which is the avoidance of tax; and

(b) the company's net assets (if any) are distributed to its members or dealt with as *bona vacantia* before the end of the relevant period or, in the case of a winding up, the end (if later) of three years from the commencement of the winding up.

14.15 The Inland Revenue have confirmed that *ICTA 1988, s 293(6)* prevents the withdrawal of relief when the company ceases to trade upon the commencement of the liquidation, even though it no longer exists wholly or mainly for the purpose of carrying on a qualifying trade. This is provided the company continues to meet the other conditions for qualification. In practice the Revenue are satisfied that *ICTA 1988, s 293(6)* applies if the cessation of trade occurs before the commencement of the liquidation, as long as the company goes into liquidation as soon as possible after the cessation of trading, that is without any avoidable delay. This view applies whether the company ceases to trade because of a decision of the directors or because of a decision by a receiver. It is unlikely that the Revenue would continue to hold this view where the cessation and winding up is used to avoid tax, and relief may be withdrawn where a hive-down is used for this purpose.

14.16 Where a winding up is within *ICTA 1988, s 293(6)*, any payment or asset received by the individual in respect of ordinary shares held by him in the company will be treated as a receipt of value within *ICTA 1988, s 300(3)*. This will cause a withdrawal of an amount of the relief equal to the amount of the payment or asset received.

Other insolvency procedures

14.17 Provided the company continues to exist wholly or mainly for the purpose of carrying on a qualifying trade, which must, under *ICTA 1988, s 297(8)* be conducted on a commercial basis and with a view to the realisation of profits, there is no reason why an administration order or a voluntary arrangement should cause a withdrawal of the relief.

Tax relief

14.18   Where a BES company is the subject of an insolvent liquidation, its shares are likely to be valueless. If the BES relief has been withdrawn from the investment because the company during the relevant period has ceased to satisfy the various conditions and requirements of the BES legislation, relief for the loss suffered in relation to the investment in the BES company may be available under *CGTA 1979, s 22(2)*. Any allowable capital loss whether under *CGTA 1979, s 22(2)*, or arising on a distribution in the course of the winding up, or on a disposal at arm's length, may also give rise to relief under *ICTA 1988, s 574*.

14.19   Provided that the BES relief has been withdrawn in full, so that neither *CGTA 1979, s 149C(2)* nor *CGTA 1979, s 149C(3)* apply, a capital loss will be available under the provisions of *CGTA 1979, s 22(2)* on the basis that the value of the shares has become negligible. The claim takes effect by treating the claimant as having sold and reacquired the asset at its negligible value. Further details as to how the claim is made and how the section operates are set out in Chapter 12. Whereas relief under the BES legislation is available in respect of an investment in eligible shares up to a maximum relief of £40,000, a claim under *section 22(2)* may be made in respect of the total amount of investment by an individual in a BES company.

14.20   Where relief has only been partially withdrawn the treatment of the capital loss will vary as follows, depending on whether the shares were issued before or on or after 19 March 1986.

(a)   For shares issued before that date, *CGTA 1979, s 149C(3)* reduces the allowable deductions by the lesser of the amount of relief still outstanding and the excess of those deductions over the disposal proceeds. This reduces the loss for capital gains tax purposes to no more than the incidental costs of acquisition. It also appears to limit the amount of indexation allowance available to increase the loss (see Taxation 24 January 1991, p 429).

(b)   For shares issued after 18 March 1986 the loss will not be an allowable loss. [*CGTA 1979, s 149C(2)*]. This applies whether the disposal or the distribution in the course of the winding up takes place within or outside the relevant period. Only if the disposal proceeds or the amount of the distribution is itself sufficient to cause the relief to be fully withdrawn, and the disposal or distribution is within the relevant period, is the restriction of *CGTA 1979, s 149C(2)* removed. In those circumstances a loss on the disposal or distribution will be an allowable loss. If the disposal or distribution takes place outside the relevant period, the loss will not be allowable, because the relief will not have been fully withdrawn.

14.21   Under *ICTA 1988, s 574*, where an individual makes an allowable loss in respect of shares in a qualifying trading company (as defined in

ICTA 1988, s 576(4)), the individual may make a claim to have the loss on those shares set against his total income. These provisions are discussed in detail in 12.4 above.

ICTA 1988, s 703

14.22 It should be borne in mind that a liquidation is a "transaction in securities" within *ICTA 1988, s 703* following *CIR v Joiner HL 1975, 50 TC 449*. The Inland Revenue have, however, said that they will not apply *ICTA 1988, s 703* to "ordinary" liquidations (see Parliamentary Answer on 21 March 1973 reproduced at Simon's Tax Intelligence 1973, p 192). This was amplified in a further Parliamentary Answer on 19 April 1973 (reproduced at Simon's Tax Intelligence 1973, p 249), a part of which was as follows:

'Until such time as there is a decision of the Court giving further guidance on this issue, the Inland Revenue is advised on the basis of recent decisions that for the purposes of *section* [*703*] a distribution to a shareholder in a liquidation is a transaction in securities. It does not propose any change of practice in relation to an ordinary liquidation, that is to say the *bona fide* winding-up of a business as a discrete entity, whether the business with its concomitant goodwill then comes to an end or is taken over by some other concern which is under substantially different control. On the other hand the Inland Revenue would not regard as "ordinary" a liquidation which is part of a scheme of reconstruction which enables the old business to be carried on as before with substantially the same shareholders, directly or indirectly, in control. *Section* [*703*] does not of course apply where a taxpayer can show that the transaction or transactions were carried out for *bona fide* commercial reasons or in the ordinary course of making or managing investments and that the main object or one of the main objects was not the obtaining of a tax advantage.

Any person who wishes to know whether the provisions of *section* [*703*] might be applied to any liquidation which he is proposing to put into effect may seek a clearance from the Revenue under *section* [*707*].'

Chapter 15

International Element

Enforcement of foreign tax claims

15.1   Under the principles of public international law, one nation will not enforce the revenue laws of another nation. This was enunciated in the context of a UK liquidation in *Government of India v Taylor HL, [1955] 1 All ER 292*. The company concerned in that case was an English company in voluntary liquidation, which, at the time its liquidation commenced, had incurred certain Indian capital gains and income tax liabilities. The House of Lords held unanimously that these claims could not be enforced in the English courts, and so were not to be included among the "liabilities" to be discharged by the joint liquidators under what is now *IA 1986, s 107*. Accordingly, the liquidators could not be compelled to admit them to proof and did not even (as Viscount Simonds put it at p 298) have any discretion to meet the Indian claims, not being ones which were legally enforceable in the UK, without the consent of those who would be prejudiced (the creditors and contributories). Though the correctness of the principle applied by the House of Lords in the *Government of India* case has recently been questioned (by Woolf LJ in *Re State of Norway's Application (No 2) CA 1987, [1988] 3 WLR 603* at p 658), it remains good law.

15.2   The same principle has been cited in a number of subsequent cases in different contexts. See, for example, *Brokaw and Another v Seatrain UK Ltd and Another CA, [1971] 2 All ER 98*, which concerned an action by the US Government to enforce a tax claim and *Williams & Humbert Ltd v W & H Trade Marks (Jersey) Ltd and others HL, [1986] 1 All ER 129*, which concerned an action by the Spanish Government to enforce appropriation of some trademarks as part of the nationalisation of the Rumasa group. It encompasses an indirect means of enforcing a foreign tax claim, for example by garnishee proceedings (as in *Rossano v Manufacturers' Life Insurance Co, [1963] 2 QB 352*) as well as other types of quasi-fiscal claims such as those for certain municipal rates (*Sydney Municipal Council v Bull, [1909] 1 KB 7*), customs duty (*Attorney General for Canada v Schulze & Co CS 1901, 9 SLT 4*), local national insurance (*Metal Industries (Salvage) Ltd v Owners of the S T 'Harle' CS, [1962] SLT 114*) and possibly also proceedings to enforce foreign exchange control regulations (*Re Lord Cable (deceased) Ch D, [1976] 3 All ER 417*). It is immaterial that the foreign state in question is a member of the British Commonwealth, as in *Government of*

India v Taylor itself. The UK courts may, however, grant an order under the *Evidence (Proceedings in Other Jurisdictions) Act 1987* for examination of a UK witness in foreign tax proceedings (*Re State of Norway's Application (No 2) CA 1987, [1988] 3 WLR 603*). The Inland Revenue may exercise its powers to call for information from taxpayers contained in *TMA 1970, s 20(1)–(8), (8C)–(9)* in relation to taxes of other EC member States. [*FA 1990, s 125*].

15.3   *Government of India v Taylor* concerned the admission of pre-liquidation claims to proof under what is now *IA 1986, s 107* but there is no authority on how liabilities for foreign tax incurred after liquidation has begun should be treated. On the basis that these liabilities cannot be enforced in the UK, the same principle would presumably apply; but the position might be different if the payment of such liabilities was necessary to enable realisation and repatriation of foreign assets, for example, or to avoid a personal liability for the liquidator and his staff, on the basis that these would be necessary disbursements of the liquidation to be discharged under *Ins R 1986, Rule 4.218(1)(m)*. Necessity will be a matter of fact.

15.4   The principle in the *Government of India* case has been held to extend to liquidations where the sole creditor was the tax authority. In *Peter Buchanan Ltd v McVey 1951 SCE, [1955] AC 516* a Scottish liquidator was unable to bring recovery proceedings in the Republic of Ireland because the sole creditor of the company was the UK Inland Revenue. The Irish judgment of Kingsmill Moore J in that case was approved by Lord Keith of Avonholm in the House of Lords in the *Government of India* case (at p 298I) and was also considered in *Re Tucker (a bankrupt), ex parte Tucker CA 1987, [1988] 1 All ER 603*, which concerned a UK tax bankruptcy, and where one of the reasons given by the English court for refusing to make an order for examination of a Belgian resident was that the Belgian courts could not be asked to assist enforcement of the order. The *McVey* case was not, however, followed in an Australian case, *Ayres v Evans FCA 1981, 39 ALR 129* where the Federal Court of Australia held that a request for aid by the official assignee of a New Zealand resident's estate made under Australian bankruptcy legislation should be complied with since the provision in question superseded the *Government of India v Taylor* principle and because there were in any event creditors of the estate other than the New Zealand Revenue.

Cross-border insolvencies

General

15.5   The liquidation or administration of a foreign resident company in the UK, or the appointment of a receiver over its UK assets, raises a host of questions posed by the conflict of laws, among them how the UK tax liability of the company (or of the individual liquidator, administrator or receiver) will be affected. So, too, does the liquidation (or receivership) of a UK resident company overseas. The following paragraphs address some points of difficulty relating to UK tax although many others are likely to be encountered in this complex area. It should be noted that, for obvious reasons, the possible application of double tax treaties is considered only briefly in 15.16 below. Such treaties will in many cases be relevant in addition to the position under UK law alone, depending on the countries involved.

15.6 A point relevant to the following paragraphs is that, under *IA 1986, s 230*, an administrator, administrative receiver or liquidator of a UK company must (unless he is the Official Receiver) be a licensed insolvency practitioner. This does not, however, mean that he will necessarily be a UK resident, though obviously the majority of qualified individuals are UK residents.

Cross-border liquidations

UK resident liquidator of foreign resident company

15.7 Since 15 March 1988, English (and Scottish) law has contained two tests to determine the tax residence of companies. Thus, a foreign incorporated company will be regarded as resident outside the UK provided its central management and control are exercised abroad (see, *inter alia*, *De Beers Consolidated Mines Ltd v Howe HL 1906, 5 TC 198* and *Bullock v The Unit Construction Co Ltd HL 1959, 38 TC 712* and, for the Inland Revenue's views on the question, SP 1/1990). A company incorporated in the UK will, however, be regarded as automatically resident in the UK under *FA 1988, s 66(1)* unless it is eligible for one of the transitional exemptions in *FA 1988, 7 Sch* in which case it will become resident in the UK on 15 March 1993 if it does not become UK resident before that date. *Section 66* may also be disapplied under the terms of a double tax treaty.

15.8 A foreign incorporated company may be wound up in the UK under *IA 1986, Pt V* whether or not it has been wound up already in another jurisdiction (*Banque des Marchands de Moscou (Koupetschesky) v Kindersley CA 1950, [1951] Ch 112*). It is no longer necessary for there to be available assets in England and Wales, provided that there is a sufficient connection with the jurisdiction and provided that there is a reasonable possibility of benefit accruing to the creditors from the winding up (*International Westminster Bank plc v Okeanos Maritime Corporation Ch D, [1987] 3 All ER 137*).

15.9 Where a company is regarded as foreign resident for tax purposes, the appointment of a UK resident liquidator is likely to cause it to become UK resident for tax purposes, under the "central management and control" test mentioned in 15.7 above, because the liquidator will exercise the powers of the company in substitution for the directors. So, too, will the appointment of a UK resident liquidator under foreign law, although this may conceivably depend on the powers which that law (and the local courts) confer. Once a company becomes UK resident for tax purposes it will become subject to UK corporation tax (*inter alia*) on its worldwide income and on chargeable gains arising in the course of the liquidation, such gains being computed by reference to the full gain realised between acquisition of the asset and its disposal, without any uplift of the base cost to take account of the company's period of non-residence other than indexation allowance and 1982 rebasing election.

15.10   This view of the effect of appointing a UK liquidator was expressed in terms by the Inland Revenue, to the ICAEW (see ICAEW TR 799, para 31) where they said:

'*The test of residence*

(a)   The Statement of Practice 6/83 should not be read as implying that, as a general rule, the Revenue have moved in any way from the test enunciated by Lord Loreburn [see 15.7 above]. A company is regarded as resident for tax purposes where central management and control is to be found because that, according to Lord Loreburn, is where the real business is carried on. (The Statement of Practice 6/83 has now been superseded by Statement 1/90 but the relevant paragraph is unchanged.)

(b)   The word "business" may have different connotations according to the context in which it is used. The Revenue does not consider that a company normally ceases to have a residence under Lord Loreburn's test on going into liquidation.

Application of the test

(c)   In law, the liquidator has management and control of the company's affairs. It is therefore not possible to confirm that a company, whether solvent or insolvent, which has hitherto been non-resident, will not become resident in the United Kingdom on the appointment of a UK resident liquidator.

(d)   However, the exercise of central management and control is a question of fact. If it is exercised abroad by the liquidator or if the liquidator acts in accordance with the wishes of non-resident shareholders so that management and control is not in fact in the UK, the company will not become resident here.'

The response is not very informative. The situation mentioned (where the shareholders effectively control the company after the liquidation begins) would not be relevant in an insolvency. It is worth noting, however, that the ICAEW mention that the Revenue have confirmed in individual cases that appointment of a UK resident liquidator who carries out his duties abroad would not cause management and control to transfer to the UK. Similarly, presumably, with a joint appointment with a non-resident liquidator provided decisions of "management and control" are not customarily made in the UK.

15.11   As has been seen in 8.36 above, the liquidator is the "proper officer" of the company for the purposes of *TMA 1970, s 108(1)*. It seems that this would include a liquidator appointed under foreign law, having regard to the interpretation put on the term in the context of registration of charges, in *NV Slavenburg's Bank v Intercontinental Natural Resources Ltd QB, [1980] 1 All ER 955. TMA 1970, s 108(2)* deals expressly with the situation where a liquidator is appointed over a foreign company. It is as follows:

> 'Corporation tax or other tax chargeable under the Corporation Tax Acts on a company which is not a body corporate, or which is a body corporate not incorporated under the [Companies Act 1985] or any other enactment forming part of the law of the United Kingdom, or by Charter, may, at any time after the tax becomes due, and without prejudice to any other method of recovery, be recovered from the proper officer of the company, and that officer may retain out of any money coming into his hands on behalf of the company sufficient sums to pay that tax, and, so far as he is not so reimbursed, shall be entitled to be indemnified by the company in respect of the liability so imposed on him.'

This provision is potentially very serious. It appears on its face to impose a personal liability on a liquidator of a foreign company to pay UK tax, subject only to a right of reimbursement out of assets coming into his hands and a right of indemnity which will rarely be enforceable in practice. It is not in terms limited to post-liquidation liabilities, but could apparently extend to any unpaid tax which is 'chargeable under the Corporation Tax Acts' (i.e. corporation tax on income and chargeable gains, but not tax chargeable under other provisions such as income tax deductions under *ICTA 1988, s 349* or the PAYE regulations). Its justification is presumably that it offers the Inland Revenue their only chance of recovering the tax, but as will be appreciated, it can cause considerable difficulties since, particularly where a receiver has disposed of UK situated assets, the amounts of tax could in many cases exceed the assets available to the liquidator. Where he is appointed under foreign law, also, the local equivalent of *Government of India v Taylor* (see 15.1–15.4 above) may preclude his admission to proof of UK Revenue claims. The provision is contrary to the thrust of the companies legislation and could operate so harshly that it must be possible that a court would apply some limit to it, although an interpretation along the lines of that given to *TMA 1970, s 108(1)* is difficult to justify.

15.12   The implications of *TMA 1970, s 108(2)* were also raised with the Inland Revenue by the ICAEW and the Revenue's response was as follows:

'The Revenue has, as you say, no stated policy with regard to the application of *Section 108(2)*, *TMA*, to liquidators of foreign companies. Where a foreign company owes tax it is the Revenue practice to proceed against the company itself, invoking the procedure in *Part V, IA 1986*, for winding up unregistered companies.' (ICAEW TR 799, para 36).

This is, again, a non-committal response that reflects the writer's experience that the Revenue's approach to foreign liquidations is normally pragmatic and reasonable, while the threat of personal liability is preserved to prevent what would otherwise be a rather blatant device for tax evasion.

15.13 One more favourable point, though, is that, where a company is in liquidation under foreign law, the rules of priority and preference of claims will depend on the foreign law. Consequently, there can be no preferential claim for UK tax in any event, and the question of the priority of tax claims arising after liquidation over liquidator's remuneration (see 8.37–8.42 above) cannot arise in that form. This is accepted by the Inland Revenue.

Foreign resident liquidator of UK resident company

15.14 The appointment of a foreign liquidator of a UK resident company will not now result in a company ceasing to be UK resident since *FA 1988, s 66(2)* provides that:

'For the purposes of the Taxes Acts, a company which . . . (b) is being wound up outside the United Kingdom, shall be regarded as continuing to be resident in the United Kingdom if it was so regarded for those purposes immediately before . . . any of its activities came under the control of a person exercising functions which, in the United Kingdom, would be exercisable by a liquidator'.

It would appear that the effect of *section 66(2)* is permanent, i.e. the company cannot migrate after the winding up begins even if it is prepared to pay an "exit charge" under *FA 1988, s 105*. Accordingly, it remains liable to UK tax in the normal way on the disposal of its assets and on its worldwide income. The UK tax liabilities may not, however, be provable in a foreign liquidation (see 15.1–15.4 above) giving rise to potential difficulties in connection with the liquidation of UK resident foreign incorporated companies.

Foreign resident liquidator of foreign company with UK branch or agency

15.15 Subject to relief under any applicable double tax treaty, a foreign resident company trading in the UK through a UK branch or agency is liable to UK corporation tax on:

(a) any trading income arising directly through or from the branch or agency, and any income from property or rights used by, or held by or for, the branch or agency, excluding distributions from UK resident companies [*ICTA 1988, s 11(1)(a)*]; and

(b) chargeable gains on the disposal of UK situated assets used in or for the purposes of the trade at or before the time when the capital gain occurred, or used or held for the purposes of the branch or agency at or before that time, or UK situated assets acquired or used by or for the purposes of the branch or agency. [*ICTA 1988, s 11(1)(b); CGTA 1979, s 12(1)*].

Tax on chargeable gains is only payable on a disposal if the disposal is made at a time when the company is carrying on the trade in the UK through a branch or agency. [*CGTA 1979, s 12(1A)*]. Thus, where a foreign resident liquidator disposes of a UK situated asset used or held for the purposes of a trade carried on in the UK through a branch or agency then even though the company is not UK resident a tax charge may arise. A charge may arise without a disposal if, instead of disposing of the asset, the asset ceases to be chargeable because it becomes situated outside the UK or the UK trade ceases. [*FA 1989, s 127*]. If the tax is not paid, then, unless there are assets left in the UK, the Inland Revenue's ability to enforce the tax claims will, in the light of the principles discussed in 15.1–15.4 above, be limited to either recovering the tax from the liquidator personally under *TMA 1970, s 108(2)* (see 15.11–15.12 above) or, if the charge arises under *FA 1989, s 127*, assessing any company which is or was within the "relevant period" (broadly, the preceding year) a member of the same group as the taxpayer company, or any person who is or was within the "relevant period" a controlling director of the taxpayer company or of a company which has, or within that period had, control over the taxpayer company. [*FA 1989, s 134*]. The cessation of the UK trade may give rise to other tax charges, such as balancing charges in respect of capital allowances based on the market value of the assets [*CAA 1990, s 24(6)(c)(v)*] but, apart from *TMA 1970, s 108(2)*, there are no special collection provisions applicable to such charges.

Double tax treaties

15.16 As will be apparent from the discussions in the previous paragraphs, there is a potential for double taxation where the appointment of a liquidator has the effect of transferring the management and control of a company out of the jurisdiction where it was formerly resident (for example, appointment of a foreign liquidator in circumstances where *FA 1988, s 66(2)* applies—see 15.14 above). Where a double tax treaty applies, this may provide relief from double taxation after the transfer if there is an appropriate tie-breaker provision (see, for example, Article 4(3) of the OECD Model Treaty) but is unlikely to relieve double taxation on capital gains.

Cross-border receiverships

UK resident receiver of foreign resident company

15.17   The appointment of a receiver resident in the UK over particular assets of a non-resident company is unlikely in most cases to cause the company to become UK resident, given the distinction drawn in the cases between central management and control normally exercised by the directors (who may remain in office after receivership), and the place where day to day management occurs, since a receiver's powers will be limited to the particular assets subject to the charge.

15.18   As noted in 15.15 above, a foreign resident company is only subject to corporation tax if it carries on a trade in the UK through a branch or agency (and subject to relief under any applicable double tax treaty). If it does not do so, it is subject to income tax at the basic rate on any income derived from a UK source such as rents derived from UK situated property or interest from a UK source debt (both of which are discussed further below). The appointment of a UK receiver will not normally create an income tax liability in respect of foreign source non-trading income since, although technically chargeable to income tax in respect of (for example) income from foreign possessions under Schedule D Case IV or V as a recipient of the income under *ICTA 1988, s 59* (see below) the assessment will be for nil (*Archer-Shee v Baker HL 1927, 11 TC 749* and *Reid's Trustees v CIR 1929, 14 TC 512*).

(i)   Branch or agency—trading income

15.19   If a non-UK resident company trades in the UK through a branch or agency then it is subject to corporation tax on any trading income arising directly or indirectly through or from the branch or agency and any income from property used by, or held by or for, the branch or agency and on chargeable gains in respect of such property as set out in 15.15 above. "Branch or agency" is defined in *ICTA 1988, s 834(1)* as 'any factorship, agency, receivership, branch or management'. This is in many situations an uninformative definition, but is unambiguous so far as receiverships are concerned. The question which does occasionally arise, however, is that of what constitutes trading in the UK by a receiver of a non-resident company. This is an impossible question to answer in generalities since the answer depends on many factors such as, for example, the manner in which the company traded in the UK before receivership, if it did so, the structure of any pre-existing UK branch or agency and what the precise activities involved are, since a receiver is more likely to be concerned with the disposal of assets than with maintaining a trade (though he has power to do so under *IA 1986, 1 Sch 14* where it applies). The present author has no hesitation in referring readers to the excellent discussions by E C D Norfolk in 'Non-Resident: United Kingdom Trade' in [1980] BTR 70 and S M Porter in Volume 2 of Tolley's Tax Planning 1991.

15.20   If there is no UK trade, a UK receiver may still be chargeable to UK income tax under *TMA 1970, s 78(1)*—see further 15.25–15.26 below.

(ii)   Rents and other income from land

15.21   As noted above, rents and other income from land derived by the UK receiver of a non-resident company from UK investment property are within the scope of income tax. Tax under Schedule A is, under *ICTA 1988, s 21*, 'charged on and paid by the persons receiving or entitled to the profits or gains in respect of which tax under that Schedule is directed by the Income Tax Acts to be charged.' A receiver of a non-resident company is thus assessable to income tax in respect of any income taxable under Schedule A which he in fact received (*CIR v Thompson KB 1936, 20 TC 422*). In respect of rents or other income taxable under Schedule D Case VI, *ICTA 1988, s 59(1)* applies similarly. The receiver will also be assessable under *TMA 1970, s 78(1)* in respect of any income, whether or not received (see 15.25–15.26 below). Where rents, etc. are paid to a UK resident receiver, or to a bank account in his name, the deduction provisions in *ICTA 1988, s 43* (discussed in 15.28 below) will not, in the author's view, apply.

15.22   A UK receiver of a non-resident company will be within the scope of the special collection provisions in *ICTA 1988, s 23* (see 5.6–5.8 above) and the argument that this provision is inapplicable mentioned in 5.8(a) above will not be relevant.

(iii)   Interest and dividends from investments

15.23   A UK receiver of a non-resident company is assessable to income tax at the basic rate in respect of interest he receives from UK sources as a 'person receiving or entitled to the income' under *ICTA 1988, s 59(1)* (*CIR v Thompson KB 1936, 20 TC 422*). Such interest will frequently be received under deduction of tax but if not *section 59(1)* (or *TMA 1970, s 78*) will apply—in particular ESC B13, which would otherwise confirm that the interest escapes UK taxation, expressly excludes this situation.

15.24   The exemption from corporation tax for dividends of UK companies in *ICTA 1988, s 208* does not apply since the foreign company is subject to income tax on its investments, not to corporation tax, nor is the company entitled to a tax credit. [*ICTA 1988, s 23*]. However, no assessment is made for basic rate income tax on the dividend and the company is not liable to tax at higher rates. [*ICTA 1988, s 233(1)*].

(iv)   TMA 1970, s 78(1)

15.25   This provision is as follows:

'*Method of charging non-residents*

Subject to [subsection (2) below and] section [43] of [ICTA 1988] (Schedule A etc.) a person not resident in the United Kingdom, whether a British subject or not, shall be assessable and chargeable to income tax in the name of . . . any branch or agent, whether the branch or agent has the receipt of the profits or gains or not, in like manner and to the like amount as such non-resident person would be assessed and charged if he were resident in the United Kingdom and in the actual receipt of such profits or gains.'

Section 78 is applied to capital gains tax by *TMA 1970, s 84*, and to corporation tax by *TMA 1970, s 85*. A person chargeable under *section 78* is, however, entitled to retain out of moneys coming into his hands on behalf of the non-resident so much thereof as is sufficient to pay the tax, and is indemnified for all such payments, under *TMA 1970, s 83(2)*.

15.26 As noted in 15.19 above, a UK resident receiver will constitute a "branch or agency" of a non-resident company. He is, therefore, capable of being assessed in its name in respect of UK tax liabilities which it incurs. *TMA 1970, s 78(1)* is not limited to trading income of a UK branch or agency but includes, for example, tax on UK source interest received gross. It may not be circumvented by payment of such interest direct to the company or a creditor (unlike the liability arising under *ICTA 1988, s 59(1)* for example—see *Archer-Shee v Baker HL 1927, 11 TC 749*), since it applies whether or not the receiver has the receipt of the profits or gains in question. It appears that *TMA 1970, s 78(1)* is not limited to tax liabilities arising after the receiver is appointed. It should be borne in mind that the indemnity in *TMA 1970, s 83(2)* may be of limited assistance if a foreign court declines to recognise it under the *Government of India v Taylor* principle discussed in 15.1–15.4 above.

Foreign resident receiver of a UK resident company

(i)   General

15.27 As noted in 15.17 above, the appointment of a receiver should normally not in principle affect the residence of a company for UK tax purposes. As with any receiver of a UK resident company, a foreign resident receiver will not be subject to corporation tax. How far he is liable for deduction taxes (e.g. PAYE) will, however, depend on the extent of his activities in the UK and whether this amounts to a "trading presence" in the UK within the principles established in *Clark v Oceanic Contractors Inc HL 1982, [1983] STC 35*. It will also depend on how far the liabilities can be enforced against him (see 15.1–15.3 above).

(ii) Deduction of income tax from rents

15.28 *ICTA 1988, s 43(1)* contains special provisions requiring the person making a payment of profits or gains chargeable under Schedule A, or certain items under Schedule D Case VI, to deduct income tax at the basic rate where 'payment is made (whether in the United Kingdom or elsewhere) directly to a person whose usual place of abode is outside the United Kingdom'. In such cases, *ICTA 1988, ss 349, 350* are applied and *TMA 1970, s 78(1)* is disapplied. This is not an easy provision to construe in an insolvency. Clearly, the test is a different one from where the company is resident, and apparently a wider one. It is considered that where a company has a foreign resident liquidator, *section 43(1)* may apply but in principle not where there is a UK resident liquidator even if the company was previously resident abroad for tax purposes. The position of foreign resident receivers of UK resident companies is unclear but possibly the better view is that the company's "usual place of abode" remains in the UK. Conversely, a foreign resident company with a UK receiver probably retains its foreign abode. Notwithstanding this, the safer course in both cases is for the tenant to deduct income tax unless he has express clearance from the Inland Revenue.

Cross-border administrations

15.29 The situation where a foreign incorporated company is put into administration in the UK is an unlikely one, though it is understood that in one unreported case the court has made an administration order over a Canadian company under *IA 1986, s 426* (co-operation between courts exercising jurisdiction in relation to insolvency). Incorporation is not the only test of residence for tax purposes, though, and it is worth briefly considering the situation where a UK administrator is appointed over a company resident abroad for tax purposes.

15.30 The appointment of an administrator over a foreign resident corporation may, it is considered, cause the company's residence to alter. Although the purposes for which an administrator may be appointed under *IA 1986, s 8(3)* are unlikely to involve the "central management and control" of the company, the administrator has extensive powers (see *IA 1986, s 14(1), 1 Sch*) and the powers of the company and its officers may not be exercised in such a way as to interfere with the administrator's exercise of these powers unless he consents. [*IA 1986, s 14(4)*]. If the company does not become UK resident but is liable to corporation tax, the position will be as described in Chapter 6, while it seems that as with a UK receiver of a foreign resident company the administrator could be liable for income tax on UK source income (see 15.17–15.26 above).

HM Treasury consents

15.31 *ICTA 1988, ss 765–767* make it a criminal offence for a person to do or be a party to the doing of certain acts in relation to the shares or debentures of non-UK resident companies under the control of UK resident companies without Treasury consent. The provision of most concern to receivers, administrators and liquidators of UK companies will be *ICTA 1988, s 765(1)(d)* which prohibits (without such consent) the transfer of shares or debentures to any person. This provision does not apply to a "movement of capital" between residents of EC member States [*ICTA 1988, s 765A*], though there are still reporting requirements in these cases. The Treasury have issued 'The Treasury General Consents 1988' which will frequently be applicable to insolvency sales to unconnected third parties (see paragraph 8(b) thereof). Where they are not applicable, the Inland Revenue and Treasury accept that an application for consent may be made on behalf of the company by its liquidator (who is its "proper officer" within *TMA 1970, s 108*) or administrator or receiver (who will normally be its agent).

Chapter 16

Interest and Penalties

Introduction

16.1   References have been made in previous chapters to interest and penalties. This chapter deals in more detail with the position in an insolvency of interest imposed on unpaid tax and penalties arising from the late or non-payment of tax, together with the altogether separate issue of the taxation of interest payable in the course of the insolvency.

Interest on income and corporation tax

16.2   Interest on unpaid income and corporation tax is at present imposed by *TMA 1970, s 86* and interest on overdue advance corporation tax or income tax on company payments is imposed by *TMA 1970, s 87*. When the Pay and File provisions come into effect, proposed to be on 30 September 1993, interest on unpaid corporation tax will be imposed under *TMA 1970, s 87A*. Since 19 April 1988, interest has been imposed on a formal determination of late payment of PAYE by employers, under *ITER 1973, Reg 29A*. Following the amendment to *ICTA 1988, s 203(2)(d)* by *FA 1988, s 128*, new regulations will be introduced to impose interest on late payments of PAYE without the need for the formal determination, but these regulations will not take effect before 1993. Where a failure to give a notice or return, or an error in any information, has led to a loss of tax for which an assessment has been made, default interest may be imposed under *TMA 1970, s 88* if the Inspector or the Board so determine, and the Board has power to mitigate or compromise this interest. [*TMA 1970, s 88(4)*]. If default interest is charged, no interest may be imposed under *TMA 1970, s 86*, but default interest will not be chargeable instead of interest under *TMA 1970, s 87A* when it comes into effect. Interest is charged from the date when the tax becomes due and payable [*TMA 1970, ss 86(3), 87A(1)*] or when it ought to have been paid [*TMA 1970, s 88(1)*] except where an appeal has been made against an assessment and *TMA 1970, s 86* applies. [*TMA 1970, s 86(3A)*]. The rate of interest is that applicable from time to time under regulations made pursuant to *FA 1989, s 178*.

Interest and penalties on VAT

16.3   Customs & Excise may impose civil penalties under *FA 1985, ss 13–17*, penalties for fraudulent evasion of VAT under *VATA 1983, s 39* and a default surcharge under *FA 1985, s 19*. Interest may also be payable on assessments under *FA 1985, s 18*. Where any person is liable to a penalty under *sections 13–17*, interest or surcharge, *FA 1985, s 21* provides that such amounts are to be collected by an assessment raised on him 'of an amount due in respect of the prescribed accounting period' concerned. [*FA 1985, s 21(2)*].

Administrative receivership

Interest and penalties on unpaid tax

16.4   An administrative receiver will normally be concerned with interest and penalties on unpaid income and corporation tax to the extent that he is concerned with the tax itself (see Chapter 5). These amounts are irrelevant for the purposes of preferential claims (see 16.9 below). He may, however, become liable for interest and penalties on unpaid VAT which arise during the course of the receivership (see 16.17 below). The position regarding VAT preferential claims is the same as in liquidations—see 16.14 below.

Interest paid by receivers

16.5   As a separate matter, where a receiver (including one appointed under a fixed charge) makes a payment of interest he may have to account for income tax under *ICTA 1988, s 349*—see 5.16–5.20 above.

Administration

Interest and penalties on income and corporation tax

16.6   An administrator will be in a similar position to an administrative receiver with regard to interest and penalties on income and corporation tax in that he will prudently not be directly concerned to pay them unless they relate to liabilities for which he may be held liable (e.g. on PAYE deductions). Such liabilities will, however, enter into consideration in relation to the appropriate "exit route" from the administration—see further Chapter 6 above.

Interest and penalties on VAT

16.7   The position of administrators regarding interest and penalties on VAT will be the same as that of liquidators.

Liquidation

16.8   When considering the taxation of interest in a liquidation, a distinction must be made between:

(a)   interest on tax and other debts itself provable as a debt in the winding up;

(b)   interest on unpaid tax for periods after the liquidation has begun; and

(c)   interest on debts arising after the liquidation has begun.

Interest before liquidation on pre-liquidation income and corporation tax

16.9   Interest is not "tax" as such (although it may be so treated for some purposes, as under *TMA 1970, s 69*). Consequently it can never rank preferentially even when it arises in respect of unpaid PAYE. Interest on tax unpaid at the date the company goes into liquidation will therefore be provable only as an unsecured claim. Before *IA 1986*, the amount of interest provable was initially restricted by *Bankruptcy Act 1914, s 66* (applied to companies by *CA 1985, s 612*) to that corresponding to a rate of 5 per cent, the balance of interest then only being provable as a postponed debt. These provisions were replaced by *Ins R 1986, Rule 4.93* which sets out the rules governing the proof of interest as part of a debt, when the debt proved in a liquidation bears interest. *Rule 4.93* does not require a demand for interest on unpaid tax, since unpaid tax already bears interest under the statutory provisions (see 16.2 above). For the same reason, *Rules 4.93(2)–(6)* are inapplicable, which means that the applicable rate or rates of interest on underpaid tax will determine the amount provable, not the *Judgments Act 1838, s 17.*

16.10   The date up to which interest may be proved in the liquidation is the date when the company went into liquidation. [*Ins R 1986, Rule 4.93(1)*]. By *IA 1986, s 247(2)* this is when the resolution for voluntary winding up is passed, or, in the case of compulsory winding up, when an order for the winding up is made by the court. This is later than the position before the *IA 1986* took effect, since it had been held under the old law in *Re Amalgamated Investment & Property Co Ltd, [1985] Ch 349* that the date for proof of interest was the date of presentation of the petition for winding up.

Interest after liquidation on pre-liquidation income and corporation tax

16.11   Before *IA 1986* took effect, creditors of an insolvent company were in a different position from creditors of a bankrupt individual, because the provisions of *Bankruptcy Act 1914, s 33(8)*, which permitted creditors to claim for interest out of any surplus, did not apply to insolvent companies. *IA 1986, s 189* has altered this position, by providing that interest is payable on debts (including debts representing interest on the principal) out of any surplus remaining after payment of the company's debts in full. The interest is paid in respect of the periods during which the debts have been outstanding since the company went into liquidation. [*IA 1986, s 189(1)(2)*]. Interest ranks equally, irrespective of how the underlying debt ranked. [*IA 1986, s 189(3)*]. The rate is the greater of that specified in *Judgments Act 1838, s 17* on the day the company went into liquidation, and the rate applicable to the debt apart from the winding up (i.e. the rate applicable under *FA 1989, s 178*). [*IA 1986, s 189(4)*]. The Inland Revenue do not in normal circumstances consider that income tax should be deducted from payments of interest under *IA 1986, s 189* as it is not considered to be annual interest. However, they state that:

> 'It is possible for the interest to constitute annual interest . . . on the basis that the period for which the interest is payable is known at the time it is paid, i.e. the period from the date of liquidation to the final date interest can run is ascertainable . . . If it is payable for one year or more it is annual interest.' (ICAEW TR 799, para 20).

Interest on post-liquidation income and corporation tax

16.12 Where interest accrues on tax on profits earned or gains made after liquidation, the position is more straightforward. There, interest on any assessment raised will be treated like other tax liabilities arising after liquidation, as a "necessary disbursement" of the liquidator (see 8.36–8.41 above).

Penalties on income and corporation tax

16.13 The Inland Revenue has wide powers to impose penalties under *TMA 1970, Pt X* and under various other statutory provisions, and also may, under *TMA 1970, s 102*, mitigate any penalty, or stay or compromise any proceedings for a penalty. A fine or penalty is a provable debt (*Re Pascoe Ch D, [1944] 1 All ER 593*). Notwithstanding *Re Hurren (a Bankrupt), ex parte the Trustee v CIR Ch D 1982, 56 TC 494*, where the Revenue indicated that in bankruptcy they did not normally prove for penalties where outside creditors were concerned, it is understood that the Revenue will normally prove for penalties as well as tax (with interest) in corporate insolvencies. However, the Revenue have stated that each case is dealt with on its own merits and there may be cases where the Revenue would elect not to prove for the whole of the Revenue debt.

Interest on pre-liquidation VAT

16.14 By *FA 1985, s 21(7)* where a person is liable for interest under *FA 1985, s 18* the amount is assessed 'as if it were tax due from him'. It is unclear whether such amounts might then be regarded as VAT 'which is referable' to the six-month preferential period, as described in *IA 1986, 6 Sch 3*. It is understood that Customs & Excise do not, however, claim interest as part of the preferential debt.

16.15   If the element of interest on preferential claims for VAT is not treated as preferential itself, it (and interest on non-preferential VAT) will be an unsecured claim, governed in the same way as interest on unpaid tax by *Ins R 1986, Rule 4.93* (see 16.4–16.5 above). Unlike interest on unpaid income and corporation tax, interest under *FA 1985, s 18* has to be assessed, and it then becomes an amount due in respect of the prescribed accounting period in respect of which the tax was due. [*FA 1985, s 21(5)(a)*]. If interest continues to accrue, further assessments may be made. [*FA 1985, s 21(5)(b)*]. It is considered that *FA 1985, s 21* is subject to *Ins R 1986, Rule 4.93(1)* which states that interest may only be claimed up to the date of the company going into liquidation and that interest after that date on VAT for pre-liquidation periods is only payable under *IA 1986, s 189* (see 16.11 above).

Interest on post-liquidation VAT

16.16   Where supplies are made by the liquidator and a delay is made in accounting for VAT, he will be liable to interest on VAT just as he is liable for the VAT itself (see 9.6 above).

VAT penalties

16.17   Penalties arising under *FA 1985, ss 13–17* are collected in the same way as interest arising under *FA 1985, s 18* by an assessment under *FA 1985, s 21*. It is arguable that the wording of *section 21(7)* would also cause any penalties relating to the six months preferential period to be themselves preferential, as with interest (see 16.14 above) but it is understood that Customs & Excise do not in practice normally prove for penalties in respect of pre-liquidation periods although they may apply a set-off under *FA 1988, s 21* (see 20.9–20.13 below). Customs stated in 1986 that they would not impose default surcharge under *FA 1985, s 19* on liquidators or administrative receivers for the accounting periods during their administrations but reserved the right to impose penalties subject to the assurance that before doing so all the circumstances would be considered, and that only in those cases where there is some evidence of negligence on the part of the practitioner would he be penalised.

Tax treatment of interest generally

16.18   The final question is how a payment of interest on a provable debt, other than one for unpaid tax, is to be treated for tax purposes. In *Re Beecham (Sir Thomas) Ch D, [1934] B & CR 138*, judicial notice was taken of a practice in bankruptcy whereby under an arrangement between the Board of Inland Revenue and the Board of Trade, creditors for annual interest were entitled to prove gross, and to appropriate dividends received in the bankruptcy in the first instance against principal. It appears that this arrangement has ceased but that the Revenue are understood not to object to the principle that a creditor should be allowed to recover his capital before any distribution to him is regarded as generating income.

Chapter 17

Compliance

Introduction

17.1 This chapter covers the practical aspects of dealing with the tax affairs of companies in receivership, administration and liquidation and discusses:

(a) reviews following appointment;

(b) notification requirements;

(c) time limits;

(d) recovering tax assets;

(e) ongoing compliance matters;

(f) job closure.

Reviews following appointment

Corporation tax

17.2 The following information should be gathered at an early stage. This will normally follow discussion with company personnel or their former tax advisers, and should be undertaken before early co-operation turns to indifference. Gaps can often be filled by discussion with the company's Inspector of Taxes.

(a) Details of tax payments for the past four years. Increasingly, companies facing insolvency will be found to have paid tax in recent years. This is largely attributable to the reduced capital allowances which have been available to companies since the enactment of *FA 1984*. Where substantial payments have been made within reach of loss carry-back claims, there will be a high probability of tax asset recovery and the costs of involving expensive tax specialist time will be justified. The claims which can be made to recover such payments are discussed further in 17.11.

(b) Status of tax affairs for past years, starting at the date when liabilities were last agreed and settled, and showing where tax computations have been submitted and agreed. The scope of work that will be devoted to finalising these matters will depend on the amounts, if any, which will be payable to unsecured creditors.

(c) Commentary on matters giving rise to preferential tax liabilities. See Chapter 2.

(d) Details of matters giving rise to tax liabilities for the company or personal obligations for the practitioner.

VAT

17.3 The increasing complexity of VAT legislation has increased the likelihood of significant errors in companies' VAT affairs and review by VAT specialists will normally be worthwhile to confirm the company's preferential VAT liability. The scope for repayment claims has been reduced since the changes made by *FA 1989*, and is discussed further in 20.5–20.6 below.

Notification

Customs & Excise

17.4 There is a requirement to notify Customs & Excise within 21 days of the appointment of a liquidator, administrative receiver or administrator who carries on the business of a VAT registered trader. [*VAT Gen R 1985, Reg 11(2)*]. See further 9.2 above. Once the notification is given, the VAT affairs of the company will be transferred to Customs' Insolvency Section at Bootle, and the insolvency practitioner will find it advantageous to deal with the specialists there who have daily involvement with insolvency cases, unlike local VAT offices.

Inland Revenue

17.5 There is no similar requirement to notify the Inland Revenue of the appointment of an insolvency practitioner to a company, but it is good practice to do so and can reduce considerably the amount of unnecessary correspondence and friction which will otherwise arise. The Revenue's practice is to send correspondence, including company corporation tax assessments, to the insolvency practitioner rather than the company's former tax agents without the submission of a Form 64–8. Therefore, a simple letter is sufficient which should include the following information:

(a) the name of the practitioner and the office address to which correspondence should be sent;

(b) the nature and date of appointment;

(c) whether the tax affairs of the company will continue to be dealt with by any other party, e.g. the former tax agents; and

(d) arrangements for dealing with groups of companies.

17.6 *Compliance*

17.6 This letter is a convenient opportunity to ask the Inspector whether there are compliance matters such as open appeals or imminent Commissioners' hearings which require the practitioner's early attention, and also whether he is aware of any matters about the disposition of the company's assets which warrant further investigation.

Group of companies

17.7 Where there is a group of companies, it is common for a number of partners from the same firm to take appointments over various companies. In these circumstances, and where no conflicts of interest will arise, it will be helpful for one partner to take joint appointment over all of the companies, so that he will have the capacity to sign claims, etc. for all of them and reduce the logistical difficulties that will otherwise arise. Unlike a liquidator, a receiver or administrator is not a proper officer of a company within *TMA 1970, s 108*, and there is some doubt whether the powers given to administrative receivers and administrators by *IA 1986, 1 Sch* give them equivalent powers. Notwithstanding this, it is the practice of the Inland Revenue to accept claims, etc. submitted by an insolvency practitioner who is conducting the affairs of a company.

17.8 It is common in large groups for various companies to remain outside the insolvency processes affecting the remainder. It will be found to be helpful to clarify, both for the Inspector of Taxes and the group's former tax advisers, which members of the group are not being dealt with by the insolvency practitioner and where the responsibility of dealing with the tax affairs of the company remains with the directors of those companies. For some of these companies, the insolvency practitioner will have an interest as "shareholder" in maintaining their value so as to maximise the proceeds of disposal of their shares. He will have no capacity to act directly for those companies, but good communications can avoid such difficulties as liabilities crystallising in formerly solvent subsidiaries because notices of Commissioners' hearings received at the practitioner's office were not forwarded in good time for the directors to arrange attendance at the hearings.

Time limits

17.9 The main time limits of concern to the insolvency practitioner are as follows.

(a) *Claims.* The various claims which could give rise to tax recoveries and reduced liabilities are discussed in 17.11 below. Most have a two-year time limit which is enforced strictly, and this may be by reference to accounting periods which ended before the practitioner was appointed. Therefore, the practitioner has to ascertain what the accounting reference date of the company is, and what changes there have been in the past two years. Where the appointment occurs soon before a month end, this should be given urgent priority as claims have to be submitted immediately. Where insolvent companies are being wound up, these limits are of lesser relevance as the liquidator can use the regulations referred to below to reduce the Inland Revenue's claims for tax. Where recoveries are sought, however, the strict time limits should be observed. The regulations referred to were originally issued pursuant to *CWR 1949, Rule 224* and were reproduced in Appendix I of the first edition of this book. A revised version is expected some time in 1991 after the date of writing. The procedure is currently available where proof has been made for tax assessed upon the company (other than certain deduction taxes) and it is claimed that the company has no liability for tax or the assessments are excessive. It involves an affidavit by the secretary or other officer of the company (if this is available) accompanied by a certificate by the liquidator, setting out the grounds for the claim. The relevant form is to be obtained from Inspectors of Taxes.

(b) *Appeals.* The practical aspects of dealing with appeals against assessments are discussed in 17.16 below. Appeals need to be made within 30 days of issue [*TMA 1970, s 31*], and the practitioner's office should have procedures to ensure that the assessments are logged when received and are dealt with timeously. In principle, it is necessary to demonstrate that there is a "reasonable excuse" for an appeal brought out of time. Although the Inland Revenue are normally sympathetic to late appeals in insolvency cases, this should not be relied upon.

(c) *VAT returns.* These are required to be submitted no later than one month after the period to which they relate. [*VAT Gen R 1985, Reg 58(1)*]. A convenient method of ensuring that VAT matters are kept up to date is to log and monitor completion of the VAT return form which is issued automatically by Customs & Excise for the relevant period, and which states the date by which the return should be submitted. Although Customs have confirmed that default surcharge under *FA 1985, s 19* will not be levied on companies in receivership, liquidation or administration whether in respect of pre- or post-appointment default in the timely submission of VAT returns, it is still necessary for practitioners to guard against the penalty provisions of *FA 1985, s 17* which can be levied against practitioners where there has been failure to furnish a return or pay tax when due. (These penalties are not assessed where a default surcharge liability has been assessed.) See further Chapter 16 below. VAT returns for post-appointment periods are signed by the insolvency practitioner in his capacity as liquidator, administrative receiver, etc. Where the practitioner submits a return for a pre-appointment period, it is customary for this to be forwarded unsigned with a covering letter indicating, where appropriate, that it has been compiled from the company's accounting records.

(d)   *PAYE and payments to sub-contractors.* See 17.30–17.34 for details of the requirements for regular returns.

Recovering tax assets

17.10   The main tax recoveries will be achieved by carry-back or surrender claims. Additional value may be extracted by way of hive-down and sale of an active trade together with its trading losses (see Chapter 18) and the packaging of capital losses (see 19.10–19.11 below).

Carry-back claims

17.11   The following carry-back claims could result in tax repayments or reduced liabilities as appropriate.

(a)   A trading company may claim that a trading loss incurred in an accounting period can be carried back to reduce taxable profits (including interest, income and chargeable gains) in the immediately preceding twelve months or, if shorter, a period equal in length to the accounting period in which the loss arose. [*ICTA 1988, s 393(2)*]. The time limit for this claim is two years from the end of the accounting period in which the loss arose. Only trading losses can be carried back under this provision. (An announcement was made in the Budget of 19 March 1991 that trading losses of accounting periods ending after 31 March 1991 will be able to be carried back against profits of the previous three years. Although no provision to this effect was contained in the Finance Bill published on 17 April 1991, it has been announced that such a provision will be introduced by the Government during the Bill's passage through Parliament.)

(b)   There is a special provision for the carry-back of losses where a company ceases to trade. Such a company may carry back a trading loss incurred in the twelve months prior to the cessation of trade against any income from the same trade in the three years prior to the final twelve months of trading. [*ICTA 1988, s 394*]. The figures for the normal accounting periods are time apportioned for the purpose of this calculation. A terminal loss relief claim must be made within six years of cessation of trade.

(c)   Any ACT which cannot be set off against the corporation tax liability for the period to which it relates can be carried back to reduce the corporation tax liability for any accounting period beginning in the previous six years. [*ICTA 1988, s 239*]. The time limit for this claim is two years from the end of the accounting period in which the surplus ACT arose.

Surrender claims

17.12 There are also a number of claims which can be made within groups of companies (where the beneficial ownership requirements are satisfied) so that the benefit of losses, etc. is transferred to companies with profits to absorb them.

(a) Certain tax losses may be surrendered as group relief by a member of a 75 per cent owned group to be set against the profits of a fellow group member. [*ICTA 1988, ss 402–413*]. There are detailed rules for apportionment of losses/profits to "corresponding accounting periods" where these do not coincide or companies join or leave the group. [*ICTA 1988, ss 408–410*]. Relief is also available in the case of consortium companies, which are broadly speaking companies which are owned by other UK resident companies who own at least 5 per cent of the share capital each.

A claim for group relief must be made, at present, within two years of the end of the surrendering company's accounting period. The present rules will, however, be replaced by a new system of revocable claims on the introduction of Pay and File [*FA 1990, s 100, 15 Sch*], and this is expected to affect accounting periods ending after 30 September 1993. Further details will be found in Tolley's Corporation Tax.

(b) Part or all of the ACT relating to an accounting period can be surrendered to a subsidiary which is more than 50 per cent owned. [*ICTA 1988, s 240*]. A claim to surrender ACT must be made within six years of the accounting period to which the ACT relates.

17.13 It is usual in insolvency cases for losses to be surrendered at a price equal to half the tax saved by the claimant company (see 5.27 above in relation to administrative receiverships). Furthermore, to avoid unnecessary administrative effort, it will often be convenient for all loss making companies in a group to agree that a single company with sufficient losses should undertake the formal agreement of losses for surrender with the Inland Revenue and that payments received by that company should be shared equally by all the loss-making companies.

Information

17.14 The main difficulty in achieving tax recoveries is satisfying the Inspector on the quantum of losses available for carry-back or surrender in the absence of audited accounts and detailed tax computations. Unless the practitioner has lost the Inspector's goodwill, it will be found in practice that a simple net assets statement is sufficient for the purpose of establishing the existence of losses. Such a statement would compare net assets in the last audited accounts with the position in the Directors' Statement of Affairs. Reduction in net assets would be treated as attributable to trading losses after adjusting for known movements on reserves including any dividends, interest, disallowable expenditure (if necessary, using round sum amounts based on past computations), and providing for the maximum claw-back of capital allowances.

Ongoing compliance matters

Corporation tax returns

General

17.15   Companies are required to notify the Inland Revenue that they have a tax liability for an accounting period within twelve months from the end of that period, unless they have already been required to make a return. [*TMA 1970, s 10*]. Returns are requested as a matter of course by the Revenue and this is done by Form CT1, which is normally issued three to six months after the end of the accounting period, and allows 30 days for completion. Except in the most straightforward cases, or where there are no profits to report, tax computations supported by accounts are normally submitted in lieu of Form CT1. Where the return, or a computation in lieu of it, has not been received by the Inspector by the time limit, he will normally raise an estimated assessment. If this is not appealed against within 30 days, the estimated liability is confirmed and becomes payable. The Inspector and the taxpayer may agree to settle any appeal between themselves. [*TMA 1970, s 54*]. In cases where agreement cannot be reached the appeal will be heard before the General or Special Commissioners. The Clerk to the Commissioners will send a notice of a hearing to the taxpayer setting out the date, time and place of the hearing. The Commissioners may postpone the hearing if there are reasonable grounds to do so. Alternatively, they may determine the appeal or issue a precept requiring certain information to be submitted to the Revenue so that the appeal can be considered further [*TMA 1970, s 51*]. The mechanism for returns will be markedly different under the Pay and File system which is expected to apply to accounting periods ending after 30 September 1993. Full details will be found in Tolley's Corporation Tax.

17.16   Following *IA 1986*, corporation tax is no longer a preferential claim for insolvency appointments after 29 December 1986. Accordingly, insolvency practitioners will deal with returns and correspondence from the Inland Revenue in like manner to other unsecured claims against the company. However, in order to maintain a practitioner's professional reputation with an Inspector (who may well be dealing with going concern clients of the practitioner) it will be important to maintain strict professional courtesy in doing so. In this regard, it is usually helpful to have correspondence with the Revenue conducted by tax personnel rather than insolvency personnel.

Administrative receivers

17.17 As corporation tax is an unsecured debt, an administrative receiver is not generally concerned with agreeing any corporation tax liabilities arising either before or after his appointment and he need only avoid prejudicing the claims of unsecured creditors. If the receiver is served with an estimated assessment, to protect the company's position he should appeal against the assessment and apply to postpone all the tax charged thereby. A final assessment showing tax payable is simply held and passed onto the liquidator when one is appointed. Other correspondence with the Inland Revenue (e.g. correspondence on open years, notices of hearings before the Commissioners, and payment demands) are simply acknowledged with a courtesy letter informing the Revenue that their claim is unsecured and falls to be dealt with by a subsequent liquidator. The receiver will not normally do anything further to prevent a liability being determined even if in an excessive amount.

17.18 The position would be different if the receiver could obtain a repayment of tax by agreeing the corporation tax liability for an open year. In this situation, he would want to deal with any correspondence with the Inland Revenue which will facilitate this repayment. Ultimately, a commercial decision has to be made as to whether the costs of pursuing a repayment claim outweigh the potential tax recovery.

17.19 Correspondence from the Inland Revenue for a company to which a liquidator has already been appointed, should be passed directly to the liquidator unless the receiver has other reasons for dealing with it.

Fixed charge receivers

17.20 A fixed charge receiver is not concerned with the day-to-day affairs of the company. Therefore, he should pass to the directors any forms or correspondence received from the Inland Revenue.

Administrators

17.21 An administrator is concerned with all claims against the company and must therefore deal with all tax liabilities. If an administration is expected to be followed by a return to solvency, the administrator will deal with Inland Revenue correspondence as if the company were a going concern company. Where, however, an administration is likely to be followed by an insolvent liquidation, he will generally deal with Revenue correspondence in a similar way to an administrative receiver by deferring matters until the liquidator is appointed. In practice, however, it is likely that it will be the same practitioner who conducts the insolvent liquidation, and it will be convenient to progress matters as far as possible as administrator. An administrator will go further than a receiver to prevent excessive liabilities being determined and should, for example, provide the information requested by Inspectors to avoid the Commissioners confirming an over-estimated tax liability.

Liquidators

17.22 A liquidator will agree all the claims against the company where there are funds to pay any part of them. He will therefore need to agree all the corporation tax liabilities up to the date of his appointment. He should appeal as necessary against corporation tax assessments for periods prior to his appointment, and reply fully to correspondence from the Inland Revenue. If an appeal for a pre-appointment period is listed for hearing before the Commissioners, a liquidator should provide the Inspector with any outstanding information required. If he is unable to obtain a postponement of the hearing, he should attend it.

17.23 Any corporation tax payable in respect of accounting periods after a liquidator's appointment is an expense of the liquidation and Inland Revenue correspondence on it should be dealt with as for a going concern company.

17.24 In a members' voluntary (solvent) liquidation, all the company's creditors will be paid in full. Therefore, all Inland Revenue correspondence should be dealt with as for a going concern company.

17.25 Companies must also make returns (using Form CT61) of certain payments from which it was liable to deduct income tax. [*ICTA 1988, s 350(4), 16 Sch*]. Returns, together with payment of the income tax deducted, must be made within 14 days of the end of the return period. Such periods end on 31 March, 30 June, 30 September, 31 December and at the end of an accounting period. Where a practitioner makes such payments on behalf of the company, he should submit the Form CT61 signed in his capacity as liquidator, administrative receiver, etc.

17.26 Credit can be claimed in a return for income tax deducted from payments received in the accounting period in which the return period falls. Where income tax suffered on receipts exceeds income tax deducted from payments, the excess is set off against the corporation tax liability for the period. [*ICTA 1988, s 7(2)*].

17.27 The CT61 procedure is also used for accounting for ACT liabilities of companies in respect of income distributions, including dividends. [*ICTA 1988, 13 Sch*]. Whereas such distributions do not normally arise for companies under an insolvency process, it should be noted that a return may be required within 14 days of the appointment of a liquidator in respect of transactions occurring in the return period then ending.

Payments

17.28   Corporation tax is payable within nine months from the end of the accounting period [*ICTA 1988, s 10*], with the following exceptions.

(a)   For a company which was trading before 1 April 1965, the payment interval which applied before corporation tax was introduced is preserved while the pre-1 April 1965 trade continues. Such companies are, however, subject to transitional provisions (introduced by *FA 1987* in preparation for the Pay and File regime— see 17.29) which are progressively reducing the payment interval until all companies will have the same nine months' payment period.

(b)   Where there is an appeal against an assessment, the full amount charged is due and payable unless application for postponement of payment is made. [*TMA 1970, s 55*]. This is normally done at the same time as the appeal. Where application is made for postponement of part of the tax charged by the assessment, the balance which has not been postponed is due and payable 30 days after the postponement application has been agreed.

(c)   Corporation tax is never payable earlier than 30 days after the date of issue of an assessment. [*ICTA 1988, s 10(1)*].

See Chapter 16 for details of interest on late payment of tax, and penalties.

Pay and File

17.29   *F(No 2)A 1987* introduced a new system, known as Pay and File, which is intended to modernise the administration of corporation tax. Pay and File will not come into effect until 30 September 1993, as proposed, so as to allow for implementation of the necessary computer support. By then, all companies will have a due date for payment of corporation tax no later than nine months after the end of an accounting period. The main features of Pay and File are summarised below. Further details will be found in Tolley's Corporation Tax.

(a)   The company will make its own estimate of the tax due and pay this, without the need for an estimated assessment, on the normal due date nine months after the end of its accounting period.

(b)   The company will be allowed twelve months from the end of the period to which it makes up its accounts in which to supply its return and accounts to the Inland Revenue.

(c)   Failure to submit the return and the accounts to the Revenue within twelve months will result in an automatic penalty, unless the company can show a reasonable excuse. The penalty will start at £100, if the return is less than three months late, increasing in stages up to £200 plus 20 per cent of any tax unpaid, where the return is more than twelve months late.

(d)   Where the final liability agreed with the Revenue is greater than the estimated payment made at the normal due date, interest will be charged by the Revenue on any additional liability from the due date until the additional liability is settled.

(e)   Where the finally agreed liability is less than the estimated payment made at the normal due date, interest will be paid by the Revenue on any payment from the due date until the repayment is made.

PAYE and payments to sub-contractors

17.30   Within 14 days of the end of a tax month, employers are required to pay to the Inland Revenue Accounts Office all monies owed for PAYE and NIC for that tax month. [*ITER 1973, Reg 26*]. This means that payment is required by the nineteenth day of each month. Similar provisions govern accounting for amounts deducted from payments to uncertified sub-contractors. [*Income Tax (Sub-Contractors in the Construction Industry) Regulations 1975, SI 1975 No 1960, Reg 7*].

17.31   No interest charges are imposed on late monthly remittances by employers, the Inland Revenue having acknowledged the practical difficulties which would be caused by such a regime (Inland Revenue consultative document—'Keith: Further Proposals', 29 July 1988, p 47). However, *F(No 2)A 1987* introduced an interest charge, with effect from 19 April 1988, on late payments where exceptionally the Inspector of Taxes has made a formal determination on an employer or on a contractor [*ITER 1973, Reg 29A; Income Tax (Sub-Contractors in the Construction Industry) Regulations 1975, SI 1975 No 1960, Reg 12A*]. The interest rate is the general rate for overdue tax. Furthermore, *FA 1988* has paved the way for the introduction of regulations imposing a general interest charge on payments of PAYE and NIC delayed beyond the end of the tax year. These provisions will not come into force before 1993 at the earliest because of computerisation constraints. Draft regulations to implement the general interest charge have been issued by the Revenue (IRPR 23 January 1990). These provide for interest (at the general rate for overdue tax) to run from 14 days after the end of the tax year (i.e. 19 April) on any PAYE unpaid at that date.

17.32   At the end of the tax year employers are required to submit an end of year return providing details of pay, PAYE and NIC for their employees (Forms P14 and P35). This return is due by 19 May. [*ITER 1973, Reg 30*]. Similarly, contractors in the construction industry must make an end of year return of payments made to uncertificated sub-contractors (Forms SC11 and SC35). [*Income Tax (Sub-Contractors in the Construction Industry) Regulations 1975, SI 1975 No 1960, Reg 10*]. Where such payments have been made by him, the insolvency practitioner signs the relevant forms in his capacity as liquidator, administrative receiver, etc. Depending on the nature of his appointment, the insolvency practitioner may also need to agree preferential claims for such sums. To do so, it is usually convenient, although there is no underlying statutory duty, to submit Forms P14, P35, etc. for the period from 6 April immediately preceding the date of his appointment to that date. Where this is done, end of year returns for the tax year in which that date falls will only contain details of post-appointment payments.

17.33 New penalties for late end of year returns were introduced in *FA 1989, s 165* and these are being introduced gradually to help employers and contractors get up to date. For the year ended 5 April 1990 no proceedings for penalties will be taken if the end of year returns were submitted by 19 August 1990. For 1990/91 and 1991/92 the deadlines are 19 July 1991 and 19 June 1992 respectively (IRPR 16 July 1990). Thereafter, the returns must be submitted by 19 May. If the end of year returns have not been submitted by these dates, the Inland Revenue will be able to take proceedings before the General Commissioners, who will have the power to award an initial penalty of up to £1,200 per 50 employees. If the failure to file returns continues, automatic and non-mitigable penalties of £100 per 50 employees per month will be charged. Further penalties, which would be tax-geared and subject to mitigation, would be charged in cases where either the delay continued beyond 19 April in the following year or where the end of year return was found to be incorrect as a result of fraud or negligence on the part of the employer. Ultimately, penalties will be charged automatically on late returns, without the need for the Revenue to take formal penalty proceedings first, but these automatic penalties will not be introduced before full computerisation of the Revenue's existing procedures. See Chapter 16 for a discussion of the ranking of such penalties and interest.

17.34 Employers are also required to submit details of employees' expenses and benefits during the tax year whether or not tax has been deducted (Forms P9D and P11D). If these returns have not been submitted by 6 June, the Inland Revenue may take proceedings to charge an initial penalty of up to £300 for each late return, and if the failure continues a further penalty not exceeding £50 for each day of continued failure can be imposed. The maximum penalty for information given fraudulently or negligently in such a return is £3,000 per return. Where benefits, etc. have been provided by him, the insolvency practitioner signs the relevant forms in his capacity as liquidator, administrative receiver, etc. Forms relating to period prior to his appointment should be signed by a director of the company concerned. If there is no such director remaining, the forms should be submitted unsigned and accompanied by a suitable covering letter.

Job closure

General

17.35 Before closing the job, the practitioner will wish to ensure that he has adequate confirmation from the Inland Revenue that there are no claims against him. The scope of "clearance" which is necessary will depend on the nature of the process involved and the type of transactions which have occurred. The following actions will provide the practitioner with a minimum level of comfort.

Liquidators

17.36 Liquidators should require confirmation that the tax affairs of the company have been concluded for both pre- and post-liquidation accounting periods. Where there are sufficient funds for tax liabilities to be discharged in full, this will involve confirmation from the Inspector of Taxes that all relevant assessments have been raised, and separate confirmation from the Collector of Taxes that no further amounts are due. The latter confirmation can sometimes also be obtained from the Inspector's office, but details of interest liabilities for late payment are usually only available from the Collector's records.

Administrative receivers, administrators and supervisors of voluntary arrangements

17.37 In the absence of any unequivocal published Inland Revenue statements to confirm that there is no personal liability for these office-holders for corporation tax liabilities arising from their transactions, it is prudent to seek such confirmation on a case by case basis. This will normally involve the practitioner sending copies of his receipts and payments accounts to the company's Inspector of Taxes and requesting confirmation that the Revenue has no claims against him personally. Such confirmation is given in practice.

Chapter 18

Hive-downs

18.1   Hive-downs were probably the best known tax planning device in insolvencies until the restrictions introduced in *FA 1986*, now contained in *ICTA 1988, s 343(4)*, greatly reduced the benefits (see 18.19–18.21 below). There are still occasions where hive-downs are carried out for tax reasons but the reasons are now more often commercial (for example, staff morale). Though simple in concept, they are fraught with tax traps for the unwary.

What is a hive-down?

18.2   Assume that X Ltd, a trading company, is in administrative receivership. To hive down the business, the receiver will incorporate a new company (Newco), all shares of which are beneficially owned by X Ltd. He will then transfer the business of X Ltd to Newco for a deferred consideration. In due course, the shares of Newco may be sold to a third party. Newco's debt to X Ltd may at that stage be discharged by or assigned to the purchaser. It is important to note that a hive-down will not be effective to transfer tax losses to Newco after commencement of the liquidation of X Ltd (see 18.13 below), and that in any event the available losses will be reduced if not eliminated by the provisions introduced in *FA 1986* now in *ICTA 1988, s 343(4)* (see 18.19–18.21 below). Hive-downs are also relevant in administrations and company voluntary arrangements and many of the points raised below will be equally valid there.

Why hive down?

18.3   The tax planning motive for a hive-down was, before enactment of the 1986 provisions, to enable the purchaser of the trade of X Ltd to take advantage of any unutilised losses which had been incurred in that trade and to set them against future profits under *ICTA 1988, s 393(1)*, using the relief available for transfers between companies in common ultimate ownership. [*ICTA 1988, s 343*]. This was potentially advantageous for the receiver, who could obtain an increased price for the business, even after taking into account any claim which might be made for repayment of tax on a cessation of the trade if the assets were sold directly. [*ICTA 1988, s 394*].

18.4   There are, however, other reasons for hiving down which are now likely to be the primary reasons. In particular, a hive-down may provide a receiver with protection in carrying on the trade due to the limited liability of Newco, a point of some importance if X Ltd goes into liquidation. Moreover, a new company provides a convenient sale package, free from the liabilities of the old, and can benefit the morale of the workforce. A receiver also has the advantage of *Transfer of Undertakings (Protection of Employment) Regulations 1981, SI 1981 No 1794, Reg 4(1)(a)* which defers the otherwise automatic transfer of employees into the hive-down company. Another motive may be that Customs & Excise will not be entitled to set off VAT input tax repayments to Newco under *FA 1988, s 21* if it registers separately, in situations where not all pre-receivership liabilities have been met (see 20.12 below) or under *VATA 1983, s 14(7)* if not all returns have been filed. In addition, providers of public utilities, such as the electricity board, may be obliged to supply Newco as a new consumer and be unable to demand payment of otherwise unsecured claims against X Ltd as a condition for continued supply. [*IA 1986, s 233(2)(b)*].

Corporation tax on a hive-down

18.5   The success of a hive-down in carrying forward the tax losses will depend on *ICTA 1988, ss 343, 344*, now subject to the statutory restriction discussed in 18.19–18.21 below. These sections apply where there is a transfer of a trade between two companies and where, on or at any time within two years after the transfer, the trade (or an interest amounting to not less than 75 per cent in it) belongs to the same persons as the trade (or such an interest) belonged to at some time within a year before the transfer. [*ICTA 1988, s 344(1)(a)*]. The meaning of "belonging" in this context is set out in *ICTA 1988, s 344*: broadly, a trade belongs to the person entitled to its profits, and, in the case of a company, will also "belong" to that company's direct or indirect parents. [*ICTA 1988, s 343(1)(2)*]. The trade must not, within the period which is relied on, be carried on otherwise than by a company which is within the charge to tax in respect of it, such as a non-resident company. [*ICTA 1988, s 343(1)(b)*]. There are apportionment provisions applicable where only part of a trade is transferred. [*ICTA 1988, s 343(8)(10)*].

18.6   The effect of *ICTA 1988, s 343* is that there is no cessation of the trade carried on by X Ltd so far as loss relief is concerned. Subject to *ICTA 1988, s 343(4)* (see 18.19–18.21 below), Newco effectively inherits the losses incurred in the trade by X Ltd, which may be carried forward under *ICTA 1988, s 393(1)* as if the trade had always been carried on by Newco. [*ICTA 1988, s 343(3)*]. *ICTA 1988, s 343(2)* also provides that no balancing charges are to be made on X Ltd on the transfer and that capital allowances computations for Newco are to be made as if a single company had carried on the trade throughout. X Ltd is precluded from making a claim for terminal loss relief under *ICTA 1988, s 394.* [*ICTA 1988, s 343(3)*].

18.7   Although *ICTA 1988, s 343* may apply on the transfer of the trade, it is important to remember that under *ICTA 1988, s 768* the losses will still be disallowed following sale of the shares of Newco if there was a major change in the nature or conduct of the trade within the three years *before* the change of ownership, or if the sale occurred at any time after the scale of activities in the trade has become small or negligible and is followed by a revival of the trade. *ICTA 1988, s 768* may also apply to disallow the losses if there is a major change in the nature or conduct of the trade within three years *after* the change of ownership. If the purchaser considers that he will have to change the nature of the trade to make Newco profitable, he should consider if he has good commercial reasons for a further hive-down (or up) through an intra-group transfer within *ICTA 1988, s 343*, as it appears that *ICTA 1988, s 768* (and in particular, *section 768(5)*) would not apply to the change of ownership of the "predecessor", which in this event would be Newco.

18.8   *ICTA 1988, s 343* does not apply to enable Newco to carry forward surplus ACT. Where under *ICTA 1988, s 240* ACT is surrendered by X Ltd to Newco, *ICTA 1988, s 245* may restrict the ability of Newco to set off the ACT against any liability to corporation tax.

18.9   It should be noted that *ICTA 1988, s 343* will apply with the consequences discussed in this chapter whenever the ownership criteria in *s 344* are satisfied and not necessarily as a matter of deliberate intention. A curious case which illustrates this is *Wadsworth Morton Ltd v Jenkinson Ch D 1966, 43 TC 479*, where the directors and shareholders of an insolvent company formed a new company and acquired as much of its assets as they could from the receiver and other purchasers, leasing the same premises and employing substantially the same staff and even tendering for its uncompleted contracts. They settled a claim by the liquidator of the company that they had dealt wrongfully with the company's goodwill and should account for their profits by purchasing an assignment of the goodwill. Although it had never formally acquired the company's business, the new company was held to have taken over the old company's trade.

Beneficial ownership

Contract for sale

18.10   In determining whether the 75 per cent ownership requirement is satisfied (see 18.5 above), it is the beneficial ownership of the shares in Newco held by X Ltd which must be considered. [*ICTA 1988, s 344(3)(a)*]. This concept is discussed in detail in 8.3–8.10 above. An important case in the context of hive-downs is *Wood Preservation Ltd v Prior CA 1968, 45 TC*

112, where it was held that a hive-down company could not take the benefit of its parent's losses where its shares were already, at the time the trade was transferred, subject to a binding contract for sale to a third party, which prohibited the declaration of dividends, etc. As Lord Donovan put it at p 132: 'the shares (in a word) were like a tree which the owner could not sell and could not cut down and of which he could enjoy none of the fruit'. See also *Parway Estates Ltd v CIR CA 1968, 45 TC 135*. By comparison, in *Burman v Hedges & Butler Ltd Ch D 1978, 52 TC 501* it was held that because the company *could* freely dispose of shares and was entitled to participate in respect of them in a winding up it was the beneficial owner of them.

18.11   The problem, in many cases, will be to identify what is or is not a binding contract. In the *Wood Preservation* case itself, the contract was expressed to be subject to a condition at the time of transfer: confirmation by a German company that they would not consider the purchase of Wood Preservation as an "important reason" entitling them to terminate their agreement with Wood Preservation for the use of a wood preservation process. The court held that this still amounted to a binding contract because it was open to the purchaser to waive it and to apply to the court for specific performance to enforce the contract at any time. A similar question was considered in a stamp duty case, *CIR v Ufitec Group Ltd QB, [1977] STC 363*. A so-called condition may be no more than a term of performance of the contract—see *Eastham v Leigh London & Provincial Properties Ltd CA 1971, 46 TC 687*. Problems may also arise where a contract is genuinely conditional, for example, where there is a binding option to sell. There is some authority which suggests that beneficial ownership may already pass where a binding option has been granted, at least where the vendor has agreed to restrict the powers he can exercise in respect of the shares (see *William Cory & Son Ltd v CIR HL, [1965] 1 All ER 917* and *United Dominion Trust (Commercial) Ltd v Eagle Aircraft Services Ltd CA, [1968] 1 All ER 104*). This area has been considered most recently in *J Sainsbury plc v O'Connor Ch D, [1990] STC 516* and, although the case is subject to appeal at the time of writing, it is worth noting the judge's conclusions. The case concerned the effect (for group relief purposes) of an agreement in which Sainsbury and a Belgian company granted each other put and call options over shares in a joint venture company constituting 5 per cent out of the 75 per cent holding of Sainsbury, this being the minimum amount which Sainsbury could beneficially own to enable group relief surrenders between the joint venture company and Sainsbury. The option price was not market value but the amount paid up on the shares, plus interest, less any dividends received by Sainsbury. The judge indicated the following.

(a)   An unfettered freedom of disposition is not an essential feature of beneficial ownership. The "beneficial enjoyment" of the shares and the income from them were, he considered, sufficient to constitute beneficial ownership.

(b)   The right to beneficial enjoyment of dividends should be distinguished from control over whether or not dividends could be declared, and the option agreement should be contrasted with a pre-existing sale as had existed in the *Wood Preservation* case, *supra*.

(c)   The hope of gain or risk of loss are not necessarily a part of "beneficial ownership", which concept has 'nothing to do with the value or the economic attributes of ownership'.

While at the time of writing it remains to be seen how far the Court of Appeal will accept these conclusions, the possibility remains that an option agreement, and perhaps even cross options, may exist without disturbing beneficial ownership. In view of the doubt in this area, however, it is prudent to avoid any arrangement of this kind until after the hive-down.

18.12   Another case in which the nature of beneficial ownership was considered is *J H & S (Timber) Ltd v Quirk Ch D 1972, 48 TC 595*, where a receiver and a would-be purchaser of a business exchanged letters agreeing to the sale of a business, the sale to be effected by a hive-down. The receiver's acceptance was unconditional, and stated that the receiver would instruct solicitors to proceed with the "legal formalities". When the hive-down had been completed, the Inland Revenue were able to argue successfully that beneficial ownership of the assets had already passed to the purchaser under a binding contract, so that relief under *ICTA 1988, s 343* was not available. In recent years, the Revenue have interpreted loss of beneficial ownership still more widely. Although the extended interpretation which they have occasionally adopted is of doubtful legal validity, it is not impossible that the principle might be extended by the court, though the High Court's judgment in the *Sainsbury* case (see 18.11 above) offers some hope that the tide may have turned. There are, of course, the implications of *Furniss v Dawson HL 1984, 55 TC 324* to be considered as well (see 18.28–18.29 below). A hive-down should ideally be effected as early in the receivership as possible and, if a potential purchaser has been identified, it is sensible to avoid detailed discussion of possible terms of sale. An early hive-down will also assist with obtaining stamp duty relief and may enable VAT inputs to be claimed at an earlier stage.

Liquidation

18.13   The beneficial ownership requirement also prevents a hive down from occurring after liquidation of X Ltd. It was held by the House of Lords in *Ayerst v C & K (Construction) Ltd HL 1975, 50 TC 651* (approving an earlier case, *Pritchard v M H Builders (Wilmslow) Ltd Ch D 1968, 45 TC 360*) that following liquidation, a company ceases to be the beneficial owner of its assets which pass into a kind of suspense. Consequently, a hive-down effected by the receiver after liquidation was unsuccessful in passing the tax losses to the hive-down company because the parent had ceased to be the beneficial owner of its assets and the requirement that the transferor should hold 75 per cent of the share capital in the hive-down company was not satisfied. Arguably, also, beneficial ownership of assets of a company in a compulsory liquidation is lost when the petition is presented (see 8.3–8.10 above). It should, however, be noted that the beneficial ownership requirement may not prevent a "hive-up" from X Ltd; nor will it preclude a "hive-over" between sister companies provided the parent is not in liquidation (see further 8.3–8.10 above).

Administration and company voluntary arrangements

18.14   While it is not considered that a company in administration thereby ceases to be the beneficial owner of its assets, this could be a consequence of an administrator's activities (see further 6.11 above and the comments referred to there on "arrangements" by the Inland Revenue). Similarly, a company voluntary arrangement which involves a hive-down would need to be implemented—and timed—very carefully if it were proposed that *ICTA 1988, s 343* should apply.

Succession

18.15   For *ICTA 1988, s 343* to apply, the trade carried on by Newco must be the same trade (or part of the same trade) as that originally carried on by X Ltd when the losses were incurred. This means that two conditions must be met: the trade of X Ltd must not have ceased before the date of the hive-down, and there must be a succession to all or part of the trade of X Ltd.

18.16   The question of cessation of a trade is discussed generally in 8.11–8.17 above. However, this area must be viewed particularly cautiously in the context of hive-downs where part of a trade has already been disposed of. As Walton J said in *Rolls-Royce Motors Ltd v Bamford Ch D 1976, 51 TC 319 at p 346:*

> 'if there is in substance a complete division of the trade of the company into two separate parts, notwithstanding that trade of the same general nature is carried on thereafter by each of the two now separate entities, it appears to me that neither of them is carrying on the same trade as the composite whole formerly carried on.'

The comments of Millet J in *Falmer Jeans Ltd v Rodin Ch D, [1990] STC 270* are also relevant. He noted that while the "very same trade" must be carried on, it is not necessary for all the activities of the trade to be carried on by Newco, but it is enough if sufficient of them are carried on for the Commissioners to make a finding of fact that the trade is the same. Nor need X Ltd's trade be carried on as a separate trade by Newco.

18.17 *Rolls Royce Motors Ltd v Bamford* is perhaps the best-known example of a hive-down which failed to achieve the desired result of protecting the company's carry forward losses because there was no succession to the trade. The receiver of the company sold its aircraft engine division and three other divisions to the Government and then hived down the two remaining divisions (comprising the much smaller original car business) to a wholly owned subsidiary, shortly before commencement of the liquidation. The subsidiary's claim to carry forward the losses incurred by the original company (all six divisions) was refused on the basis that the continuing business was so different that the trade had been discontinued. Walton J put the position as follows at pp 344–345:

'it appears to me that there is all the difference in the world between an organic growth of a trade and a sudden and dramatic change brought about by either the acquisition or the loss of activities on a considerable scale. Let me illustrate what I mean by the case of a company owning a single village grocer's shop. Over the years it acquires, a few at a time, additional shops; it then organises a central system of bulk buying for them; it may then possibly organise manufacturing facilities in respect of various lines for its chain of shops to sell; and it may well move into the realms of transport and run its own fleet of vans. If it can do all this without ever having discontinued one trade and commenced another—which is the assumption which has to be made in the present case and which may well be correct—well and good. The final trade of that company will, however, as a matter of business activity, bear but little relationship to its original beginnings. Then if, as a result of some crisis, that company has to get rid of all its activities by selling them off, leaving it with only the original village shop, I would myself be under no doubt whatsoever but that there had been a violent change in the trade of that company.'

18.18 Relief was, however, held to be available under the same provisions in *Wadsworth Morton Ltd v Jenkinson Ch D 1966, 43 TC 479*, and in the course of his judgment at p 487, Cross J summarised the features which led him to decide that the relief should be available:

'There is no doubt that it does just the same sort of work as was done by the old company, that it operates from the same premises with substantially the same staff, and its principal customers are the same and that it began business by taking over and carrying out a number of contracts or orders which had been made with or given to the old company.'

Other factors taken into account by the courts in other cases on succession to trades include whether the books and accounts are transferred, as well as lists of customers of the old business. However, a court will be unlikely to hold that a succession has occurred where there has been a discontinuance of the trading activities, such as an actual closure of the premises, while clearly there must be no question of a cessation for tax purposes (see 8.11–8.17 above and in particular the selective list of relevant factors in 8.17). The discussion of what property should be included in the hive-down in 18.25 below is also material. Slightly different issues will be raised where the successor company already carries on a trade and these were considered by Millett J in *Falmer Jeans Ltd v Rodin Ch D, [1990] STC 270* but this situation is relatively unlikely in an insolvency hive-down.

Restrictions on relief

18.19   The relief available to Newco under *ICTA 1988, s 343* may be restricted by *section 343(4)*, when X Ltd has insufficient assets to cover its liabilities. The loss available for relief is reduced by the amount by which X Ltd's "relevant liabilities" exceeds the open market value of its "relevant assets" in both cases ascertained immediately before the hive-down.

18.20   "Relevant liabilities" are defined in *ICTA 1988, s 344(6)(8)–(10)*, as liabilities which were outstanding and vested in X Ltd immediately before the hive-down and which were not transferred to Newco. They do not include liabilities representing X Ltd's share capital, share premium account, reserves or loan stock, unless these result from conversion of relevant liabilities within the year preceding the hive-down, or are loan stock where the loan stockholder was carrying on a trade of lending money (e.g. a bank) when the liability was incurred. By *ICTA 1988, s 344(8)* if X Ltd transferred a liability to Newco but the creditor accepted settlement of part of the liability as settlement of the whole, only that part is treated as transferred to Newco, so the remainder is within X Ltd's "relevant liabilities".

18.21   "Relevant assets" are defined in *ICTA 1988, s 344(5)* as assets which were vested in X Ltd immediately before the hive-down and which were not transferred to Newco (e.g. capital assets), together with the consideration given by Newco to X Ltd in respect of the hive-down, but excluding liabilities assumed by Newco for X Ltd. Thus any group indebtedness resulting from the hive-down should be discharged rather than sold, to increase the "relevant assets" and minimise the reduction in relief. By *ICTA 1988, s 344(10)* if a liability representing loan stock is secured on a "relevant asset" the value of the asset is reduced by the amount of the liability.

Timing and structure

18.22   It will be apparent from the points discussed in the preceding paragraphs that the hive-down should be effected as early in the receivership or administration as possible—certainly before liquidation begins, preferably before a purchaser has been found. If a purchaser has been identified, then it is most inadvisable to conduct detailed discussions with him and any form of agreement (even one "subject to contract") could create problems with the "beneficial ownership" requirement, irrespective of the position under *Furniss v Dawson* (discussed in 18.28–18.29 below). Ideally, of course, a hive-down should be carried out *before* formal insolvency, to avoid the restrictions discussed in 18.19–18.21 above, but this is unlikely in practice and could create problems with the *Transfer of Undertakings (Protection of Employment) Regulations 1981, SI 1981 No 1794*.

18.23 The obvious problem with this is that it is difficult to know what the consideration for the transfer should be. There are three ways of structuring the transaction which avoid this problem to a greater or lesser extent. They are as follows.

(a) *Transfer in exchange for shares.* X Ltd transfers the relevant assets to Newco, in consideration of an allotment of shares in Newco. On the face of it, there is no need to allocate a consideration to the shares, but in actual fact this will be required because a return of allotments would need to be filed with the Registrar of Companies which must, under *CA 1985, s 88(2)(b)*, be duly stamped, if not relieved under *FA 1930, s 42* (see 11.22–11.25 above). This may necessitate adjudication, which will inevitably result in unnecessary delays. The capital gains position would also require consideration. This course is not, therefore, one very frequently adopted.

(b) *Transfer in exchange for cash left outstanding as intra-group loan.* X Ltd transfers the assets to Newco for a stated consideration, which is not paid, but left outstanding as a debt. The difficulty here is arriving at the consideration. If market value is used, this will prejudice negotiations with the purchaser, while if book value is used and exceeds market value, the hive-down company may start life as an insolvent company. Moreover, if the company is in administration and the Newco is sold for greater than the amount subscribed for the shares, a capital gain will be generated. (This will be irrelevant to a receiver.)

(c) *Transfer in exchange for a consideration to be certified.* X Ltd transfers the assets to Newco for a consideration which is to be certified by an independent party (say, its auditors) as market value, at a future date. This leaves the door open for negotiations with the purchaser, and in due course the hive-down agreement can be varied by negotiation with the purchaser of X Ltd's shares to provide for a definite figure as required. Such a variation should not, in a normal case, result in a rescission of the first agreement—see *Magnavox Electronics Co Ltd (in voluntary liquidation) v Hall Ch D, [1985] STC 260*, where the *Ramsay* principle (and not this point) won the day for the Inland Revenue. This is the structure most frequently used.

18.24   Whatever the structure adopted, the receiver will enter into a second agreement with the purchaser for sale of the shares, and simultaneously of any loan. Alternatively, the purchaser may discharge the indebtedness or procure that Newco does so itself. The former structure can be arranged to avoid the purchaser needing to pay stamp duty on the consideration he gives since the discharge of Newco's indebtedness may be treated as stampable consideration under *SA 1891, s 57*. This is achieved if the loan is a promissory note or "loan capital" within *FA 1986, s 79*. The latter course will now be the more efficient since it will increase the "relevant assets" for the purposes of the restriction (see 18.19–18.21 above). It is not thought that Newco would thereby be involved in giving financial assistance for the purchase of its shares (which would be in breach of *CA 1985, s 151*)—see *obiter dicta* in *Armour Hick Northern Ltd v Armour Trust Ltd Ch D, [1980] 3 All ER 833*. If the purchaser buys the debt, the allotment of the consideration will have to be considered: the purchaser may well want to ensure that his base cost for the shares is kept as high as possible. The receiver, on the other hand, will not (save in exceptional cases) be concerned with any tax on chargeable gains which remains the company's liability—see Chapter 5. (This may, however, be a relevant consideration for an administrator or in a company voluntary arrangement). An apportionment should, however, be *bona fide* and reflect the respective commercial values of the assets (*West London Syndicate Ltd v CIR CA, [1898] 2 QB 507; Re Hollebone's Agreement CA, [1959] 2 All ER 152*).

What property should be included?

18.25   In principle, substantially all the assets of the trade (including goodwill) should be transferred by X Ltd to Newco. To preserve the losses, it is essential that Newco carries on the same trade or part of the trade of X Ltd, which might not be the case if only a part of the assets were transferred (see 18.15–18.18 above). This may also be necessary to transfer the business as a going concern for VAT purposes (see 9.36–9.46). Special difficulties do, however, arise with other capital assets, notably land and buildings (including fixtures) and intellectual property (patents, trade-marks, know-how and copyright). If such assets are transferred to Newco, a tax charge may arise under *ICTA 1970, s 278* if the shares of Newco are sold within six years. This is calculated by reference to the base cost of the assets to X Ltd and applies so that Newco is treated as if immediately after its acquisition of the asset it had sold, and immediately reacquired, the asset at market value at that time. A tax liability may therefore pass to the purchaser who may well require the receiver to reduce the price or to indemnify him, so facing the receiver with a liability for corporation tax on chargeable gains which would not normally be met out of the funds under his control (see Chapter 5).

18.26   There are two solutions to this problem. One (the more risky) is that the purchaser may be able to avoid the capital gain when Newco joins his group. (He will not, of course, be able to use group relief in view of *ICTA 1988, s 409.*) Alternatively, as is almost invariable practice, the capital assets (other than goodwill) may be kept by X Ltd and appropriate licences granted to Newco. The capital assets can then be sold on to the purchaser directly by X Ltd, subject to the licences. Although a liability for tax on any chargeable gains would result from this, it will not normally be the receiver's responsibility and is in any event an inevitable consequence of the sale. The point will, however, be a concern for administrators. The transfer of the goodwill to Newco is the transfer of a chargeable asset but in an insolvency the value of the goodwill at the time of transfer to Newco is likely to be negligible. A useful case showing that the sale of a major asset, which is then used under licence, does not of itself bring about a cessation of a business, is *CIR v Daniel Beattie & Co CS 1955, 36 TC 379*, where a coal company continued under licence to work a mine nationalised and sold to the National Coal Board, and was held not to have ceased its trade until the licence expired.

Unscrambling hive-downs

18.27   One risk in effecting a hive-down early in a receivership or administration is that it may prove impossible to sell the company. It should normally be possible to unscramble the hive-down without serious tax consequences (although, if employees remain, there are likely to be problems resulting from the *Transfer of Undertakings (Protection of Employment) Regulations 1981, SI 1981 No 1794*). This would normally be effected by revocation of the hive-down agreement. Provided X Ltd is not in liquidation, this should not have any tax consequences since *ICTA 1988, s 343* would apply, and any transfer of capital assets would normally also be relieved under *ICTA 1970, s 273*. The VAT registration of Newco would then be cancelled. Any stamp duty previously paid should normally be recoverable under *SA 1891, s 59(6)*.

Anti-avoidance

Ramsay principle

18.28   There is arguably some risk that the *Ramsay* principle could be relevant to hive-downs, on the basis that it might be said that the hive-down formed part of a pre-ordained series of transactions having no commercial purpose other than the avoidance of tax. As has already been noted, it is possible to minimise any element of pre-contrivance if the hive-down is effected early in the receivership, at a time when there is no certainty that a sale will be carried through. But it is in any event unlikely that a hive-down will be effected solely for tax avoidance purposes (see 18.4 above). On either count, it is doubtful that the principle would apply although in view of the developing state of this area of law, the possibility cannot be entirely disregarded in some situations.

18.29 In practice, the Inland Revenue have indicated publicly that they will not normally regard a hive-down as subject to the *Ramsay* principle. Although a prudent purchaser will bear in mind that exceptions can be made (doubtless noting the somewhat guarded tone of the statement), and will ensure that adequate attendance notes and other evidence relating to the transaction are available to him in case of any dispute, the cases where problems are now likely to arise are few. The Revenue's statement was made in response to a letter from the ICAEW on 20 September 1985. Both sides of the correspondence are reproduced as ICAEW TR 588 in Appendix 1. The statement contrasted the Revenue's position on hive-downs with that regarding brought-in capital losses. Since then, the recent decision in the taxpayer's favour in *Shepherd v Lyntress Ltd, News International plc v Shepherd Ch D, [1989] STC 617*, which concerned bought-in capital losses (see 19.10–19.11 below) would seem to have restricted the *Ramsay* principle even further, although the decision of the Revenue not to appeal that case does not necessarily indicate that they will not pursue their position further, possibly through legislation.

Value-shifting

18.30 In determining the value to be placed on Newco, the value-shifting provisions of *CGTA 1979, s 26* should be borne in mind. In particular the exception in *section 26(7)* for intra-group transfers has been restricted by *CGTA 1979, s 26B* introduced by *FA 1989* for disposals after 13 March 1989. The effect of *CGTA 1979, s 26B* is that where the transfer of assets is less than market value and less than cost, *section 26* will deem the consideration to be increased to a just and reasonable figure unless the disposal was for *bona fide* commercial reasons and was not part of a scheme or arrangement of which one of the main purposes was the avoidance of tax. This will be of little concern to an administrative receiver, but it will be of concern to an administrator unless the hive-down is followed by the liquidation of X Ltd, and to supervisors of company voluntary arrangements.

Chapter 19

Tax Planning—1. Corporation and Income Tax

General

19.1   Opportunities for tax planning can occur before commencement of a liquidation or appointment of a receiver although, in the nature of things, tax planning will rarely be high on the list of priorities of those concerned. There is perhaps more to be done in administrations. This chapter briefly mentions a few of the steps which can be taken if the chance arises. It is concerned solely with tax planning matters specific to insolvency: no mention is made of wider measures primarily useful in other areas.

Timing opportunities

19.2   Following abolition of the preferential claim for assessed tax by *IA 1986*, the timing of appointment of a receiver of a UK company which is not in liquidation is of no relevance to its corporation tax position (although his actions may be). The timing of commencement of a liquidation is, however, of great importance since tax liabilities arising after the liquidation begins may still rank pre-preferentially, as opposed to being merely unsecured claims.

19.3   As has been seen in Chapters 1 and 6, there are two crucial dates in relation to the priority of claims for tax in the liquidation of a trading company. These are as follows.

(a)   *The date on which a company's trade ceases.* This is the date when balancing charges may be made and by reference to which a terminal loss claim must be computed. Following that date, the special rules concerning post-cessation receipts and losses will apply.

(b)   *The date of commencement of the liquidation.* Tax liabilities after that date will be expenses of the liquidation and will rank pre-preferentially, including any liabilities resulting from the activities of any receiver or mortgagee. Tax liabilities before the date of liquidation will be unsecured claims in the insolvency.

It will be apparent that from the tax perspective (and subject always to other implications such as the directors' personal position) it is likely to be advantageous for the commencement of a liquidation to be deferred for as long as possible, certainly until after the trade has ceased and preferably until after any disposals capable of giving rise to capital gains have been made. The point is of great significance in relation to administrations, as an administrator may realise a company's assets and the tax thereby resulting will only be provable in a subsequent liquidation as an unsecured claim and not pre-preferentially as would be the case where a liquidator realised the assets. An administration will frequently, from the tax viewpoint, be more advantageous than an immediate liquidation and this is illustrated by the example discussed in 6.27–6.29 above.

Trading losses

19.4   The need to obtain the maximum benefit from available trading losses is self-evident. Upon a cessation of its trade, an insolvent company will be eligible for relief on the restricted basis set out in *ICTA 1988, s 105* (see 8.25 above). This precludes relief for trading losses against chargeable gains. Group relief claims cannot be made in respect of post-liquidation periods (see 8.31 above). A claim for terminal loss relief may, however, be made and is frequently advantageous (see 17.11 above).

19.5   As described in 17.9(a) above, time limits for claims and elections are strictly enforced in insolvencies, save that in a winding up the Inland Revenue allow a liquidator to make claims out of time to reduce corporation tax liabilities which would otherwise have arisen. (This procedure for companies in compulsory liquidation was set out in regulations made by the Department of Trade and Industry and Inland Revenue issued pursuant to *CWR 1949, Rule 224* reproduced in Appendix I of the first edition of this book. A revised version is expected some time in 1991 after the date of writing.) Care should therefore be taken to make the appropriate claims within the relevant limit if a recovery is intended.

19.6   Payments for loss relief provide a useful means of reducing the capital value of a subsidiary where liquidation is proposed, so as to reduce the chargeable gains resulting from any subsequent distribution of assets to shareholders. The Inland Revenue have stated that they 'would not expect ordinary commercial group relief transactions to fall within *CGTA 1979, s 26*.' This applies to payments which are 'no more than the value of the group relief' (CCAB June 1977, Tolley's Official Tax Statements 1990–91, 28.405).

Tax-free investments

19.7   Where trading losses are not available to set against capital gains after liquidation, it may be possible to arrange investments so that no chargeable gain results from disposals. *CGTA 1979, s 67(1)* exempts gilt-edged securities and qualifying corporate bonds from corporation tax on chargeable gains.

Pre-liquidation dividends

19.8   Payment of pre-liquidation dividends may have the advantage of reducing the taxable gain on the subsequent disposal of shares when remaining assets are distributed. Having regard to the Inland Revenue's comments on dividends paid before sale of a company made in the letter to the Institute of Chartered Accountants in England and Wales reproduced as ICAEW TR 588 in Appendix 1, the Revenue would presumably accept that this would not fall within the principle in *W T Ramsay Ltd v CIR HL 1981, 54 TC 101*. However, *CGTA 1979, s 26A* now allows the Inspector to adjust the disposal consideration by reference to the amount of the dividend if it is made out of chargeable profits caught by that section. *ICTA 1988, s 703* must also be borne in mind and *ICTA 1970, ss 280, 281* if an allowable loss would otherwise be generated.

Use of sub-groups

19.9   As noted in 8.31 above, the commencement of a company's liquidation will bring to an end its grouping for certain tax purposes with any subsidiary. A step open to receivers and administrators where liquidation is impending is the transfer of assets to sub-groups within which group relationships may be maintained.

Capital losses

19.10   Before the series of cases starting with the *Ramsay* case it was common for receivers and liquidators to dispose of companies having capital losses available to set against capital gains (perhaps as a result of their own disposal) to third party purchasers who were able to set these losses off against subsequent sales by the company of assets having substantial gains. Alternatively an asset pregnant with loss might be transferred to a newly formed subsidiary before liquidation and the shares would be sold so crystallising the loss under *ICTA 1970, s 278*. The Inland Revenue statement reproduced as ICAEW TR 588 in Appendix 1 subsequently indicated that such transactions would be attacked under the *Ramsay* principle. In *Shepherd v Lyntress Ltd, News International plc v Shepherd Ch D, [1989] STC 617*, however, the Revenue were unsuccessful in attacking under the *Ramsay* principle the use of a bought-in loss company to shelter capital gains which had accrued in the purchaser's group, which has again opened the door to the use of bought in losses. The Revenue have in the event not appealed this decision.

19.11   It may perhaps be stating the obvious to mention that where capital losses are available in a group these will be available to shelter capital gains if disposals of assets are routed through the company with the loss. This may, it seems, be done without fear of attack under the *Ramsay* principle (see Revenue statement in Appendix 1).

Negligible value claims

19.12   Where an asset or assets in the group is or are worthless it may be worth considering a negligible value claim under *CGTA 1979, s 22(2)* or, in the case of a qualifying corporate bond, under *CGTA 1979, s 136A(2)*, either before or after any necessary group transfer to ensure that the gains and losses are realised in the same company. Where a holding of securities is concerned it may be possible to fragment the loss between the different companies with the gains by transferring different securities to different companies before the claim is made. This may provide a stronger defence to an attack based on *Ramsay* than routing the sale through a capital loss company since the intra-group transfer of the valueless securities will not need to be part of a "pre-ordained series" of transactions.

Chapter 20

Tax Planning—2. VAT

The VAT review

20.1   Following appointment, a receiver who is carrying on the company's business, an administrator or a liquidator, will need to conduct a review of the company's VAT affairs. These will frequently be in a chaotic state: companies may not be registered which should be, or may be registered which should not be. Records may be non-existent. The wrong companies may have issued invoices, or none may have been issued at all. VAT may have been charged when it should not have been, or may not have been charged when it should have been. To comply with his own VAT obligations, and where appropriate to ascertain the preferential or unsecured claims, the receiver or liquidator must put matters in order.

Registration

20.2   If the company is not VAT registered, for example, he must consider whether a registration is required. As discussed in Chapter 9 above, an administrative receiver, administrator or liquidator is obliged to comply with the company's legal requirements as regards VAT and cannot rely on the fact that a company may not have been registered in the past if during the period when it will be under his control a registration is required under *VATA 1983, 1 Sch.* This is complicated somewhat by the new basis for determining liability to register introduced by *FA 1990, s 10.* It should be noted, however, that both the old and the new bases involve an element of retrospectivity. As a result, a receiver or liquidator cannot simply look at the value of the supplies which he is proposing to make while the company is under his control and conclude (for example, where it is known that the business will shortly be sold) that registration is not required. He must consider whether the value of taxable supplies in the previous year exceeded the relevant limits, and if necessary register the company.

20.3   A receiver, administrator or liquidator may also wish to consider whether he should seek to register himself for VAT. This is now provided for expressly under *VAT Gen R 1985, Reg 11* (see 9.2 and 9.5 above). He is unlikely to wish to do this since he will wish to minimise any possible personal exposure, but it is a course sometimes worth considering although if the only reason for the application is the possibility of recovering input VAT, Customs & Excise would be likely to refuse to grant the request.

Group registration

20.4   Other steps may also be necessary to protect the company's position regarding VAT during the insolvency. One is the cancellation of any group registration (except possibly where a receiver is appointed by the same debenture-holder over the other members, or conceivably where intra-group supplies are to continue) since the company will, under *VATA 1983, s 29(1)*, be jointly and severally liable for VAT owed by other members of the group while it remains registered. The existence of a group registration may, it seems, also affect the treatment of supplies it makes (*Kingfisher plc v C & E Commrs, MAN/90/344 & MAN/90/527 (5366)*).

Recovery of VAT overpayments

20.5   If or when the company is properly registered, a receiver, administrator or liquidator must (under the duty owed to debenture-holders or the company, as the case may be) take steps to recover any VAT which has been overpaid by the company before his appointment, so far as he can. A case illustrating this is *Betterware Products Ltd v C & E Commrs QB, [1985] STC 648* (subsequently approved by the House of Lords in *C & E Commrs v Fine Art Developments plc HL, [1989] STC 85*) in which joint receivers established that the company had overpaid tax of nearly £1,000,000, as it had been accounting incorrectly for VAT for nearly a decade.

20.6   The ability to recover overpaid VAT is now limited by *FA 1989, s 24*. Except where the amount is £1,000 or less, a claim must be made separately from the VAT return and is subject to a limitation of six years after the date of the overpayment (except in the case of tax paid by mistake when the six years runs from the date when the mistake was discovered or could with reasonable diligence have been discovered). Interest is not payable under the 1989 Act although Customs & Excise may pay interest under legislation proposed in the 1991 Finance Bill where their conduct has contributed to the overpayment. The right conferred by *section 24* is limited to tax overpaid to Customs themselves— VAT overpaid to another taxpayer can only be recovered in an action for money "had and received" and then only if it was not paid under a mistake of law.

Output tax in the insolvency

VAT-exclusive contracts

20.7   A receiver, administrator or liquidator must ensure that VAT is properly collected on any supplies made by the company. It is therefore essential to ensure that contracts for the sale of assets provide expressly for VAT to be paid by the purchaser. In the absence of an express provision, or extrinsic circumstances, making clear that the contract should be construed as for a VAT-exclusive price the price will normally be VAT inclusive under *VATA 1983, s 10(2)* unless the tax arises because of a change in the law. [*VATA 1983, s 42*]. See also *Franks and Collingwood and Another v Gates QB, 21 September 1983* (unreported). Should no provision have been made in the contract, an assessment for VAT could well result and this might have severe consequences in view of the penalty and interest provisions in *FA 1985*. Conversely, where tax is charged which should not have been, a purchaser could be faced with the disallowance of his input tax credit and may well then seek to recover any overpayment, something almost certain to be an embarrassment if only because the money is likely to have been paid already to Customs & Excise. There may be a defence available of "mistake of law" but in view of the uncertainty in this area it would not be safe to rely on such a defence.

Transfer of a business as a going concern

20.8   It will frequently be advantageous to structure disposals as transfers of a going concern where this is possible, as described in 9.36–9.49 above, as this may enable an exempt or partly exempt purchaser to increase his price. Such transfers are outside the scope of VAT under *Value Added Tax (Special Provisions) Order 1981, SI 1981 No 1741, Art 12* but the input tax attributable to the disposal will normally be recoverable. See 9.15(c) above. On the other hand, where the purchaser is fully taxable, a sale structured so that VAT is properly chargeable may give a cash flow advantage to the seller.

Refunds of input tax

20.9   As previously noted, Customs & Excise may now, in place of arguments based on Crown set-off, seek to withhold input tax repayments due in an administrative receivership or administration in respect of periods subsequent to appointment of a receiver or administrator where tax remains unpaid for pre-receivership periods, under *FA 1988, s 21*. This provision is as follows:

'*Set-off of credits*

In any case where—

(a)   an amount is due from the Commissioners to any person under the Value Added Tax Act 1983 or Chapter II of Part I of the Finance Act 1985; and

(b)   that person is liable to pay a sum by way of tax, penalty, interest or surcharge,

the amount referred to in paragraph (a) above shall be set against the sum referred to in paragraph (b) above and, accordingly, to the extent of the set-off, the obligations of the Commissioners and the person concerned shall be discharged.'

It replaces a separate provision, similar in effect, formerly in *VATA 1983, s 14(7)*, with effect from 29 July 1988. *VATA 1983, s 14(7)* does, however, remain in existence where VAT returns have not been submitted for earlier periods, in which case it enables Customs to withhold payment of input tax claimed subsequently.

20.10   *FA 1988, s 21* was considered in *Re Potco Realisation Ltd Ch D 1988, [1989] STC 429*. In what was originally intended as a test case, the joint receivers applied for judicial review of Customs' action in withholding a VAT repayment under *VATA 1983, s 14(7)*, but before the case was heard that section was repealed and *section 21* replaced it. Scott J held that *section 21* is clear in its terms and applies equally to tax unpaid before and after the date it took effect. He considered that because *VATA 1983, s 14(7)* was amended, and the relevant part repealed, when *section 21* took effect, the new section had to be taken as providing the same remedy in respect of the same amounts. It is apparent from the judgment that he regarded the new section as at least as wide in effect as the old one.

20.11   *FA 1988, s 21* is, as Scott J said, clear enough in its terms and requires a set-off between tax repayments (e.g. excess input tax under *VATA 1983, s 14(5)* or overpayments under *FA 1989, s 24*) owed by Customs & Excise to a taxpayer and amounts he owes to Customs. It is significant that *section 21* works both ways—it entitles a taxpayer to set off an amount he is owed against an amount which he declares as payable on a VAT return. Customs consider (probably rightly) that *section 21* applies across the date of "out of court" administrative receiverships or administration. They initially took the view that it applied in company voluntary arrangements and liquidations but recently revised their policy and decided not to use the provision in these circumstances (see CEPR 6 February 1991). Customs also consider that the decision in *Re Unit 2 Windows Ltd Ch D, [1985] 3 All ER 647* discussed in 3.13 above, which determines the order of set off against preferential and non-preferential claims for the purposes of Crown set-off under *Ins R 1986, Rule 4.90* is inapplicable but this view is less easy to justify since what is equitable for the purposes of one statute is surely no less equitable for the purposes of another. It also seems that *FA 1988, s 21* (and *VATA 1983, s 14(7)*) will override the rights of a chargee of book debts no matter when the charge took effect, on the grounds that the chargee takes his rights subject to these provisions.

20.12 *FA 1988, s 21* will, as has been noted, allow a taxpayer as well as Customs & Excise to apply a set-off and is to this limited extent more favourable than *VATA 1983, s 14(7)*. It can be circumvented in some other ways also. The receiver, administrator or liquidator may register himself for VAT (see 20.3 above). It may be possible to ensure that rights to repayment of input tax in the insolvency (e.g. on the insolvency practitioner's own professional fees) are matched in any period by taxable outputs. The problem with this is that inputs in receiverships are generally by their nature suffered at the end of the period by which time the business which generates the outputs will have been sold. A better solution is to hive down the business to a subsidiary (a course frequently undertaken from other motives—see Chapter 18 above). The hive-down could be arranged as a transfer as a going concern, as described in 9.36–9.49 above. The subsidiary would not (provided it re-registered in its own right and did not take over its parent's VAT registration) be the same taxable person, and would not therefore be liable for its parent's VAT default. It would not have to exceed the registration limits in its own right as *VATA 1983, s 33(1)* should apply. The disadvantage of this would be cost, and legal and other expenses might not make the proposition economical. Customs might also ask for security for the payment of tax under *VATA 1983, 7 Sch 5*.

20.13 Another possibility is a group registration. Arguably, if a group registration is effected after the receivership, and the representative member is a different company, any supply of goods or services to the insolvent company would be treated as made to the representative member which would itself be treated for VAT purposes as carrying on the business formerly carried on by the receivership company, under *VATA 1983, s 29(1)*. The "taxable person" would thus have changed. This is likely to be a practical possibility in very few cases, although it is also an alternative to separate registration following a hive-down. One problem is that Customs & Excise could refuse to register the representative member for the protection of the revenue, under *VATA 1983, s 29(5)*. It is less clear whether *VATA 1983, s 29* has the same effect in the opposite circumstances where the company was already a member of a group registration at the time of receivership. If the group registration is broken the company would again be a separate taxable person but it seems that (unlike the position under *VATA 1983, s 14(7)*) it will be liable for an amount of tax, albeit jointly and severally, which can be set off against repayment under *FA 1988, s 21*.

Partial exemption

20.14 Customs & Excise's approach to the recovery of input tax by partially exempt insolvent companies is outlined in 9.15 above. As will be apparent, recovering input tax which is reclaimable only under the "residual" category may be improved where in the relevant period a sufficient level of taxable supplies can be achieved or the input tax may on closer examination be attributable to matters which Customs will accept as giving rise to a recovery.

Appendix 1

ICAEW TR 588 — Furniss v Dawson

Extracts from a memorandum submitted by the Institute of Chartered Accountants in England and Wales to the Inland Revenue and the text of their response, and published as a guidance note in September 1985.

Capital losses

4.   This is perhaps the most important area; it was referred to in the Ministerial statement which mentioned 'straightforward transfers of assets between members of the same group' and there is also earlier guidance following the Ramsay case where it was stated at our meeting on 6 January 1982 that the decision would not generally be applied to 'the routing of assets through a company within the same Group which has allowable capital losses and had not been acquired after these had arisen'. You indicated at the meeting that this statement is still regarded as valid following Furniss v Dawson.

5.   Although this guidance is of considerable help in a clear cut case problems can still arise. We touched upon some at our meeting. For example, a significant group might be acquired for demonstrably commercial reasons but one of the companies in that group has capital losses. We remain unclear whether the routing of assets from a member of the acquiring group to use that loss would be attacked.

6.   We indicated in our discussions that we would have preferred the Furniss v Dawson doctrine to be identified as applicable under this heading only where a company with a capital loss was acquired with that loss being its sole or main asset and with a motive of acquisition to utilize the loss in question. We believe that confirmation of this approach would do much to clarify the area of what constitutes 'straightforward transfers of assets between members of the same group'.

Hive-downs

7.   One of the first priorities of a receiver appointed under a floating charge is to establish whether part or the whole of the business can be disposed of as a going concern. If this is viable it will invariably produce a greater return (and incidentally, preserve jobs) than a piecemeal sale of the assets. It will also, subject to the provisions of sections 252 and 483,

ICTA 1970 [see now sections 343 and 768, ICTA 1988], enable the tax losses of the business to be preserved and made available to the purchaser, the value of which will be taken into account in arriving at the sale price.

8.   For this purpose it is the normal practice, having established the position, to hive down part or all of the business and relevant assets into a newly-formed subsidiary the shares in which are disposed of. There are sound commercial reasons for disposing of the business in this way, and it is of course important to effect the hive down as soon as possible and certainly before a liquidator is appointed; once that happens the company is no longer the beneficial owner of its assets and section 252 will not apply.

9.   The reasons for the hive-down are therefore founded on sound insolvency practice so that the benefit of the tax losses, representing additional funds, is available to creditors. We have encountered cases where inspectors have stated that they will seek to apply section 483 but if this fails invoke the doctrine in Furniss v Dawson. Since the disposal of a business by a receiver is governed by commercial considerations it would be helpful if an assurance could be given that the Furniss v Dawson principle will not be applied and that the transaction only requires consideration under existing law and practice as outlined above.

Dividends paid before sale of a company

10.   If a subsidiary company is to be disposed of outside the group it is often normal practice, prior to disposal, to declare a dividend to eliminate the undistributed profits of the subsidiary. This reduces the value of the shares for the purposes of arriving at the chargeable gain on disposal and effectively avoids double taxation since the profits which are being distributed have already been subject to corporation tax. Furthermore, the depreciatory transactions provisions contained in section 280, ICTA 1970 only prohibit the creation of capital losses in this way—they do not apply to the reduction of capital gains. Again, in some groups it is normal practice to pay as dividend to the parent each year the distributable profits of each subsidiary. We consider that the Furniss v Dawson principle should not apply to the payment of intra-group dividends as described above.

Extract from a reply dated 20 September 1985 from the Board of Inland Revenue.

I am writing in reply to your letter of 8 July.

As you know, the Board very much welcomed the recent opportunity to discuss with the Institute of Chartered Accountants and the Law Society the implications of the judgments handed down by the House of Lords in the cases of Ramsay, Burmah and Dawson.

Clearly, the interpretation of the Ramsay and Dawson judgments is a matter for the Courts. It will be for the Courts, not for officials, to determine the law. However, you have explained that, meanwhile, there are a number of points on which practitioners and businesses would find it helpful to have a note of how the Revenue understands the position, and in this letter I try to respond accordingly.

We start with much common ground between us. Perhaps the shortest and simplest explanation of the "new approach" was given by Lord Wilberforce, when he said that 'legislation cannot be required . . . to enable the Courts to arrive at a conclusion which corresponds with the parties' own intentions'. I think many of us accept that this "new approach" brings interpretation of the law in this area closer to the reality, or if you like the substance, of the transactions with which it has to deal. We are also conscious that it has also brought with it a measure of uncertainty: partly because by its nature it requires us all to take a rather broader view of the legal implications of a transaction or series of transactions; but partly also because the approach is "new" and (as the House of Lords themselves have emphasised) will no doubt be refined further, as the Courts come to consider more cases.

I do not want to get this out of proportion. It is commonplace that the Courts in North America and a number of European countries have been following somewhat similar approaches for many years. And even in this country a number of fundamental questions for tax purposes—for example, the existence of a "partnership", of "employment", of "income" itself—have always been left undefined in the taxing statutes: there is such a wide and complex variety of facts and real-life relationships that, accepting some inevitable uncertainty at the margin, the tax code does not attempt to capture them in a mechanical formula but leaves them to be determined in the last resort by the courts, having regard to the actual facts of the particular case. Having said that, we are all agreed that the line of reasoning in Ramsay and subsequent cases represents a new and important development.

When we discussed these issues with the Institute and the Society, we in the Revenue confirmed our readiness to co-operate with you in reducing uncertainties of this kind and (where possible) removing them. Taxpayers should not be burdened by unnecessary uncertainty in judging the likely tax consequences of their actions; and I might add that uncertainty of this kind can also make more difficult the work of those who are responsible for administering the Taxes Acts

On your side, the Institute recognised that, whilst we could try to help with guidance and clarification of the Revenue's attitude in the normal or more straightforward case, we are not in a position to give categorical assurances. In particular, we might well take one view of a transaction standing on its own; we might take another view—and I think this follows necessarily from the approach described by Lord Wilberforce—where a similar transaction was one step in a series of transactions apparently designed to avoid tax. You have therefore said that the Institute appreciates that any response which we are able to give must be subject to the caveat that, even where it is agreed that the Revenue would not as a rule seek to invoke the Ramsay and Dawson principle, there may well be individual cases where, because of the circumstances, the Revenue would nevertheless feel it was obliged to follow the Ramsay and Dawson approach. In particular, we may need to look at all the facts of the case in order to establish the nature and legal implications of the transaction. What follows is to be read in that spirit.

I thought that it would be helpful to spell out all this, even at the cost of some length. And it is against this background that I now try to give you as positive and helpful a response as we can, at this stage, to the . . . specific questions which the Institute has raised with us.

Capital losses

I agree that this is an important area where, in our view, the Ramsay principles are likely to have considerable application. Let me say at once that the Board stands by the assurance given on 6 January 1982, about straightforward transfers of assets between members of the same group. By contrast, as you are no doubt aware, Inspectors have advanced Ramsay contentions in a number of cases where the effect of a series of transactions has been to transfer the benefit of capital losses from one group to another. Whether the "new approach" is thought to be applicable will depend on the facts of particular cases bearing in mind, for example, the relationship between the amounts of the loss involved, the period for which the company with the loss has been within the group and on the circumstances in which the losses have arisen. On this approach it would seem unlikely that the judgment would be invoked where the losses were a relatively insubstantial element in the acquisition, as evidenced by the circumstances in which they were utilised and the commerciality of the circumstances surrounding the acquisition.

Hive-downs

This is one of the topics on which it is particularly difficult to see at present where exactly the new approach might apply, if at all. On the face of it, the new approach might have some relevance in cases where little more than the tax losses are being hived down, though even then it would be necessary to demonstrate that there was a composite transaction and the insertion of a "non-commercial" step in that transaction. However, we would not normally expect the new approach to be relevant in cases where an entire trade, or part trade, together with its related assets and liabilities, are hived down with a view to its being carried on in other hands—although of course in those circumstances Section 483 might apply.

Dividends paid before sale of a company

We would not normally expect the new approach to apply here. There is, of course, nothing objectionable about a parent taking out profits of a subsidiary as a dividend. And, as regards Section 280 ICTA which you specifically mention, we would not regard there being a depreciatory transaction under that provision where dividends are paid out of post-acquisition profits.

Appendix 2

ICAEW TR 799—Tax Aspects of the Insolvency Act 1986

Memorandum submitted by the Institute of Chartered Accountants in England and Wales to the Inland Revenue and the text of their response, and published as a guidance note in June 1990.

Introduction

1.   The Insolvency Act 1986, together with the related Insolvency Rules, has introduced two new insolvency procedures and both modified and consolidated existing insolvency law. While the basic principles of receivership and liquidation are largely unchanged, the major features of the new law include the Administration and Voluntary Arrangement procedures. During 1987 and 1988, in England and Wales, there were 330 Adminstration Orders, 70 Corporate Voluntary Arrangements and 1,200 Voluntary Arrangements for Individuals. However, the tax consequences of these new procedures remain unclear and this causes considerable difficulty in practice. No guidance appears to have been laid down by Inland Revenue to local districts or Enforcement Office on how to deal with the new procedures and there is general unfamiliarity in tax offices with the new Insolvency law.

2.   This Memorandum sets out a number of aspects of the Insolvency Act 1986 concerning companies where the tax consequences need to be clarified or where we believe concessions should be made. Some of these matters have been mentioned to the Department of Trade and Industry who have expressed concern informally that the interests of creditors (which the DTI is seeking to protect) might be prejudiced by the tax side effects of the new insolvency legislation. It will be necessary for the Department of Trade and Industry and Inland Revenue to agree their approach and it may be that the proper forum for an agreed approach would be Regulations and Notes for Guidance of Insolvency Practitioners in a form similar to the regulations which were issued under the provisions of Rule 224 of the Companies Winding-up Rules 1949 for the guidance of Liquidators appointed in a Court winding-up, and for Trustees in Bankruptcy. (The last regulations under these provisions were issued on 1 October 1977, and are no longer applicable for insolvency procedures commencing after 29 December 1986).

Inland Revenue response

(a)   The Inland Revenue deal with every Administration Order and Voluntary Arrangement proposal on its own individual merits, taking into account all known features of the case. When deciding how to vote, the Revenue give consideration to, amongst other things, the way in which the taxpayer has attended to his tax obligations, the level of uncertainty over assets and liabilities and whether a voluntary arrangement is the appropriate course for the Revenue to approve as a creditor. The Revenue are also very much aware of the interests of other parties and of the purpose of the voluntary arrangement procedure.

(b)   Both the Inland Revenue's Enforcement Office and its Collector's Offices have instructions on how to deal with matters within their own areas of responsibility. But because every case is different, rather than adhering to strict guidelines, these instructions provide for the exercise of judgement upon the facts and background of each particular case. There have been no Inland Revenue Press Releases or Statements of Practice dealing with any aspects of the new insolvency legislation.

(c)   The Revenue are presently liaising with the Department of Trade and Industry over revised Regulations and Notes for Guidance of Insolvency Practitioners on the lines of those issued in 1977.

Detailed comments

Administrators

Introduction

3.   The Administrator procedure is an entirely new concept within the framework of insolvency legislation in Great Britain. The purposes for which an Administration Order may be made are set out in the Act as follows:

(i)   the survival of the company, and the whole or any part of its undertaking, as a going concern;

(ii)   the approval of a Voluntary Arrangement;

(iii)   the sanctioning of a compromise or arrangement under Section 425 of the Companies Act 1985;

(iv)   a more advantageous realisation of the company's assets than would be effected on a winding up.

4.   The new procedure provides an immediate suspension of payments and court protection ahead of any scheme to compromise debts.

5.   Once an Administration Order has been made, the Administrator is required to formulate his proposals as to how the purposes specified in the court order may be achieved. Until such time as the order is discharged he is responsible for managing the company's affairs through his power of agency.

6.   It is clear from both the Act and the tenor of the parliamentary debate that preceded it, that the overall purpose intended for the Administrator is company rescue. There are, however, a number of uncertainties as regards the taxation consequences of the making of an Administration Order which do not help in achieving that objective, and which are causing difficulty in practice in ascertaining what the outcome for creditors will be. The following are the matters which require clarification.

Liability to tax

7.   The Administrator acts throughout as agent of the company and without incurring personal liability. On his release he is specifically 'discharged from all liability both in respect of acts or omissions of his in the Administration and otherwise in relation to his conduct as Administrator'. (Section 20(2) Insolvency Act 1986). It remains to be confirmed that it is the Revenue's view that tax liabilities arising as a consequence of the Administrator's transactions will be treated as liabilities of the company and not the Administrator personally, and will rank pari passu with the claims of other unsecured creditors in a subsequent insolvency process.

Inland Revenue response

(a)   In most circumstances tax remains the company's liability.

(b)   However, notwithstanding this, the administrator can discharge the liability of the company under:

   (i)   his general powers in S.14(1) Insolvency Act 1986;

   (ii)   his specific power 13 in Schedule 1 of that Act.

(c)   Moreover, he is liable to account for PAYE/NIC deductions. As agent of the company (Section 14(5)) he pays emoluments to its employees. He thereby becomes an employer within the 1973 PAYE regulations (Reg 2; also Regulation 3 SI 1973 No 334) and thus liable to deduct the appropriate tax.

(d)   Although, under Section 20(2), the administrator is discharged from liability arising post his release and from liability outstanding at the date of his release, if a winding up order is made he may be liable under Section 212(1)(b) in respect of the period for which he was, effectively, the employer.

Consequences of the appointment of an Administrator

8.   There is no apparent reason why an accounting period of a company should end for the purposes of corporation tax on the making of a Administration Order. As this can have a material bearing on the ability of the company to set-off trading losses against chargeable gains, it would be helpful to have the position confirmed generally.

9.   Whereas the beneficial ownership tests of the various group relationships of a parent company are no longer satisfied (apart from the capital gains group) after the commencement of liquidation, there is no apparent reason why such relationships should be disturbed on the making of an Administration Order. As the availability of group relief may have a material bearing on the tax liabilities of a company in Administration it would be helpful for the position to be confirmed.

Inland Revenue response

Accounting period

(a)   Section 12 ICTA 1988 sets out the circumstances in which an accounting period ends. These include the commencement of a liquidation (S.12(7)); the cesser of a trade (S.12(3)(c)).

(b)   It is considered that neither the filing of an administration order petition, nor the making of an administration order, would bring about the end of an accounting period.

Beneficial Ownership tests

(c)   Whilst the Revenue would not normally regard an Administration Order itself as affecting the beneficial ownership tests of the various group relationships of a parent company, it is possible that proposals by the administrator which are approved under Section 24, Insolvency Act 1986, might well do so.

(d)   Arrangements by the administrator for the sale of the shares in subsidiaries, even if they did not have the effect that the company subject to the Order lost beneficial ownership of the shares in the subsidiaries, would by virtue of Section 410(1)(b) and Section 240(11), ICTA 1988, respectively cut off entitlement to group relief and to set-off by the subsidiaries of surrendered advance corporation tax.

Voluntary arrangements

10.   A Voluntary Arrangement is based upon a 'proposal to the company and to its creditors for a composition in satisfaction of its debts or a

scheme of arrangement of its affairs'. (Section 1 Insolvency Act 1986). The proposal must provide for a licensed insolvency practitioner to supervise its implementation.

11. The success of Voluntary Arrangements is being jeopardized by uncertainty as to the tax consequences of them for the debtor company and for creditors. The following matters have a material bearing on the outcome of Voluntary Arrangements and require urgent clarification if the procedure is to succeed.

12. It is not clear whether a composition in satisfaction of debts under a Voluntary Arrangement would lead to those debts being treated as "released" for the purposes of Section 94 ICTA 1988 (or Section 103(4) ICTA 1988 where trade has ceased). Under that section, if the debts in question had given rise to a deduction in computing trading profits of the debtor company, the amount released would be treated as a taxable receipt arising in the period in which the release is effected. Where losses are not available to shelter such a receipt, the consequence would be to create further liabilities for the debtor company, which the Arrangements would then have to take into account. The amended Arrangements could then give rise to further charge to taxation under those provisions, and so on.

13. Such a charge to tax would not have arisen if the debtor company had gone into insolvent liquidation, and government policy should not be to seek to achieve a windfall gain for the Exchequer at the expense of creditors in these circumstances.

14. If a charge to tax does arise, it remains to be confirmed what is the status of any such tax liability in the Voluntary Arrangement. In particular, it is not certain whether the Board of Inland Revenue regard Rule 1.28(b) and Rule 5.2(b), The Insolvency Rules 1986 as prescriptive of the Supervisor's duties as regards taxation. These Rules allow there to be incurred for the purposes of the Voluntary Arrangements such fees, costs, charges and expenses which are sanctioned by the terms of the Arrangement, or would be payable:

(i)   for individuals, in the debtor's bankruptcy;

(ii) for companies, in an administration or winding-up.

15. There is a further difficulty for creditors who wish to obtain a bad debt deduction for corporation tax purposes in respect of the debtor company. Whereas no such deduction would be available in respect of any amount of the indebtedness which is repaid, there is uncertainty as to whether the amount of the debt which is "satisfied" by the Voluntary Arrangement remains eligible for relief.

16. Such relief could be available to the creditor on the balance of his claim if the debtor company went into insolvent liquidation, and if the net

outcome under the Voluntary Arrangement is not as good for the creditor as it would be under insolvent liquidation, the creditor will not accept the proposals.

Inland Revenue response

Tax treatment of debts

(i)   *The debtor*

(a)   The taxation treatment of debts which have been released is dealt with by Section 94 ICTA 1988 (formerly S.136 ICTA 1970). This provides that where, in computing for tax purposes the profits or gains of a trade, profession or vocation, a deduction has been allowed for any debt incurred for the purposes of the trade etc, then if the whole or any part of the debt is later released the amount released is to be treated as a receipt of the trade etc arising in the period in which the release is effected.

(b)   Section 94, ICTA 1988, originated in Finance Act 1960, Section 36, the aim of which was to rectify an anomaly whereby a trader incurred a debt, obtained a tax deduction for the amount of the debt, and subsequently got his creditor to release him from all or part of the debt. The Courts had held that the amount released could not be taxed even though the trader had obtained a deduction for the debt. The legislation in what is now Section 94 therefore imposes a charge in these circumstances.

(c)   It is a feature of the legislation that it only applies where a debt is formally released by the creditor. Thus the mere failure to pay or even the bankruptcy or liquidation of the debtor will not give rise to a charge under Section 94.

(d)   There *is* a release where there is a formal arrangement with creditors. The position is similar where there is a scheme approved by the Court, notwithstanding that there were some creditors who did not want to agree but were obliged to do so because the necessary majority agreed. A comprise in satisfaction of debt under a voluntary arrangement would therefore give rise to a "release" which would be treated as a taxable receipt of the debtor by virtue of Section 94.

(ii)   *The creditor*

(e)   The creditor will not be entitled to relief in respect of any part of a debt which is to be paid to him under the terms of an arrangement. But the release of a debt (or part of a debt) by virtue of a voluntary arrangement may not necessarily entitle the creditor to a deduction. In particular, a deduction may only be allowed by virtue of section 74(j) for bad debts proved to be such and doubtful debts to the extent that they are respectively estimated to be bad. A release in excess of an amount arrived at on that basis is unlikely to be an allowable deduction.

(f) Inspectors will usually need to consider all the facts of a particular case before deciding whether a deduction is due in respect of any part of a debt which has been released.

Status of tax liability (S.94 ICTA 1988)

(g) Both Rules 1.28(b) (company voluntary arrangements) and 5.28 (individual voluntary arrangements) provide what "fees, costs, charges and expenses" may be incurred for the purpose of a voluntary arrangement. Apart from those sanctioned by the voluntary arrangement itself, those permitted are defined as those which either would be payable, or would correspond to those which would be payable, (1) in an administration or winding up (companies) or (2) in the debtor's bankruptcy (individuals)—see Rule 1.28(1)(b)(ii) and Rule 5.28(b)(ii). The relevant Rules for this purpose are Rules 4.218 and 6.224—Order of Payment of Costs etc out of estate. The only relevant provision in Rule 4.218 is at Rule 4.218(1)(b) 'expenses incurred or disbursements made by the Official Receiver or under his authority, including those incurred or made in carrying on the business of the company'. Clearly the release of a debt by a creditor giving rise to a taxable receipt under Section 94 cannot be within Rule 4.218(1)(b). The same applies to the corresponding Rule for individuals at Rule 6.224(1)(b) which is in similar terms. The Section 94 tax liability, therefore, is outside the ambit of the Insolvency Rules.

Interest payments under Section 189 Insolvency Act 1986

Introduction

17. Section 189 Insolvency Act 1986 provides for payment of interest on the claims of creditors who prove in the winding-up in respect of the period since the company went into liquidation. Interest up to the date of insolvency is included in the creditor's claim for which proof is lodged. Payment of post-insolvency interest can only occur if there is a surplus after all creditors claims are met in full (including claims for pre-insolvency interest).

18. If the contract with the creditor specified a rate of interest, that rate would be payable in respect of the post-insolvency period, provided that

the rate is greater than the statutory rate applicable to judgment debts, which is currently 15%.

Deduction of tax and charges on income

19.　There is considerable difficulty in determining what is the correct character of this interest payment for the purposes of Section 349 ICTA 1988. Individual practitioners have been advised that the Revenue regards interest paid under Section 189 Insolvency Act 1986 as short interest and therefore that deduction of tax is not required. Where, however, interest payments would otherwise qualify as a charge on income, treating the payment as short interest will deny the opportunity for relief in the paying company. We recommend that in cases where interest payments made before liquidation would have qualified as a charge on income, the same treatment should prevail after commencement of liquidation.

20.　Practical difficulties arise in obtaining relief for charges on income paid in liquidations. Where such interest payments are made out of the income of earlier periods, no relief will be available against the taxable income of the earlier period. We believe that concessionary relief from the strict application of Section 338 ICTA 1988 should be allowed in these circumstances, so that relief may be obtained.

Inland Revenue response

(a)　In normal circumstances interest paid under Section 189, Insolvency Act 1986, is not considered to be annual interest. There would, therefore, be no obligation or right for the payer to deduct tax.

(b)　However, it is possible for the interest to constitute annual interest. This is on the basis that the period for which the interest is payable is known at the time it is paid, ie the period from the date of liquidation to the final date interest can run is ascertainable. Therefore, if interest is payable for less than a year it is short interest, but if it is payable for one year or more it is annual interest.

(c)　Interest is allowable as a charge if it meets the conditions of Section 338, ICTA 1988. It appears, however, that your paragraph 20 on obtaining relief for charges goes wider than the Section 189 interest matters dealt within the rest of this Section. Charges on income, so far as paid out of the company's profits brought into charge to corporation tax, are allowed only as deductions from the profits for the period in which they are paid. It is not clear from paragraph 20 the grounds on which you feel that there should be a departure from the statutory basis.

Disclaimer

21.   It is likely, in practice, that a group company which is in potential receipt of interest under Section 189 IA 1986 will wish to disclaim its entitlement. Otherwise the situation could arise in a group of companies that taxable income is generated without corresponding opportunity for a tax deduction by way of group relief. It would be helpful if the Inland Revenue would accept that such a disclaimer is effective for tax purposes, and may be made at any time before the liquidator makes payment to the creditor. Such a disclaimer would not operate to turn income into capital, but rather would prevent turning capital into income.

Inland Revenue response

The charge to tax under Case III Schedule D is on the income arising. Income arises when it is paid or made available. Therefore, provided that the interest is not paid or made available there would prima facie be no Case III charge.

The interaction of Insolvency Act 1986 and Taxes Management Act 1970

22.   It has been confirmed to individual practitioners by the Inland Revenue that where tax liabilities are claimable in a liquidation, then interest under Section 189 Insolvency Act 1986 will only arise from whichever is the *later* of the date of commencement of the liquidation or the reckonable date for interest under Taxes Management Act 1970. It would be of assistance if this position could be confirmed generally.

Inland Revenue response

(a)   Interest under the Taxes Management Act 1970 will not accrue beyond the date of commencement of the liquidation (Compulsory/ Members Voluntary Liquidation). Interest under Section 189, Insolvency Act 1986, may arise on tax debts claimed in the liquidation, and in addition on interest under the Taxes Management Act 1970.

(b)   Where tax is claimable in a liquidation, interest under Section 189, Insolvency Act 1986, may arise from either the date of the liquidation or the reckonable date for interest under the Taxes Management Act 1970, whichever is the later.

(c)   Interest under Section 189, Insolvency Act 1986, may arise from the relevant date (as in (b) above) to the date of payment of the liability, no matter what the method of payment.

(d)   The Revenue's view would remain the same for assessments made after the liquidation date. For post-liquidation accounting periods, interest under Section 189, Insolvency Act 1986, would not be applicable.

Liquidation of non-resident UK companies

Introduction

23.   With the coming into law of the Insolvency Act 1986, only a UK licensed insolvency practitioner (or the Official Receiver) can now be appointed as liquidator of a UK incorporated company (Section 230, IA 1986).

24.   In the past, the appointment as Liquidator over UK incorporated but non UK tax resident companies was usually taken by locally resident individuals rather than UK practitioners. A company officer or employee was frequently involved where the company was solvent. As this procedure is no longer available, it is necessary to consider whether the appointment of a UK resident Liquidator serves to transfer the place of residence of the company to the UK and subject it to possible charge to UK corporation tax. This matter will be of increasing significance in the transitional period up to 15 March 1993 provided by FA 1988 as regards the residence status of UK incorporated companies which were not UK resident for tax purposes on 15 March 1988.

The present position

25.   Under existing case law the generally accepted test of company residence is that enunciated by Lord Loreburn at the beginning of this century in *De Beers Consolidated Mines v Howe* (5 TC 198) as follows:

'A company resides, for the purposes of income tax, where its real business is carried on; and the real business is carried on where the central management and control actually abides'.

26.   It has been pointed out by the Board of Inland Revenue in its Statement of Practice 6/83, that 'nothing which has happened since has in any way altered this basic principle· under current UK case law a company is regarded as resident for tax purposes where central management and control is to be found'.

27.   It is noteworthy that this proposition moves away from Lord Loreburn's original formulation that the place of residence of a company is where its real business is carried on; he applied the test of central management and control to identify the place where "real business" is carried on.

28.   In the context of the winding-up of the company, this difference is important. Under the revised formulation it is hard to see that central management and control is exercised by anyone other than the Liquidator. Under the original formulation, however, it would be hard to find evidence of "real business". Indeed, the Revenue generally argue that a company in liquidation which has ceased to trade has no business and that its activities are directed solely to the realisation of its assets.

The future position as we would like to see it

29.   The licensing provisions were introduced by the government primarily to protect creditors. It would be paradoxical if by their operation a windfall gain accrues to the Inland Revenue to the detriment of creditors generally.

30.   In previous correspondence with the Inland Revenue on the Finance Bill 1988 when this subject was raised, the Inland Revenue's view was given that the problem of becoming UK resident can be avoided as 'it would . . . be possible for companies to rearrange their affairs in ways other than liquidation, such as by shifting assets to a company incorporated elsewhere leaving behind only a shell'. Where companies are insolvent, however, such steps would not be available and we believe the position should be re-examined with a view to confirming generally that the appointment of a UK liquidator to an insolvent company which was non-UK resident will not transfer its residence to the UK.

31.   If the Board feel unable to extend such confirmation to solvent companies as well, it would nonetheless be helpful to have a general statement of the position that has been confirmed on occasion to individual insolvency practitioners, that management and control would remain abroad where a UK resident liquidator carries out his duties abroad in relation to that company, or in the case of a private company whose shareholders were the directors and the liquidator acts in accordance with the wishes of the non-resident shareholders.

Inland Revenue response

The test of residence

(a)   The Statement of Practice 6/83 should not be read as implying that, as a general rule, the Revenue have moved in any way from the test enunciated by Lord Loreburn. A company is regarded as resident for tax purposes where central management and control is to be found because that, according to Lord Loreburn, is where the real business is carried on. (The Statement of Practice has now been superseded by Statement 1/90 but the relevant paragraph is unchanged.)

(b)   The word "business" may have different connotations according to the context in which it is used. The Revenue does not consider that a company normally ceases to have a residence under Lord Loreburn's test on going into liquidation.

Application of the test

(c)   In law, the liquidator has management and control of the company's affairs. It is therefore not possible to confirm that a company, whether solvent or insolvent, which has hitherto been non-resident, will not become resident in the United Kingdom on the appointment of a UK resident liquidator.

(d)   However, the exercise of central management and control is a question of fact. If it is exercised abroad by the liquidator or if the liquidator acts in accordance with the wishes of non-resident shareholders so that management and control is not in fact in the UK, the company will not become resident here.

Liquidation of foreign companies

32.   Foreign companies which have been carrying on business in Great Britain may be wound up under the Insolvency Act 1986, so that UK creditors including the Inland Revenue may have the protection of a local licensed insolvency practitioner dealing with the assets for their benefit.

33.   UK practitioners are, however, wary of such appointments as the effect of Section 108(2) Taxes Management Act 1970 may be to make them personally liable in respect of the company's UK tax liability. Such liability is apparently not limited to the funds in the liquidation estate.

34.   A similar difficulty arises from UK practitioners who are asked to conduct the liquidation of foreign companies under foreign law, if their appointment was to make the foreign company UK resident for tax purposes.

35.   There is no statement of the Board of Inland Revenue's policy on the application to a liquidator of Section 108(2) TMA 1970, and it would be of assistance if the Board would make clear the circumstances in which the provision would be invoked, if at all.

36.   Liquidators wish to compete freely in the international market for their specialist skills, and they are at present disadvantaged by uncertainty of their position to the detriment of the UK economy.

Inland Revenue response

The Revenue has, as you say, no stated policy with regard to the application of Section 108(2), TMA, to liquidators of foreign companies. Where a foreign company owes tax it is the Revenue practice to proceed against the company itself, invoking the procedure in Part V, IA 1986, for winding up unregistered companies.

Other matters

37. Included in the matters which were dealt with in the former Regulations and Notes for guidance of Liquidators in Compulsory Liquidation, and for guidance of Trustees in Bankruptcy, were:

(i) regulations detailing how the Inland Revenue will forego excessive claims for taxation. (These provided relief where time limits had been missed);

(ii) regulations setting out the conditions which will apply where before the date of the winding-up order a Collector of Taxes has levied a distress against goods.

38. The requirement for agreed practice in such matters remains, and it should be extended to cover all insolvency procedures of the Insolvency Act 1986.

39. There should also be published those concessions which have been agreed with the insolvency profession in the past, including such matters as the Revenue's policy not to seek to recover notional ACT chargeable under Section 419 ICTA 1988 in respect of loans to participators when the lending company was already insolvent or where the participator is adjudged bankrupt.

40. There are also numerous detailed procedural matters which should be included and these should be the subject of discussion with the Inland Revenue. It is noteworthy that unlike HM Customs & Excise, the Inland Revenue does not centralise the conduct of cases involving insolvency procedures, nor are there clearly identified technical or policy specialists with whom the insolvency profession can have regular discussions about matters of concern to them, not all of which have been detailed in this memorandum. We would welcome such liaison arrangements and would be pleased to cooperate in them.

Inland Revenue response

Notes for guidance

(a) As mentioned earlier, amendments to the Department of Trade

Regulations 1977 are currently under consideration by the Inl.
Revenue and Department of Trade and Industry.

Liaison arrangements

(b)   Because of the extremely wide-ranging nature of matters affected by
the Insolvency Act, it is not considered practicable for the Inland
Revenue to have clearly identified technical or policy specialists.
However, if any point of difficulty are referred, in the first instance,
to Compliance and Collection Division, they will consult with the
necessary specialists to ensure that a reply is sent.

Index

Tolley's Commercial and Company Law Service

Tolley's Company Law (looseleaf)

The highly successful Tolley's Company Law is now being published in looseleaf format to ensure a quick and accurate service covering changes resulting from legislation, case law and the directives issuing from Europe as they occur. The emphasis of this practical book is on how the law operates on a day-to-day basis.

Supplements will comprise complete chapters only to facilitate quick and easy updating.

1870 pages
ISBN 0 85459 375-6 **£65.00**

Tolley's Commercial Loan Agreements

James Lingard LLB, Solicitor (Norton Rose)

This book discusses the major issues likely to arise in negotiating a Loan or Multiple Option Facility Agreement. The consequences of the reforms introduced by the Companies Act 1989 and the Insolvency Act 1986 are examined.

136 pages
ISBN 0 85459 453-1 **£29.95**
Hardback

Tolley's Practical Guide to Company Acquisitions (2nd edition)

A practical guide to acquisitions, covering acquisition strategy and tactics, legal aspects, tax planning, accounting requirements, employment responsibilities and pension schemes. Up-to-date to the Finance Act 1990 and the Social Security Act 1990.

220 pages
ISBN 0 85459 510-4 **£29.95**

Tolley's Companies Legislation

This new title contains the full text of current companies legislation including the Companies Acts 1985 and 1989, Business Names Act 1985, Company Securities (Insider Dealing) Act 1985 and the Company Directors Disqualification Act 1986. Also included are the relevant provisions of the Fair Trading Act 1973 and the Financial Services Act 1986. Extensive annotations incorporate the full text of superseded provisions in these Acts and comprehensive cross-references.

1108 pages
ISBN 0 85459 391-8 **£19.95**

Tolley's Corporate Insolvency Handbook

Shashi Rajani, Solicitor

Based partly on extracts from Tolley's Company Law, this new handbook covers the major issues, both legal and tax-related, of corporate insolvency in a single easy-to-use volume.

508 pages
ISBN 0 85459 509-0 **£27.95**

Tolley
HOTLINE

081-686 0115

The above Hotline number is a direct line to our Customer Liaison staff and can be used for a faster, more convenient service when ordering any Tolley publication.

(Outside office hours an answering machine is in operation)

Tolley Publishing Co. Ltd.,
Tolley House, 2 Addiscombe Road, Croydon, Surrey, CR9 5AF